RELUCTANCE IN WORLD POLITICS

Why States Fail to Act Decisively

Sandra Destradi

BRISTOL
UNIVERSITY
PRESS

First published in Great Britain in 2023 by

Bristol University Press
University of Bristol
1–9 Old Park Hill
Bristol
BS2 8BB
UK
t: +44 (0)117 374 6645
e: bup-info@bristol.ac.uk

Details of international sales and distribution partners are available at bristoluniversitypress.co.uk

British Library Cataloguing in Publication Data
A catalogue record for this book is available from the British Library

ISBN 978-1-5292-3023-9 hardcover
ISBN 978-1-5292-3024-6 paperback
ISBN 978-1-5292-3025-3 ePub
ISBN 978-1-5292-3026-0 ePdf

Cover design: Lyn Davies Design
Front cover image: Alamy/Zoonar GmbH

To Max, who asks so many beautiful
'why?' questions

Contents

List of Figures and Tables

Figures

Tables

About the Author

Sandra Destradi is Chair for International Relations and a Professor in the Department of Political Science at the University of Freiburg. Previously, she was Professor of International Relations and Regional Governance at Helmut Schmidt University, a Senior Research Fellow at the German Institute for Global and Area Studies in Hamburg, and a Jean Monnet Fellow at the Robert Schuman Centre of the European University Institute. Her current research interests include the international implications of populism and democratic backsliding, (trans)regional security dynamics, and the role of the Global South in global governance.

Acknowledgements

I remember the moment when I first had the idea to develop a project about reluctance in world politics almost a decade ago. I was sitting in an apartment in New Delhi, where I was doing field research for a project on India's Afghanistan policy, and it occurred to me that India's approach to its region was in many ways not too different from Germany's approach to Europe, which had, in the 2010s, been discussed as being that of a 'reluctant hegemon'. It was with that idea that I applied for a Jean Monnet Fellowship at the Robert Schuman Centre of the European University Institute (EUI), where I first developed my conceptualization of 'reluctance' in 2014–15. And it was at that same institute that I wrote down large parts of this book during sabbatical leave in 2022. This project on reluctance has therefore become a decade-long endeavour, and there are so many people I would like to thank for supporting me over the years. Ulrich Krotz at the EUI was the first to believe in my idea, and I wish to thank him for hosting me at the EUI. My article on the conceptualization of reluctance, published in the *European Journal of International Relations*, was an outcome of that first phase of research, and benefited greatly from his comments. Large parts of that article are reproduced in Chapter 2 under the terms of the Creative Commons Attribution 4.0 License.

I presented various parts of this book, including selected case studies, at a number of conferences and seminars, including at the EUI, Robert Schuman Centre for Advanced Studies (research area: 'Europe in the World'), the Swedish National Defence College (December 2014), the International Studies Association Annual Conventions in New Orleans (February 2015) and Atlanta (March 2016), the conference 'Changing Asia: Perspectives on Regional and Global Cooperation' at the German Institute for Global and Area Studies (GIGA) in Hamburg (April 2015), the congress of the German Political Science Association in Duisburg (September 2015), the workshop 'Asia's Challenges to Liberal Norms in the Contemporary International Order' at the University of Warwick (January 2017), the European Workshops in International Studies in Cardiff (June 2017), a workshop on regional powers at GIGA in spring 2018, and an online seminar at Shiv Nadar University in India (April 2022). I am grateful to all the participants in those seminars for their helpful feedback at different stages of the project, especially to Ulrich Krotz, Kjell Engelbrekt, Ronnie Hjort, Chiara Ruffa, Miriam Prys-Hansen, Fabrizio Coticchia, Richard Maher, Michal Onderco, Katerina Wright, Katharina Meissner, Christina Stolte, Annette Ranko, Christoph Harig, Ian Hall, Shaun Breslin, Derrick Frazier, Medha, Siddharth Mallavarapu, Swarati S., Robert Kappel, Magnus Schoeller, Jeffrey T. Checkel, Patrick A. Mello, Sebastian Harnisch and Moritz Weiß.

This book would also not have been possible without the support of many brilliant research assistants over the past years, who helped me in various capacities and at various institutions, including the Helmut Schmidt University and the University of Freiburg. I am most grateful to Cordula Tibi Weber and Reko Jeske for excellent research assistance! The same applies to Konrad Ringleb, who also gave me helpful suggestions about psychological approaches to decision making under pressure. Victória Silveira Novaes helped me greatly with research on the Brazilian case, Vihang Jumle with research on India, and Klara Leithäuser, Lukas Schmid, Niklas Kehrle and Hanna Dennett supported me with Citavi and research on the German case.

This project was also made possible thanks to 35 experts from India, Germany, Brazil and other countries, who agreed to share their knowledge and insights with me. I carried out those interviews over a long time span, from 2013 in India until 2015 in Germany and 2022 online with experts on Brazil and India. I chose to anonymize all interviews, but I want to emphasize how grateful I am to each and every one for their time and their trust. I would also like to thank some of my colleagues who helped me during my field research and in organizing many of those interviews, especially Robert Kappel, Meena Singh Roy, Christoph Harig, Kai Michael Kenkel and Erica Resende.

I was able to write this book thanks to an inspiring research stay as a Visiting Fellow at the Schuman Centre of the EUI in February–October 2022. I am grateful to Stephanie Hofmann for hosting me, and to my colleagues and my team at the University of Freiburg for making this stay abroad possible while still serving as a Dean of Studies and Head of Department in Freiburg. I would also like to thank Stephen Wenham of Bristol University Press for supporting this book project, and the four anonymous reviewers for giving extremely helpful feedback on my book proposal and the final manuscript.

The biggest 'grazie!', however, is for Dino and Max, for their love and support, and for every precious minute we spend together.

1

Introduction

> We believe that Germany has reacted too reluctantly to this
> dangerous situation, to these growing threats. We already warned
> [Germany] two months ago. We pointed out that this muscle
> flexing and these troops that are sent from all corners of Russia ...
> to the borders of Ukraine, that all this shouldn't be taken lightly.

These were the warning words of the Ukrainian ambassador to Germany, Andrij Melnyk, in a radio interview on 13 February 2022 (Deutschlandfunk, 2022), a few days ahead of Russia's attack against Ukraine.[1] This would not be the last time that a representative of the Ukrainian government asked Germany to do more to support Ukraine. In the following weeks and months, as the unthinkable – a fully-fledged war of aggression in Europe – was unfolding, Germany adopted a series of policies that disconcerted its international partners with their lack of coherence, frequent delays and lack of responsiveness. In the weeks immediately preceding the Russian attack of 24 February 2022, the German government was debating the delivery of 5,000 helmets to the Ukrainian army (FAZ, 2022), much to the bewilderment of its international partners (Dempsey, 2022b), which were providing substantial military aid. Germany, by contrast, long refused the delivery of weapons or other equipment, citing political and legal constraints on the provision of military equipment to conflict zones (BMWK, nd). Moreover, the German government was extremely slow in agreeing to the extension of sanctions. For example, when it came to the exclusion of Russia from the Swift payment system, the German government reacted late to mounting international pressure, being the last country in the European Union (EU) to agree to such a step (*Zeit Online*, 2022). Similarly, it only agreed to

---

[1] For all original language sources, the English translation is mine.

suspend the Nord Stream 2 gas pipeline project a few days before the start of the Russian invasion (Ischinger, 2022). An observer described Germany's approach as follows:

> ... this federal government is really highly talented in missing the right moment to act. Whether it dithers over sanctions against Nord Steam 2 or it fails to at least deliver quickly those ... ridiculous 5,000 helmets to Ukraine: desperate calls for help from Kyiv were not sufficient [to induce Germany] to become active. It was only due to the pressure by the Western community of nations that the federal government finally felt obliged to act. (Uken, 2022)

After being so recalcitrant vis-à-vis the requests of the Ukrainian government and international partners, on 26 February, the German government finally decided that it would provide 1,000 anti-tank weapons and 500 Stinger surface-to-air missiles (Bundesregierung, 2022). The following day, Chancellor Olaf Scholz made a sudden U-turn: in the Bundestag (the German federal parliament) he announced a sea change in Germany's defence policy, pledging to create a €100 billion special fund for the German Bundeswehr (Germany's armed forces) and to increase defence spending so as to meet the NATO (North Atlantic Treaty Organization) spending goal of 2 per cent of GDP (Scholz, 2022). This announcement came as a surprise to most observers, and was reportedly prepared by Chancellor Scholz without broad consultations within the governing coalition of his Social Democratic Party (SPD) with the Green Party and the Liberals (Amann et al, 2022). However, this major policy change on the part of Berlin was not followed by swift implementation. In May 2022, Germany's approach was described as follows:

> German Chancellor Olaf Scholz continues to procrastinate and prevaricate. ... The Bundestag has insisted that the chancellery deliver heavy weapons – which it promised to do some time ago. The armament companies are ready to do so. But Scholz continues to block their delivery. Just as he blocks Ukraine's ambitions to join the EU. (Dempsey, 2022a)

Similarly, in July 2022, the news emerged that Germany had not yet lived up to its promise to provide weapons to countries such as Poland, Slovakia or the Czech Republic to replace their donations of Soviet-era weapons to Kyiv (Ischinger, 2022).

During the months following the start of Russia's war of aggression, international partners time and again criticized Germany's policies. Polish Prime Minister Mateusz Morawiecki pointedly remarked: 'Ukraine drove the enemy back faster than the Germans were able to make decisions', and he added, 'Berlin's hesitation, its inaction, seriously calls into question the value of the alliance with Germany. And we are not the only ones saying that. I am hearing this from quite a few other heads of government in Europe, as well' (quoted in Puhl, 2022). The USA also put increasing pressure on Germany, with Ambassador Amy Gutmann asking Germany to 'do more' (Reulmann, 2022). Overall, Germany's policies ahead of Russia's attack against Ukraine and in the months following it have been variously described as ambiguous (Dempsey, 2022a), hesitant (Puhl, 2022) or as 'foot-dragging' (Ischinger, 2022). Quite obviously, the German government was reacting to mounting international pressure by pursuing a piecemeal approach, grudgingly making concessions at the last moment, suddenly promising ambitious change, but then not following up on it. How can we make sense of this muddling through, these inconsistent policies, the sudden turnabouts?

This book aims to make sense of the phenomenon of 'reluctance' in world politics – a concept that seeks to capture precisely this indecisiveness, hesitation and lack of coherence and responsiveness that we frequently observe in world politics, as well as in other policy fields and at other levels of analysis. This phenomenon is certainly not confined to Germany's approach to the war in Ukraine during the first half of 2022. The USA has sometimes been dubbed a 'reluctant' great power, highlighting its inconsistent approach towards the provision of global public goods (see, for example, Haass, 1997; Fehl, 2012). And countries that are predominant in their regions have also sometimes been called 'reluctant' leaders or hegemons, for example India or South Africa (Mitra, 2003; Esterhuyse, 2010). Deeply connected to the notion of reluctance is the failure of these countries to meet others' expectations of them, for example smaller regional neighbours that wanted them to contribute to the solution of regional problems or to share the costs of the provision of public goods.

In 2015, it was argued in the *Munich Security Report* (Bunde and Oroz, 2015: 22) that the crisis of the post-Cold War international order was deeply connected to 'the increasing reluctance of its traditional guardians'. The notion of reluctance describes the policies of actors who are indecisive, who try to buy time and thereby delay important decisions, who follow a zig-zagging course, backtracking on previous promises, sending contradictory and confusing signals, who are unwilling or unable to take a clear stand on important matters and instead end up 'muddling through'. It inevitably involves disappointed expectations on the part of other actors who would hope for a clearer and more predictable course of action, and it therefore makes international cooperation more difficult to achieve.

In many ways, reluctance is a widespread phenomenon in world politics: we frequently observe international actors not entirely opting out of crisis management, regional or global governance or international cooperation, but at the same time not being fully supportive, proactive or decisive. Yet reluctance has not been studied in a systematic way in the field of International Relations (IR) so far. This is all the more surprising if we think about its potential consequences. If important international actors pursue hesitant and indecisive policies, basically 'muddling through' in world politics, this will certainly hamper international cooperation: those actors will not reliably fulfil their international commitments, they will be recalcitrant when it comes to providing for their share in any collective effort at problem solving, and they will drag their feet or simply be of little use in the management of crises. Indeed, many failures in international cooperation do not necessarily derive from a straightforward refusal to act on the part of states or non-state actors, but rather from indecisiveness and hesitation in the processes of decision making or in the implementation of policies. Such indecisive and inconsistent policies will end up weakening international institutions and hampering the provision of (global) public goods. Responding to global challenges becomes more difficult if reluctant actors are involved.

At the same time, as we will see, it is important to develop a better understanding of the causes of reluctance in world politics: sometimes, reluctance emerges as a result of genuinely democratic processes of reorientation and readjustment in a country's foreign policy, and it is therefore an inevitable albeit temporary feature. In other cases, it is the result of deep-seated structural weaknesses that make it impossible to pursue consistent policies. Moreover, reluctance is a highly contingent phenomenon and can be limited to specific issues or crises.

Against this backdrop, this book seeks to answer the following question: *Why are international actors, including powerful states, often reluctant in their foreign policies?* To provide an answer, I proceed in three steps. First of all, I discuss the specifics of reluctance and develop a conceptualization of this phenomenon. Then, I move on to discuss the conditions under which international actors are reluctant, and thereby to theorize the causes of reluctance in world politics. In the empirical section of this book, I assess the explanatory power of the theory by carrying out an in-depth qualitative analysis of varying degrees of reluctance in regional crisis management on the part of three powerful regional countries – India, Germany and Brazil.

A gap in the literature

Indecisiveness, delaying, responsibility shirking, disappointing the expectations of partners – these and similar attitudes are commonplace in international politics and can actually also be observed in other fields of policy making. But reluctance has been largely ignored in academic writing on world politics– both in terms of the conceptualization of the phenomenon and in terms of a theorization of its causes. In fact, all mainstream theories of IR more or less explicitly assume straightforward behaviour on the part of international actors. Realism sets the assumption that states are unitary, rational actors that focus on their own utility maximization, either in the form of relative security maximization (Waltz, 1979) or power maximization (Mearsheimer, 2001). In both cases, states are presumed to pursue their strategic interests based on cost–benefit calculations without much hesitation. In a similar vein, liberalism, which seeks to trace the origins of preference formation within states by looking at domestic actors (Moravcsik, 1997), does not explicitly address the issue of reluctance – even though its opening of the 'black box' offers the best preconditions to trace the often complex processes through which actors within a state come to devise a certain foreign policy course for their country, and how they negotiate over it with their international partners. However, liberalism also does not focus on the zig-zagging and muddling through that often accompanies these processes. Similarly, other theories in the fields of political science or social sciences more broadly leave out the phenomenon of reluctance. For example, negotiation theory or studies on strategic interaction address issues such as deadlocks or constrained rationality, but they do not place particular emphasis on the hesitation and lack of clarity that sometimes accompany these processes (e.g., Scharpf, 1997; Lake and Powell, 1999; Zartman and Faure, 2006). Constructivist approaches in IR, in turn, expect actors to be driven by norms, identities or ideas (e.g., Risse-Kappen, 1995; Katzenstein, 1996; Checkel, 1997; Finnemore and Sikkink, 1998). These can change over time and through discursive processes, but are generally assumed to lead rather straightforwardly to the adoption of certain policies – all the indecisiveness that might ensue in this process is usually left out of the analysis, or at least it does not constitute an object of inquiry in its own right. And even critical and post-positivist approaches, which often focus on the processes and dynamics of the emergence of certain discourses and practices with a view to challenging common-sense assumptions about them (e.g., Der Derian, 1987; Diez, 1999), are not primarily interested in reluctant policies as an outcome of those processes.

Beyond these grand theories, a range of subfields in IR has looked for explanations for policies that deviate from standard expectations of straightforward policy making. For example, cognitive approaches that focus on decision making under uncertainty (Jervis, 1976; Mercer, 2005) and theories of risk aversion and bounded rationality (McDermott, 1998; O'Neill, 2001), even though not explicitly addressing reluctance, offer very useful insights for theory building. The literature on Foreign Policy Analysis (FPA) is best placed to study reluctance given its focus on the very processes of foreign policy making, which are conventionally not at the core of IR grand-theorizing. However, FPA has also not systematically addressed the issue of reluctance. In her seminal article conceptualizing the subfield of FPA as the 'ground' of IR, Hudson (2005: 2) mentions that FPA might focus on analysing 'a single decision or indecision', but she does not delve further into what such an analysis of 'indecision' might imply. Indeed, phenomena that could be subsumed under reluctance have been addressed in FPA more as pathologies and unwanted side effects rather than as fully-fledged objects of inquiry. The FPA literature has extensively discussed what 'effective' foreign policy decision making should look like: it should, overall, be 'rational' and include the definition of goals, the collection and processing of information, the consideration of available alternative courses of action, a clear cost-benefit analysis and ultimately the formulation of a roadmap for implementing decisions, monitoring them, and implementing a plan B in case of inconveniences emerging during the process (t' Hart, 1990: 18; Schafer and Crichlow, 2010: 5; Verbeek, 2017: 4). Decision-making processes that do not conform to these criteria are equated with 'poor-quality decision making' (Schafer and Crichlow, 2010: 7) and are considered to lead to 'policy failure' (t' Hart, 1990).

Indeed, case studies of foreign policies that 'went wrong' abound in FPA, and some scholars have recently started developing an interest in policy failures as a subject in its own right (Oppermann and Spencer, 2016). The literature on 'fiascos' or 'mistakes' in foreign policy makes such blunders the main object of analysis, yet it frequently takes a similar approach to the existing literature, ultimately focusing on failed goal attainment (in its objectivist variant) or addressing perceptions of failure and the issue of blaming (in its intersubjective variant) (Kruck et al, 2018a). By contrast, the very hesitation and muddling through that are so typical of reluctance are not an explicit focus of such analyses of policy failure. Some sections of the FPA literature interested in coalition governments have associated foreign policy ineffectiveness with the failure to act, with inconsistent actions or with 'fragmented action or deadlock' (Kaarbo, 2012: 33) as well as with immobilism (Kaarbo, 2012: 34). These are some of the approaches on which I will build in Chapter 3 while developing a theorization of the drivers of reluctance.

Only recently have some studies started taking into account more explicitly the fact that even powerful states often pursue hesitant and confusing policies – and that 'such inconsistent, or even contradictory, international behaviour is very common, including in high-profile issue areas' (Jones and Hameiri, 2021: 2). Basrur (2023), for example, points to domestic constraints on foreign policy in India, which have led to hesitations and delays that have the potential to hamper the country's rise in international politics. In their analysis of China, Jones and Hameiri (2021: 3) argue that inconsistencies are explained by the fact that China is not a unitary actor and that 'Decades of state transformation, involving the fragmentation, decentralisation, and internationalisation of party-state apparatuses, mean that many Chinese actors, with often differing interests and agendas ... now operate internationally with considerable autonomy and limited coordination and oversight'. These are important insights that provide one possible explanation for why even great powers, despite their huge capabilities, might resort to reluctant policies.

What is reluctance and how can we explain it?

One of the main problems with the notion of reluctance is its frequent, but mostly extremely diffuse, usage, both in everyday language and in academic analyses. In order to proceed to a conceptualization of reluctance, it is important to map its 'semantic field', that is, to reconstruct how this notion is usually employed (Sartori, 1984: 41–50) and to discuss related concepts. On this basis, it becomes possible to identify the constitutive components of a concept as well as its 'negative poles', that is, what the concept is not (Goertz, 2006). I will carry out these steps in detail in Chapter 2.

In a nutshell, reluctance can be understood as a specific type of policy making that entails two constitutive dimensions: hesitation and recalcitrance. *Hesitation* refers to the domestic process of policy making, and emerges as a result of difficulties in preferences formation. It can be operationalized by focusing on flip-flopping, delaying and/or a lack of initiative. In its most visible form, hesitation involves pursuing inconsistent policies, with rapid policy changes and contradictory moves or statements (flip-flopping). Delays to a previously set time frame are also an indicator of hesitation as they reveal difficulties in achieving a clear decision, or possibly efforts at buying time. Finally, a lack of initiative can amount to hesitation, especially if we are talking about powerful actors that would have the capabilities to address certain issues or crises in a decisive manner. *Recalcitrance* refers to the international component in foreign policy since it relates to the expectations and requests articulated by international actors. It amounts to a lack of responsiveness and can be operationalized as ignorance or rejection of others' requests, and also, to some extent, as obstructionism of others' initiatives, which can emerge in connection to delays and flip-flopping. In sum, reluctance in world politics describes a distinct way of doing foreign policy that entails both hesitation and recalcitrance, which are necessary and jointly sufficient conditions for the existence of reluctance.

How can we explain the occurrence of reluctance in world politics, and possibly beyond? In this book, I propose a theoretical framework that is clearly problem-driven (see Sil and Katzenstein, 2010) and builds on the insights of various strands of research in IR, FPA, Social Psychology and Psychology. It starts from the very understanding of foreign policy as a field at the crossroads of the 'domestic' and the 'international'. At the domestic level, foreign policies are the outcome of complex processes of preference formation in which a number of actors are involved. Hesitation will emerge if there are difficulties in this domestic process of preference formation. As we will see in detail in Chapter 3, these difficulties can be a result of political weakness, limited capacity, cognitive problems or normative struggles.

At the same time, foreign policies are always part of an international context, and the consideration of interactions with other state- and non-state actors in the international sphere will play a decisive role in devising foreign policies. In particular, the expectations articulated by other actors are an important factor that contributes to shaping foreign policy. Recalcitrance, the second constitutive component of reluctance, will emerge if a government is faced with (competing) expectations by international actors. Such international pressure will most likely exacerbate existing problems of domestic preference formation and will therefore contribute to the emergence of reluctance.

Based on the conceptualization of reluctance as entailing both hesitation and recalcitrance, the theoretical framework developed in Chapter 3 elaborates on possible drivers of these two constitutive components and brings them together. The main argument is that states will be reluctant if they face difficulties in the process of domestic preference formation and, at the same time, are confronted with competing international expectations.

Empirical analysis: varying reluctance in regional crisis management

In order to assess the explanatory power of this theory of reluctance, I carry out an empirical analysis of a set of cases of regional crisis management on the part of powerful regional countries. This approach was chosen for a number of reasons. Reluctance is frequently mentioned with reference to powerful countries as this is where the phenomenon is most puzzling. We should expect countries that have the power capabilities to solve problems and address crises to do so without much hesitation or recalcitrance, without all the muddling through and indecisiveness that are typical of reluctance. This is all the more true for the management of security crises (broadly understood) that take place in their regional neighbourhood. These crises are proximate and therefore have the potential to destabilize the region or even to spill over across boundaries and to affect the powerful countries under scrutiny. When security threats are close and imminent, we would expect powerful states to react decisively, without much hesitation, and to pursue a consistent course of action. However, this is not always the case.

In the empirical chapters of this book, I focus on varying instances of reluctance in regional crisis management on the part of India in South Asia, Germany in Europe's extended neighbourhood, and Brazil in Latin America. I focus on recent crises that took place during the 21st century, carefully choosing phases in which each country was unequivocally a powerful actor in its respective region, and also had a stable government. This focus on periods of domestic political stability is helpful to exclude the first (and most obvious) possible explanation for difficulties in preference formation, namely political instability. Yet, the three countries analysed were embedded in radically different regional contexts, from the least integrated region in the world, South Asia, to the most densely institutionalized one, Europe.

For each country, the analysis focuses on its engagement in two of the most severe crises in its extended regional neighbourhood. In the case of India, I analyse crisis management in South Asia under the government led by Prime Minister Narendra Modi of the Hindu nationalist Bharatiya Janata Party (BJP). During both terms in government (2014–19, 2019 until the time of this writing, in 2022), the government was very stable and faced no substantial challenge from a divided opposition or small coalition partners. The analysis focuses on two very different crises to which India was not itself a conflict party: on the conflict in Afghanistan between 2014 and the takeover by the Taliban in 2021, and on a serious domestic political crisis related to the introduction of a new constitution in Nepal (2015–17). By applying the conceptualization of reluctance to India's policies in those crises, I find that India's approach to both was unequivocally reluctant.

For the case of Germany, I focus on the management of crises in the European neighbourhood after 2009, that is, from the moment in which the Eurozone crisis catapulted Germany back into the centre of European politics. Given the widespread calls for German leadership and the pre-eminent position of Germany in European politics at that time, it is particularly insightful to focus on Germany as a powerful country in Europe from which a decisive and responsive approach to crisis management was expected. In particular, the analysis focuses on Germany's role in the Libya crisis (2011) and the Ukraine crisis (2014–15). While Germany's approach to Libya, with its ill-conceived abstention in the vote on United Nations Security Council (UNSC) Resolution 1973 and its subsequent hesitant and recalcitrant policies is a clear-cut case of strong reluctance, Germany's crisis management in Ukraine during the years 2014–15 is different (UNSC, 2011b). With the benefit of hindsight, taking into account Russia's war of aggression against Ukraine that started in February 2022, Germany's mediation efforts during the Ukraine crisis of 2014–15 appear naïve, but this case displays an interesting shift in German policies towards lower degrees of reluctance and an increasingly determined and responsive approach.

Finally, for Brazil, I identify two instances of non-reluctance in crisis management. The analysis focuses on the years of the first Lula presidency (2003–10), which were a period of political stability and intense international engagement for Brazil (as opposed to later years). In this case, I analyse Brazil's approach to the two most severe crises in its extended regional neighbourhood: Brazil's leadership of the United Nations Stabilization Mission in Haiti (MINUSTAH), and its approach to the Colombian civil war between FARC (Fuerzas Armadas Revolucionarias de Colombia, Revolutionary Armed Forces of Colombia) and the Colombian government. In both cases, Brazil's approach was not reluctant: in the case of MINUSTAH, it took over military leadership of the mission and pursued a straightforward course of action, displaying neither hesitation nor recalcitrance. In the case of the civil war in Colombia, the Brazilian government pursued a low-key approach that mainly focused on the provision of offers of mediation and some support with logistics. Since this approach was pursued in a very consistent manner over the years, and since it was responsive to what the Colombian government and other actors expected from Brazil, these very limited policies can nevertheless be considered as non-reluctant.

For each instance of crisis management, in Chapters 4–6 I will assess the explanatory power of my theoretical framework. As outlined in the respective chapters, in all instances of reluctance, this could be related to a combination of (competing) external expectations and difficulties in preference formation. Brazil, by contrast, could pursue non-reluctant policies in the case of MINUSTAH because there was a high degree of domestic agreement on the usefulness of playing a leading role in crisis management in Haiti, and nearly all domestic actors saw advantages in it. The government managed to silence critics and to put an end to normative struggles by arguing that the mission had primarily a peaceful intent and a humanitarian character. At the same time, all relevant international actors, from the USA and France, to fellow Latin American countries, were encouraging or at least supporting Brazil's leadership of the mission – in other words, the Brazilian government was not faced with competing expectations. In the case of Colombia's civil war, Brazil's non-reluctant policies can mainly be explained by the extremely low-key nature of its engagement. Offering support and mediation, and occasionally helping with the logistics of hostage rescue missions, was nothing that would lead to major debates or fights within the Brazilian government. At the same time, a certain estrangement between the Brazilian and Colombian governments contributes to explain why there were no major expectations vis-à-vis Brazil in the management of this crisis. This is how a low-key but non-reluctant policy became possible.

For each country chapter, I introduce the political situation and discuss in detail why the period analysed was a phase of domestic political stability. Then I move on to analyse each case of crisis management, providing an introduction into the specific case and applying the operationalization of reluctance to the analysis of the respective country's foreign policy, in order to determine to what extent it was reluctant. I then move on to assess the explanatory power of my theory by focusing on the possible drivers of hesitation as well as on the issue of competing expectations. All the in-depth qualitative case studies draw on a range of primary sources, including in the respective local languages. These comprise official documents by the respective governments and by international organizations, reports by think tanks and non-governmental organizations (NGOs) as well as newspaper articles and other press reports.

In order to reconstruct the domestic dynamics of decision making as well as the ways in which governments reacted to external pressures, I complemented this data with expert interviews. More specifically, I carried out 35 semi-structured expert interviews with decision makers, observers, journalists and academics from India, Brazil and Germany as well as from some of the countries in which the crises analysed took place and from neighbouring countries (for example, with a scholar based in Chile, as I was interested in learning more about regional neighbours' expectations vis-à-vis Brazil). These data were collected in a long time span, between 2013, when I carried out fieldwork in India on the subject of India–Afghanistan relations; 2015, when I did fieldwork in Berlin and Hamburg on the issue of Germany's crisis management; and in 2022, when I conducted a set of additional online interviews on Brazilian as well as Indian foreign policy.

What emerges from the empirical analysis is that reluctance occurs when various factors make it difficult for a government to reach clear foreign policy preferences, and if that government is subjected to competing expectations by external actors. This hampers efforts at devising a clear course of action and sticking to it. At the same time, reluctance should not be equated with an unwillingness or inability to exercise 'leadership'. This is how the notion of reluctance has sometimes been used in the literature, but this association is not helpful. This becomes clearer in Chapter 7, where I apply my theory of reluctance to a range of different cases. In particular, I seek to assess its explanatory power by focusing on various types of crisis; on different types of countries such as small states and great powers; and on different types of actors beyond the nation-state. I find that, in principle, the drivers of hesitation and recalcitrance – difficulties in preference formation and competing expectation – remain the same and also explain reluctance in those very different contexts.

Reluctance can therefore be in place even where leadership is not necessarily expected. It does not equate to a rejection of leadership, as the negative poles of the concept are determination and responsiveness. These can be features of leadership, but they don't have to be. Rather, reluctance can occur at all levels and in all political (and even social or interpersonal) contexts, and a better understanding of this concept and of its causes is helpful if we want to make sense of the muddling through and indecisiveness we often observe in the world 'out there'.

2

Conceptualizing Reluctance

Before we move on to developing explanations for the varying occurrence of reluctance in world politics, we need to develop a sound conceptualization of reluctance.[1] So far, this term has been used in a rather casual manner, and such unspecific usage has made the term not particularly useful beyond mere description. By contrast, if appropriately conceptualized, 'reluctance' can yield analytical benefits by helping us to make sense of the widespread indecisiveness and muddling through that can frequently be observed in contemporary international politics. Conceptual clarity is indispensable if we want to make sense of this phenomenon and to adequately operationalize it for empirical analysis.

The conceptualization of reluctance builds on and combines different approaches to concept reconstruction and concept building, which are briefly discussed in the next section. The actual conceptualization exercise proceeds as follows. First, based on a qualitative content analysis of selected International Relations (IR) literature that explicitly uses the notion of reluctance, I inductively identify the key issues usually associated with this term. This helps as a first approach to delineating the broader semantic field of reluctance, and thereby contributes to concept reconstruction, as suggested by Sartori (1984: 41–50). Based on this broader semantic field, in a second step I move on to discussing the related but distinct notions of exceptionalism, isolationism, under-aggression, under-balancing, buck-passing and free-riding – and I highlight why we need reluctance as an additional concept to make sense of a distinct set of phenomena. Based on

---

[1] Large parts of this chapter are reproduced from the following article: Destradi, S. (2017) 'Reluctance in international politics: A conceptualization', *European Journal of International Relations*, 23(2): 315–40. This article is distributed under the terms of the Creative Commons Attribution 4.0 License (https://creativecommons.org/licenses/by/4.0), which permits any use, reproduction and distribution of the work without further permission provided the original work is attributed and a link to the Creative Commons License is included.

the insights gained from situating the concept of reluctance in the existing IR literature, I proceed with the actual concept-building exercise, which follows the guidelines outlined by Goertz (2006) in his work on social science concepts. I therefore discuss the negative poles of reluctance – that is, what reluctance is not; I develop two core 'secondary', constitutive dimensions of reluctance; and I operationalize these two dimensions, developing indicators for empirical analysis. In a nutshell, I conceive of reluctance as a specific way of doing foreign policy that involves a hesitant attitude and a certain recalcitrance about conforming to the expectations articulated by others.

Mapping the field: reconnecting concept reconstruction and concept building

While the importance of concepts in the social sciences cannot be underestimated, extensive reflection on the process of defining and clarifying concepts remains rare, with notable exceptions (see, for example, Sartori, 1970, 1984; Goertz, 2006; Collier et al, 2012). Among the few studies that explicitly deal with the issue of concept formation in the social sciences, there is disagreement on the first step to take. Sartori suggests that this first step should always be 'concept reconstruction', which amounts to tracing the use of the concept in previous works in order to assess how others have defined it, and to extract and systematize underlying characteristics (Sartori, 1984: 41–50). As a subsequent step, Sartori recommends 'allocation of the term', that is, the choice of a specific word to be associated with the concept that one intends to study. To do this, the term that designates the concept needs to be related to its semantic field to make sure that reconceptualization does not lead to a loss of meaning of other terms, or to an increase in ambiguity instead of greater clarity (Sartori, 1984: 51–3). By semantic field, Sartori (1984: 52) refers to 'a clustering of terms such that each of its component elements interacts with all the others, and (as with all systems) is altered by any alteration of the others'. Only after concept reconstruction and allocation of the term can we proceed to the main step of reconceptualization or concept building, according to Sartori. In a similar fashion, Adcock and Collier (2001: 531) argue that conceptualization – that is, the formulation of a systematized concept – must be based on an assessment of what they call the 'background concept': the existing 'broad constellation of meanings and understandings associated with a given concept'.

Much more than Sartori, Goertz (2006: 4) highlights that thinking about concepts involves going well beyond semantics – it implies carrying out a 'theoretical and empirical analysis of the object or the phenomenon' that is being conceptualized. Correspondingly, Goertz (2006: 5) thinks of concepts

(1) in ontological terms, since conceptualizations imply focusing on what constitutes a phenomenon; (2) in causal terms, since the central dimensions of concepts have causal powers, which, in turn, shape theories that employ these concepts; and (3) in what he calls 'realist' terms, since concepts always relate to empirical phenomena.

To adequately deal with these aspects, it is important to address the structure of concepts and the relationships between the different dimensions and levels within concepts in the concept-building exercise. According to Goertz (2006: 27), developing a concept amounts to 'deciding what is important about an entity'. However, how can we make this essential decision? In other words, how do we know what is important about an entity? In order to avoid at least some of the arbitrariness that might be associated with starting the concept-building exercise without appropriate groundwork, it is useful to start with concept reconstruction, as suggested by Sartori – or to assess the 'background concept', as Adcock and Collier (2001: 530–1) put it, or to apply what Goertz and Mazur (2008: 19–20) call the 'context guideline'. The need to build on previous uses of a concept seems particularly compelling for notions like reluctance, which are already frequently employed in the literature but in a confused and unspecific manner – that is, when concept building is used to clarify the meaning of an existing term.

Concept reconstruction

The broader semantic field

As a first step, it is therefore useful to map the field, that is, to analyse existing literature that uses the concept of reluctance in order to find out how the concept is defined, what notions and types of behaviour are usually associated with it, and its 'set of associated, neighboring terms' (Sartori, 1984: 52). While the notion of reluctance is not specific to IR or to Political Science, and is, indeed, frequently used in a range of fields, from Medicine to Sociology and Psychology, to analyse specific forms of behaviour, a striking commonality across disciplines is an absence of definitions or sophisticated operationalizations of reluctance. For example, clinical studies that deal with patients' reluctance to take preventive medication, to undergo preventive tests or to seek treatment either simply equate reluctance with a choice not to do something (Quaid and Morris, 1993) or, in a slightly more sophisticated manner, with a general resistance to taking medication (Port et al, 2001) or with the notion of not seeing a doctor despite knowing they should do so (Meltzer et al, 2000). Studies in the field of Sociology simply operationalize reluctance by looking at different degrees of stated (un)willingness (Bielby and Bielby, 1992). Or, to mention another example, in a study on reluctance to communicate undesirable information, reluctance is operationalized as a time lag in the transmission of information or as the transmission of incomplete information (Rosen and Tesser, 1970).

In studies that focus on the reluctance of states in foreign policy, that is, in the fields of IR and History, we observe a similar lack of definitions. Most studies that prominently mention reluctance in their titles do not explicitly discuss the concept, and in the case of books, do not even include the term in the index (see, for example, Lowe, 1967; Haass, 1997; Dueck, 2006; Fehl, 2012). Nevertheless, these studies address a specific type of state behaviour or way of doing foreign policy that has distinct and identifiable characteristics. In order to gather more systematic information on how reluctance is understood in the field of IR, I have carried out a qualitative content analysis of selected studies that prominently use this term, proceeding inductively, that is, approaching the text corpus without a pre-defined set of categories. I have explicitly avoided building my text corpus on works that just refer to the reluctance of powerful regional countries in order to exclude circular reasoning while applying the concept of reluctance to the same group of states in later sections of this study. Most works in the field of IR that explicitly address 'reluctance' refer to the USA or other great powers, probably because of the puzzling and paradox coexistence of resource abundance or 'hegemony' with hesitant foreign policies and responsibility shirking. However, the analysis also included works on smaller reluctant states (see, for example, Gstöhl, 2002). The results of the analysis are displayed in Figure 2.1.[2]

Reluctance is usually associated, among other things, with a highly ambivalent attitude, hesitant behaviour and a selective commitment. For example, as Fehl (2012: 10) highlights, a reluctant USA was the main proponent of an International Trade Organization after the Second World War, but later stopped supporting the idea; it signed most human rights conventions, but then did not ratify them during the Cold War. In the post-Cold War world, according to Haass (1997), the USA has become a 'reluctant sheriff', struggling with the costs of providing order and with decreasing domestic interest in and consensus on foreign policy issues. This reluctance is associated with ad hoc, short-term approaches, and with a lack of 'clarity and soundness of purpose' (Haass, 1997: 3). Schweller (2006: 6) similarly sees a danger in the attitude of the USA, which risks becoming an 'elephant on

---

[2] The analysis proceeded in a 'data-driven way', that is, by 'letting [the] categories emerge from the data' (Schreier, 2012: 25). The text corpus was analysed by looking specifically for expressions associated with the notion of reluctance or used to describe behaviour defined as 'reluctant'. This approach is suitable given the descriptive aim of the exercise (Schreier, 2012: 43): the identification of the broader semantic field of concepts that are associated with reluctance in the literature.

Figure 2.1: Notions associated with reluctance in international politics

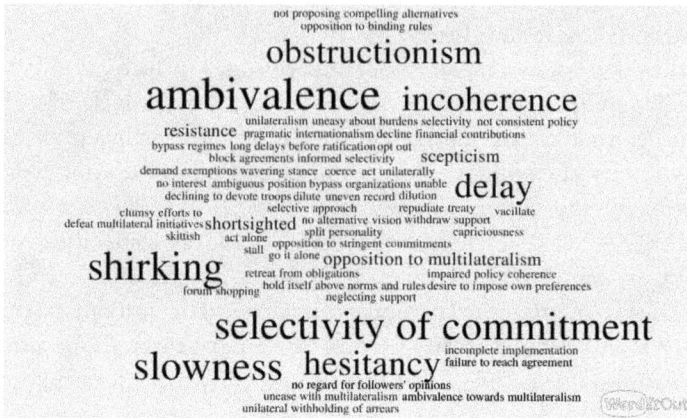

not proposing compelling alternatives
opposition to binding rules

obstructionism

ambivalence incoherence

unilateralism uneasy about burdens selectivity not consistent policy
resistance pragmatic internationalism decline financial contributions
bypass regimes long delays before ratification opt out
block agreements informed selectivity scepticism
demand exemptions wavering stance coerce act unilaterally
no interest ambiguous position bypass organizations unable delay
declining to devote troops dilute uneven record dilution
clumsy efforts to selective approach repudiate treaty vacillate
defeat multilateral initiatives shortsighted no alternative vision withdraw support
skittish act alone split personality capriciousness
stall opposition to stringent commitments
go it alone opposition to multilateralism

shirking retreat from obligations impaired policy coherence
forum shopping hold itself above norms and rules desire to impose own preferences
neglecting support

selectivity of commitment
incomplete implementation
slowness hesitancy failure to reach agreement
no regard for followers' opinions
unease with multilateralism ambivalence towards multilateralism
unilateral withholding of arrears

Note: This figure was created using worditout.com

the sidelines, a potential but reluctant hegemon unwilling to lead'. An analysis of Norway's, Sweden's and Switzerland's approaches to European integration identifies reluctance with scepticism towards integration. A preference for more limited forms of integration and the adoption of hesitant policies are seen as distinctive of this reluctant attitude (Gstöhl, 2002: 3–4). Related to ambivalence, hesitation and selectivity of commitment is a high degree of incoherence in a reluctant country's policies – as Patrick puts it, Washington 'has often seemed skittish about committing itself to proposed international legal regimes', for example on the International Criminal Court (ICC) or on human rights conventions (Patrick, 2002: 5). Similarly, Britain in the second half of the 19th century has been termed a 'reluctant imperialist', with reluctance amounting to caution and aloofness from European affairs (Lowe, 1967: 9) and, interestingly, to a certain 'amateurishness' in foreign policy making (Lowe, 1967: 13).

Other elements associated with reluctance are obstructionism towards others' initiatives and a certain slowness in implementing policies, with delays and sometimes even the adoption of 'time-buying' tactics. For example, during the 1990s the US Senate contributed to the USA's reluctance as it 'stalled, diluted, or defeated' a range of multilateral initiatives in the field of control of weapons of mass destruction, with the most evident case being the rejection of the Comprehensive Nuclear-Test-Ban Treaty (Patrick, 2002: 3).

In sum, an assessment of the broader semantic field of reluctance reveals that this notion is related to policies that are ambivalent and at times even obstructionist towards the initiatives of others, which involve shirking responsibility, a hesitant attitude, delays in implementation, selectivity of commitments and incoherence.

Related theoretical approaches

Based on this assessment of the broader semantic field of reluctance, a further useful step in concept reconstruction relates the concept to existing theoretical approaches in the field, in this case, in the subject area of IR. In particular, there are six notions that are explicitly or implicitly related to the concept of reluctance as it has developed from the analysis of the broader semantic field: under-aggression, under-balancing, isolationism, exceptionalism, free-riding and buck-passing. Obviously, these notions come from different theoretical traditions, but what they have in common is that they describe various types of foreign policy that powerful states can adopt, and that have some commonalities with the already-mentioned features of reluctance. These concepts are all related to reluctance, and are closely related among each other and sometimes even overlapping. Under-balancing and under-aggression are concepts rooted in the realist tradition of IR and refer to conflictive settings and to conditions of anarchy and self-help. Exceptionalism and isolationism usually refer to less conflictive settings and to particularly powerful countries. Buck-passing and free-riding are more frequently applied to smaller and weaker states, and refer to problems of collective action; free-riding specifically addresses the issue of public goods provision, which implies that it is mostly used with reference to multilateral settings and global governance.

The literature on under-aggression or under-expansion has its roots in realism in IR, and tries to make sense of the fact that in many cases powerful states do not conform to the expectations of realism, particularly of its offensive variant (Mearsheimer, 2001). Rising powers, for example, do not automatically translate an increase in power capabilities into an aggressive and expansionist foreign policy, and this has led to a number of studies in the neoclassical realist tradition trying to explain this phenomenon. Among the typical cases analysed in this literature is the 'imperial understretch' of the USA after the Civil War, which Zakaria (1998), for example, explains by focusing on the weakness of US state structure. Dueck (2006: 2) relates the notion of under-expansionism to the concept of reluctance by asking why Americans have been 'reluctant crusaders': 'crusaders in the promotion of a more liberal international order' but 'reluctant to admit the full costs of promoting this liberal international vision'. He comes to the conclusion that the essence of such 'reluctance' lies in a disjuncture between ambitious liberal goals and the employment of 'disproportionately limited means' to pursue them (Dueck, 2006: 2). The reason for such disjuncture is found in strategic culture (and in competing ideational legacies within it), seen as an intervening factor that modifies the impact of the structural drivers of foreign policy (Dueck, 2006: 4–5). Meiser (2015) has added to the literature on US under-expansionism (or, in his words, 'restraint') by focusing, again, on why the rising USA did not expand territorially between 1898 and 1941, with his explanation mostly focusing on domestic institutions and the path-dependency effects of restraint. Among the authors who look beyond the case of the USA is Schweller, who investigates what he calls 'the suboptimal reluctance to use force or to build up military power' (Schweller, 2006: 105) on the part of most great powers in the 20th century. His contentious conclusion is that only fascist regimes could develop the '"ideologized" power politics for mass consumption' (Schweller, 2006: 21) that are required for expansionism in the modern world and involve a substantial mobilization of the population. The notions of under-aggression and under-expansion therefore refer to policies of countries that are not necessarily inward-looking, but for different reasons do not realize their outward-looking potential in military terms.

As we have seen, some authors refer to these 'under-aggressive' policies as reluctance, but the connection to reluctance is rather remote. In fact, what scholars in this tradition focus on is actually rather consistent inactivity on the part of the 'under-aggressive' state. This means that they exclude all the more subtle nuances mostly associated with the concept of reluctance, which involves a whole array of indecisive, hesitant, flip-flopping policies. At the same time, some works in this tradition acknowledge the contradictions inherent in under-aggression. Most approaches explain under-aggression as an 'unwillingness' to expand, but some also take into account the 'inability' or, more generally, the constraints faced by powerful countries. Among the main limitations of approaches that focus on under-aggression or restraint is that they have their roots in counterfactual thinking: they are interested in explaining why something that would have been expected has not taken place (see, for example, Meiser, 2015). By contrast, the notion of reluctance, if appropriately conceptualized and operationalized, refers to actual foreign policy.

A closely related notion is that of under-balancing: the attitude of countries that do not respond to threats in conflictive settings by mobilizing military power or by forging alliances (Schweller, 2006). Unlike under-aggression, this concept does not focus on a lack of initiative or on why states are 'timid' (Schweller, 2006: 20). Instead, it focuses on why states do not react to dangerous aggressors or to dangerous changes in relative power as expected by balance-of-power theory. Like under-aggression, under-balancing is a concept used in neoclassical realism. In describing under-balancing, Schweller (2006: 63) comes close to the understanding of reluctance developed in this chapter, as he explicitly acknowledges that under-balancing can take the form of 'half measures, muddling through, and incoherent grand strategies', and thus reflects the incoherence and ambivalence that is frequently associated with reluctance. However, under-balancing addresses only a very specific context for reluctant behaviour, namely the situation of being threatened by another country – a situation in which reluctance, according to this realist reading, is a 'mistake' (Schweller, 2006: 10) that potentially affects a state's survival. Therefore, it does not refer to a broader spectrum of foreign policy contexts and situations that go beyond the particular setting of being threatened. Moreover, by focusing on under-balancing as a 'mistake', it ignores cases in which buying time, preferring not to commit too heavily or shirking responsibility might be rational and strategically employed choices to deal with different types of pressure and expectations.

The notions of isolationism and exceptionalism also refer to great powers that do not behave as expected, but in a less conflictive context. The literature on isolationism focuses on powerful countries that decide to pursue a 'minimalist' foreign policy characterized by limited goals, a high degree of restraint[3] and a limited amount of resources devoted to foreign policy (Haass, 1997: 55). Isolationism not only involves an unwillingness to use military force; isolationist countries prefer not to get engaged abroad at all – they are clearly inward-looking and therefore limit the resources devoted to different instruments of foreign policy, including diplomacy and foreign aid (Haass, 1997: 57). Correspondingly, isolationism is mostly equated with a policy of non-entanglement and with abstention from commitments. Authors like Legro (2005: 51) prefer to talk about 'separatism', understood not as strict isolation but as 'nonengagement, aloofness, and detached unilateralism'. Among the typical examples of isolationist countries are Japan between the 18th century and the Meiji Restoration – a case of strict isolationism (Legro, 2005: 128–31) – and the USA between the world wars, which was certainly not fully isolated, but refused to get engaged abroad and was characterized by strong isolationist ideas, which were only slowly replaced by an internationalist approach (Legro, 2005: Chapter 3).[4] The notion of isolationism also means that states do not make use of cooperative opportunities. The close relationship between the concepts of isolationism and reluctance is highlighted, for example, by Dueck (2006: 27), who explicitly equates a 'preference for nonentanglement' with reluctance. At the same time, there are differences between the two concepts. For example,

---

[3]   A separate, but mostly prescriptive, strand in the literature on US foreign policy revolves around the notion of restraint (or self-restraint), understood as a moderate and subtle policy focused on few threats and thereby opposed to 'expansiveness' (Posen, 2014: xiii) and interested, instead, in reassuring others about one's benign intentions (see, for example, Ikenberry, 1999). While the concept of restraint is clearly related to the concepts discussed here, it is conceptualized as a straightforward policy that does not entail the elements of hesitation and recalcitrance, which are typical of reluctance.

[4]   At the same time, isolationism is closely related to and sometimes equated with exceptionalism. As mentioned, some of the borders between the six concepts are blurred, and these notions are sometimes overlapping.

the element of hesitation, which is mostly associated with reluctance, does not necessarily form part of an isolationist policy: consistent and resolute isolationism (Nordlinger, 1996: 9) has little in common with the indecisiveness that is typical of reluctance.

The concept of exceptionalism refers to a body of literature that studies the foreign policy of states that have a particular sense of entitlement or a perception of being exceptional and therefore not subject to the rules, constraints and commitments binding other states (Nymalm and Plagemann, 2019). This leads, on the one hand, to policies aimed at 'liberating' others in the name of some messianic belief or some special responsibility (Holsti, 2010) – an activist and decisive policy clearly opposed to reluctance. With reference to the USA, underlying this approach to exceptionalism is the notion that an exceptional country 'should be exempted from the international rules that bind other nations' (Halperin and Boyer, 2007: 2). On the other hand, exceptionalism entails efforts to achieve freedom of action by shedding the burden of cooperation in multilateral institutions and regimes (Halperin and Boyer, 2007; Holsti, 2010). Exceptionalism is therefore usually employed with reference to powerful countries unwilling to engage. It is related to ambivalence and a general unwillingness to commit, which are important elements generally associated with the notion of reluctance. The potential decisiveness of exceptionalist powers in bilateral settings, in turn, distinguishes exceptionalism from reluctance, which is usually associated with hesitant, indecisive action.

The two notions in the IR literature that are used most frequently to describe an unwillingness to contribute to the costs of collective action, and therefore a tendency to undermine international cooperation, are free-riding and buck-passing. Free-riding is usually employed with reference to global governance and the provision of global public goods. Buck-passing comes from realist approaches to the study of alliances and refers to shunning the costs of a country's own defence. These concepts are frequently (but not exclusively) applied to less powerful actors. In political debates, they are often associated (and confused) with reluctance.

Free-riding implies an unwillingness to contribute to the provision of public goods. This behaviour is made possible by the very characteristics of such goods (non-excludability and non-rivalry in consumption), which make it rational for single actors to leave their provision to others while still enjoying the benefits (Kaul et al, 1999: xxi). We therefore have a collective action problem (Olson, 1965), which is particularly acute in world politics, where there is no authority that can enforce rules about the provision of such goods. Especially weak and poor states do not have the capabilities to contribute to the provision of public goods in a significant manner and are therefore free-riding, but powerful actors also have limited incentives to engage in the provision of (global) public goods.

Departing from this dilemma, the entire literature in the tradition of the hegemonic stability theory (Kindleberger, 1973) has argued that a 'hegemon' is needed to overcome such collective action problems – a state that takes a leading role and is willing to contribute more than others to the provision of public goods because it would benefit most from the stabilization of the system or from the other positive externalities generated by the provision of public goods. This theme was taken up by a broad strand of literature that focused on the USA as a 'hegemon' in world politics, but also on the limits of US hegemonic power and on hegemonic decline (see, for example, Rosecrance, 1976; Snidal, 1985).[5] This literature tended to equate the provision of public goods by the hegemon with international 'leadership',[6] and therefore lamented the USA's presumed unwillingness to provide such leadership. In the 2000s, with the rise of China and other emerging powers, the debate about global public goods provision and free-riding experienced a revival: this time, policy makers and academics (see, for example, Schweller and Pu, 2011: 42) accused rising powers of not taking a share in global public goods provision commensurate to their increased power capabilities, in line with the principle that 'with power comes responsibility' (for an overview of the debate, see Kenkel and Destradi, 2019).

Free-riding was therefore often associated with 'irresponsibility' (see, for example, Patrick, 2010), and thereby given a strong normative connotation (Culp, 2016; Kenkel and Martins, 2016; Gaskarth, 2017). The notion of free-riding is therefore closely related to that of reluctance as it refers to an unwillingness to contribute to the provision of (global) public goods. In the case of powerful states, this is, in turn, often equated with an unwillingness to lead. The concept of free-riding is certainly useful to understand some aspects of reluctance, but it is narrower: it focuses on a specific behaviour that involves the non-provision of public goods and their contemporary enjoyment. As becomes evident from the accusations of 'irresponsibility' described above, free-riding clearly disappoints expectations by other actors and obviously involves a high degree of recalcitrance. However, the concept of free-riding is not able to capture the elements of hesitation and uncertainty, the back-and-forth, the zig-zagging and meandering in policy making that is typical of reluctance. The two phenomena can go hand-in-hand, but this does not always have to be the case: states that explicitly and consistently refuse to participate to the costs of public goods provision should not be considered 'reluctant', but just plain free-riders.

---

[5] For critiques of this debate, see, for example, Russett (1985) or Strange (1987).

[6] For a discussion of different traditions within hegemonic stability theory, see Lake (1993).

Finally, the concept of buck-passing is close to that of free-riding.[7] It was developed in the realist tradition in IR to describe one of the possible strategies that states adopt to cope with security concerns (see, for example, Christensen and Snyder, 1990). Buck-passing essentially means outsourcing balancing to others, relying on allies for one's own security, and thereby radically reducing the costs one has to bear. In line with realism's understanding of states as unitary and rational actors, buck-passing is considered a rational strategy to pursue as it allows states to shun the high costs associated with balancing. It is considered a particularly useful strategy to follow for states that can count on mighty allies or that are in a relatively secure geostrategic position. As becomes evident, buck-passing is only loosely associated with the notion of reluctance as it emerged from the analysis of the broader semantic field: it is limited to the field of security and is ultimately a strategy dictated by rational choice. It entails a conscious lack of commitment, but, like most of the notions discussed here, it does not involve the elements of hesitation and indecisiveness that are typical of reluctance.

The concept of reluctance therefore touches on each of the six concepts discussed, yet differs from each of them in important respects. What the six concepts of under-aggression, under-balancing, isolationism, exceptionalism, free-riding and buck-passing all share is the (more or less explicit) notion of *not* doing something that is considered appropriate or necessary, of being forms of behaviour that do not conform with certain expectations. Under-aggressive or under-balancing states do not follow a certain systemic logic, exceptionalist and isolationist countries don't engage in world politics in a way commensurate to their potential influence, free-riders disappoint other members of the international community by taking advantage of public goods without paying for them, and buck-passing countries choose to rely on others for their security. This notion of not fulfilling the expectations of others is an important element associated with reluctance. Expectations might involve either calls to adopt a different policy course or exhortations to stop implementing certain policies, and both can be met with recalcitrance.

At the same time, the concept of reluctance stands between under-aggression, under-balancing, isolationism, exceptionalism, free-riding, and buck-passing since it can refer to different kinds of actors, to all kinds of settings regardless of whether they are cooperative or conflictive, and to any policy field (see Chapter 7). The question –'reluctance to do what?' – can therefore be answered in very different ways. For emerging or regional

---

[7]   A similar, but less frequently used, notion is also that of shirking responsibility: Schweller and Pu (2011: 42) define 'shirkers' as actors that 'want the privileges of power but are unwilling to pay for them by contributing to global governance'.

powers and for contexts of crisis like those analysed in this book, it can be the reluctance to meaningfully contribute to crisis management. For other kinds of actors and other settings, it can be the reluctance to cooperate or to contribute to public goods provision or to conform to the expectations of others, for example by aligning with their preferences or supporting them. In other words – and this is an important caveat to make – reluctance does *not* necessarily just refer to an unwillingness to lead or to pursue hegemonic policies, as suggested by studies that resort to notions such as 'reluctant hegemony'. And it is not necessarily just 'reluctance to do something', but can also refer to a hesitant and recalcitrant approach with regard to not doing something or discontinuing existing policies. Reluctance therefore constitutes a peculiar type of foreign policy that can be found across issue areas and settings. In the following sections, I proceed to flesh out what this concept entails exactly.

Reluctance: concept building

The identification of the broader semantic field of reluctance in IR and our discussion of related theoretical approaches has allowed us to obtain some insights into the 'background concept' (Adcock and Collier, 2001: 531) of reluctance. This is a useful starting point: 'concept reconstruction is a means whose ultimate purpose is to provide a cleaned-up basis for construction – that is, for the formation of concepts' (Sartori, 1984: 50). In other words, concept reconstruction helps us to grasp 'what is important about an entity' (Goertz, 2006: 27). On this basis, we can now proceed with concept building, and to that end we will follow the guidelines proposed by Goertz (2006) as this work provides important ideas on how to think about the structure of concepts.

The negative poles

The first step in concept building consists of identifying the 'basic level' of a concept, that is, the concept 'as used in theoretical propositions' (Goertz, 2006: 6). In our case, the basic-level concept is reluctance. A useful way to sharpen our understanding of a basic-level concept entails thinking explicitly about the negative pole of that concept, that is, about what the concept is not. For the case of reluctance, there is not a single obvious negative pole. Within the broader idea of 'non-reluctance', however, we can think of two dimensions that constitute the opposite of reluctance on two different continuums: (1) determination, and (2) being responsive to demands made by others.

Determination amounts to a resolute, decisive and consistent attitude, which involves the ability to make decisions without displaying much hesitation.

The concept of determination therefore encompasses the opposite of the ambivalence, incoherence, hesitancy and slowness that characterize reluctance. Responsiveness to others' demands means reacting readily and sympathetically to appeals and requests by other actors, particularly by less powerful actors in a hierarchical setting, such as that existing between emerging or regional powers and smaller neighbouring states. Potential followers can ask the rising power to participate in common initiatives, to deliver public goods, to support a certain cause, to act in a less intrusive manner – and many other things. A country that is responsive to such demands will not shirk responsibility, will not be unwilling to commit fully and will not display an obstructionist attitude towards the demands made by others – in other words, a responsive country will not be reluctant.

Determination and responsiveness therefore constitute different dimensions of the negative pole of reluctance. They can help us to clarify the actual 'constitutive' or 'secondary-level' dimensions of the concept of reluctance.[8]

Constitutive dimensions and concept structure

As illustrated in Figure 2.2, reluctance has two constitutive dimensions: hesitation and recalcitrance. These dimensions are 'constitutive' in the sense that they tell us what the basic-level concept of reluctance consists of: 'Concepts are theories about ontology: they are theories about the fundamental constitutive elements of a phenomenon' (Goertz, 2006: 5). As such, concepts are not just important as constructs that help us to grasp empirical reality, but they also have an impact on theorizing and hypothesis testing. As a consequence, concepts and the ways they are constructed have huge implications for all the successive phases of a research project (think of the implications of conceptualization for case selection); elements of causality are often inherent in concepts, and need to be appropriately acknowledged.

Hesitation is, along a continuum entailing different degrees of resolve in an actor's behaviour, the polar opposite of determination. It involves an ambivalent, incoherent attitude. Reluctance is therefore much more than just under-aggression or under-expansionism. Nor does reluctance necessarily amount to the adoption of a 'hands-off' policy, that is, to inactivity (see the discussion on isolationism and exceptionalism). A consistent refusal to get involved in a military dispute, for example, is

---

[8] Goertz (2006: 35) argues that the secondary-level dimensions of a concept will 'almost always refer to the positive concept', and that only in a second step will we have to think about the negative pole of each secondary-level dimension. In this case, however, I proceeded inversely by first thinking about what the constitutive dimensions of reluctance are not, before moving on to define them. This approach is extremely helpful in order to clarify the secondary dimensions themselves.

Figure 2.2: Negative poles, constitutive dimensions and indicators of reluctance

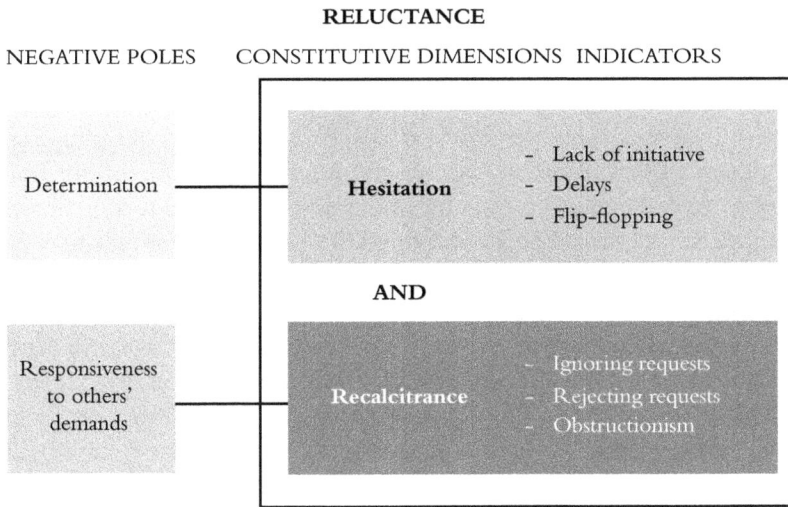

RELUCTANCE

NEGATIVE POLES   CONSTITUTIVE DIMENSIONS   INDICATORS

Negative Poles	Constitutive Dimensions	Indicators
Determination	**Hesitation**	- Lack of initiative - Delays - Flip-flopping
	AND	
Responsiveness to others' demands	**Recalcitrance**	- Ignoring requests - Rejecting requests - Obstructionism

not reluctant behaviour understood as hesitation, since it actually amounts to a clear and coherent policy course. For example, Japan's and Germany's security policies after the Second World War have often been characterized as 'reluctant to resort to the use of military force' (Berger, 1996: 318). However, this would not be a case of reluctance as I understand it in this study because these countries' policies were coherent and consistent and therefore lacked the element of hesitation. However, in cases where we start observing contrasting and incoherent statements on the need to become active, or possibly even some engagement followed by backtracking, these will be indicators of hesitation.

Recalcitrance is the second core dimension of reluctance, and it is the opposite of being responsive to others' demands – along a continuum referring to the degree of openness towards the wishes of others, especially of potential followers. It involves opposing the wishes articulated by others. For example, Fehl (2012: 4) highlights that the USA displayed a 'scepticism or outright opposition to multilateral treaty initiatives strongly favoured by European states'. The latter demanded a stronger commitment on the part of Washington, which, however, was recalcitrant – that is, unresponsive to the demands articulated by its European partners.

An essential step in building concepts is the clarification and discussion of their structure, which has huge consequences for their extension and intension (Sartori, 1970). In fact, depending on whether one adopts a necessary-and-sufficient conditions structure or a 'family resemblance' structure that does not entail any necessary conditions (Goertz, 2006: 35–46), the number of secondary dimensions will have an impact on the categories of phenomena that are covered by the concept. The concept of reluctance as developed here follows a traditional necessary-and-sufficient conditions structure: the two secondary dimensions, hesitation and recalcitrance, are necessary and jointly sufficient to define reluctance – and are therefore connected by the logical operator 'AND'.

A family resemblance structure is not suitable for a conceptualization of reluctance since it implies that all conditions are sufficient, but none is necessary. Adopting such a structure would have meant connecting hesitation and recalcitrance with the logical operator 'OR' and arguing that either hesitation or recalcitrance would be sufficient for characterizing foreign policy as 'reluctant'. However, in that case, the concept's extension would grow indefinitely since recalcitrance – a lack of responsiveness to the demands made by others – is an almost omnipresent feature of foreign policy: states are continually confronted with expectations articulated by very different actors, be they other countries, international organizations, transnational NGOs, their own public or other domestic actors. As these expectations and pressures will in most cases be contradictory, given the very different structural positions and interests of the actors articulating them, any foreign policy decision will invariably ignore or reject the demands made by some of these actors. Therefore, if recalcitrance were a sufficient condition to conceptualize reluctance, any foreign policy decision could be considered 'reluctant' and the concept itself would take a very different connotation as compared to its usage identified through concept reconstruction.

Recalcitrance alone cannot therefore count as a sufficient condition to define reluctance: it needs to be paired with hesitation. Similarly, hesitation itself is not identical with reluctance because it does not automatically entail a lack of responsiveness vis-à-vis the expectations articulated by others – even though incoherent and contradictory statements and policies will usually disappoint at least some expectations. By conceptualizing foreign policy reluctance as constituted by the necessary and jointly sufficient conditions of hesitation and recalcitrance, we avoid the ambiguities inherent in much of the literature, which amplify the concept's extension by treating reluctance in a loose and unspecified manner.

These thoughts on the concept structure of reluctance have theoretical implications. For example, the inclusion of recalcitrance in the concept will have an impact on the development of a theory of reluctance in international politics. The simple observation of an indecisive, flip-flopping foreign policy on the part of a government could in principle be easily termed reluctance, but the inclusion of the element of recalcitrance with its refusal to conform to the expectations of other actors has important consequences. For example, if we focus on the reluctance displayed by emerging and regional powers in their own regions, we should expect recalcitrance to matter when it comes to regional cooperation. In fact, a recalcitrant attitude vis-à-vis the wishes articulated by smaller regional countries will most likely lead to disillusionment and disaffection among them, and thus contribute to hampering regional cooperation. For example, India has long been recalcitrant in its approach to its smaller neighbours in South Asia, refusing to make concessions on matters such as trade. This has fuelled the suspicions of small countries of New Delhi, and has induced them to see China as an attractive alternative partner – with disastrous consequences for regional cooperation in South Asia (Destradi, 2012a). On a different note, in Chapter 3 we will see that competing expectations is an important factor that contributes to explaining the emergence of reluctance.

Operationalization

The third level of concepts is constituted by indicators to be applied in analysing empirical phenomena. An operationalization of reluctance in terms of hesitation and recalcitrance has the advantage of allowing us to avoid counterfactual arguments such as those used in publications that refer to the untapped leadership potential of 'reluctant' powers (see, for example, publications on Germany as a reluctant hegemon or, more generally, on Germany's role in the Eurozone crisis: Jones, 2010: 26; *The Economist*, 2013). In fact, those usages of the term 'reluctance' imply that something has not been done – for example, that Germany has not taken over a leadership role in Europe. Like the studies on 'under-aggression', which use counterfactuals to explain why something that would have been expected ('aggression') has not taken place (Meiser, 2015), most works that refer to 'reluctance' vaguely associate this notion with a lack of leadership or purpose. From such a perspective, reluctance would need to be thought of in terms of a counterfactual, that is, of what would have happened if an actor had not been reluctant – an approach that, of course, bears analytical difficulties. By contrast, this chapter develops indicators of hesitation and recalcitrance that refer to observable foreign policy behaviour and to expectations explicitly articulated by other actors. Thereby, these indicators allow us to identify reluctance on the basis of actual foreign policy and to avoid counterfactual reasoning.

Hesitation can be identified by the following indicators:

- Lack of initiative: this indicator implies that an actor does not make any decisions to react to a certain situation or crisis affecting it, or that it does not attempt to actively shape future events despite potentially having the ability to do so. Instead, it stays on the sidelines, is indecisive and leaves the initiative to others. A lack of initiative might entail free-riding, but it does not necessarily refer to a complete unwillingness to shoulder a fair share of the costs of public goods provision; it rather refers to a more passive policy and lack of ideas on how to deal with a situation. With a particular focus on powerful countries such as emerging or regional powers, the initiative is left to smaller states, which develop and implement suggestions and solutions on a specific issue or crisis that is relevant not just to them but also to the emerging power.

- Delaying: hesitation can take a more explicit form if an actor buys time and does not stick to a previously agreed time frame, thereby postponing important decisions in dealing with a specific issue or crisis. This indicator is not limited to a specific cause of the delay, which can be either purposeful, that is, employed as part of a bargaining strategy, or unintended, for example due to specific procedures or obstacles in the decision-making process. This reflects the fact that reluctance can be both the result of an unwillingness or inability to pursue a determined and responsive policy.
- Flip-flopping: this is the most evident form of hesitation. It can be observed if an actor pursues inconsistent policies, that is, policies that are not coherent, but keep changing rapidly.[9] Moreover, flip-flopping can also be assessed by looking at an actor's statements. These might change frequently, reflecting an inconsistent approach to an issue; or there might be contradictions, for example in statements on a specific issue made by different members of the executive or other representatives of the same government, or members of a governing coalition.

Recalcitrance, which is a lack of responsiveness towards the demands made by others, can be assessed through the following indicators:

- Ignoring requests made by others: the recalcitrant actor (in our case, the government of the emerging or regional power) does not react to calls made by other actors, and its policies do not reflect the preferences articulated by them.
- Rejecting requests: the recalcitrant actor explicitly refuses to comply with the wishes articulated by other actors.
- Obstructing others' initiatives: the recalcitrant actor hampers the activities promoted by others. This does not necessarily happen through an explicit

---

[9] Flip-flopping differs from policy changes that emerge through learning, which can be observed in sequential decision making, that is, when policy makers have to make a series of decisions about an issue over time, but in between they deal with other matters (Hermann, 2012: 5). By contrast, reluctance refers to single issues that are addressed continuously, without decision makers turning their attention to other matters. Within such a context, policies that keep changing back and forth are considered as flip-flopping. They differ from learning as they do not develop in a linear manner or display just one or a few major turnabouts, but rather entail repeated changes of direction.

veto or other formal procedures, but can take place informally, for example in the context of multilateral decision-making processes (Sartori, 1984).

Among the indicators of both hesitation and recalcitrance, there is a logical 'OR', which implies that for each dimension it is sufficient to observe at least one of the three indicators in order to classify foreign policy as hesitant or recalcitrant, but that more than one indicator can be observed at the same time. For example, a hesitant country can display both a lack of initiative in the management of serious crises and at the same time it can delay initiatives proposed by others. Similarly, a recalcitrant country can both ignore requests made by others and at the same time hamper their initiatives.

Importantly, both hesitation and recalcitrance can occur to different degrees, implying that each of these dimensions entails a continuum. In his work on social science concepts, Goertz (2006: 34) highlights the usefulness of treating 'all concepts as continuous'. This allows us to reduce measurement error by acknowledging that particular cases can lie at the weaker or stronger end of a conceptual continuum; it thereby also helps to avoid theorizing on the basis of very special cases (Goertz, 2006). Relatedly, Goertz argues in favour of an ontology that explicitly acknowledges 'borderline cases' or 'grey zones'. Grey zones include cases at the fuzzy border between positive cases, which correspond to a certain concept (in our study, cases of reluctance), and negative cases (in our study, cases of non-reluctance). Grey zones often involve 'transitions': for example, Goertz (2006) mentions democratic transition as a typical grey zone between democracy and autocracy. The existence of such grey zones needs to be 'openly confront[ed]' (Goertz and Mazur, 2008: 30) since it has huge implications for both measurement and case selection. In the following paragraphs, I will discuss the notions of a continuous concept and grey zones with reference to reluctance.

The concept of reluctance is continuous since both its secondary dimensions, hesitation and recalcitrance, can occur to different degrees. The indicators of recalcitrance are arrayed along a continuum, ranging from a mere ignoring of requests to the rejection of requests and active obstructionism of initiatives promoted by other actors. Depending on the combination of these indicators, on the frequency with which they appear, and on the salience of the issues on which a state is recalcitrant, we can classify recalcitrance as low, medium or high, with an appropriate weighting to be applied in specific empirical analyses. The same is true for hesitation, where a lack of initiative is a less explicit form of hesitation as compared to the delaying of decisions, while flip-flopping is the most evident type of hesitant behaviour.

These different intensities and the possible different combinations of lack of initiative, delaying and flip-flopping can therefore lead to varying

Table 2.1: Intensities of reluctance

		Hesitation (Lack of initiative/delaying/flip-flopping)			
		None (= determination)	Low	Medium	High
Recalcitrance (*Ignoring requests/rejecting requests/blocking initiatives*)	None (= responsiveness)	No reluctance	No reluctance	No reluctance	No reluctance
	Low	No reluctance	Low reluctance	Medium reluctance	High reluctance
	Medium	No reluctance	Medium reluctance	Medium reluctance	High reluctance
	High	No reluctance	High reluctance	High reluctance	Medium reluctance

degrees of hesitation (see Table 2.1). For example, a country whose foreign policy is strongly flip-flopping in crucial decision processes will obviously count as more reluctant than a country whose foreign policy displays little flip-flopping, strong initiatives, but some delays in the implementation of policies. As illustrated in Table 2.1, the combination of indicators of hesitation and recalcitrance leads to the identification of different degrees of reluctant behaviour. This more fine-grained assessment of reluctance, which goes beyond a mere dichotomous understanding of the concept, can prove helpful in the assessment of variation in foreign policy reluctance. Moreover, it will prove useful in tracing processes of policy change by highlighting shifts in the intensity of reluctance.

Table 2.1 also highlights that hesitation and recalcitrance are both necessary conditions for reluctance. That is, a recalcitrant but determined (non-hesitant) attitude – for example a coherent refusal to comply with smaller regional countries' wishes on the part of a dominant regional power – would not amount to reluctance. Brazil's policies in the 1960s and 1970s, for example, were recalcitrant but not hesitant – and therefore non-reluctant. After the military coup of 1964, Brazil was not at all responsive towards the expectations of smaller Latin American countries (recalcitrance). Brazil pursued, instead, a rather intrusive policy in the region, for example by intervening in support of a coup that brought to power a Brazil-friendly government in Bolivia in 1971, or by letting its secret services carry out 'anti-subversive activities' on Uruguayan territory (Hurrell, 1992: 42). While some elements of incoherence were in place – for example the mixing of an aggressive 'talk of "moving frontiers" and historical missions to regional predominance' with a parallel rhetoric on the 'need for Latin American unity' (Hurrell, 1992: 27) – Brazil's approach to the region during the 1960s–70s was overall certainly not hesitant, and therefore not reluctant, but rather openly assertive.

Similarly, a hesitant but responsive attitude would not correspond to reluctance: while it might be hard for an actor to be fully responsive while pursuing an entirely incoherent, flip-flopping policy, a delayed reaction to the wishes of others or conforming to their wishes while not developing own initiatives would not qualify as reluctance.

The 'grey zones' of reluctance include cases of transition between reluctant and non-reluctant policies. Two interesting grey zones emerge at the upper end of each continuum, that is, in cases of high recalcitrance or of high hesitation. If an actor is hesitant and highly recalcitrant, this recalcitrance might become so strong as to prevail over hesitation: the blocking of others' initiatives will become more and more determined, up to the point of leaving hesitation behind and becoming a coherent and consistent policy. For example, India was so recalcitrant about deepening cooperation within the South Asian Association for Regional Cooperation (SAARC) (see Michael, 2013) that this was no longer a reluctant policy – quite to the contrary, it was a rather determined and consistent approach. A consistent refusal to lead despite calls to do so would entail high recalcitrance, but no hesitation. This is why countries that consistently refuse to lead would not be considered 'reluctant' according to the understanding of reluctance adopted in this book. This clarification is particularly important against the backdrop of much commentary use of the term 'reluctance' to imply a straightforward refusal to lead.

If recalcitrance is combined with high hesitation, we have another 'grey zone': indecisiveness can be so strong that the reluctant actor becomes unable to make a choice and is temporarily 'paralysed'. The transition towards non-reluctance is completed when the paralysis turns into consistent inaction, since that very inaction ultimately amounts to a determined attitude. An empirical illustration of policies that are moderately recalcitrant but highly hesitant is provided by the case of the EU and its approach to the Libya crisis of 2011. In fact, the EU was very hesitant in its approach. Long after the beginning of military operations by French, US, British and other forces, and 'With [NATO's] "Operation Unified Protector" well under way, the EU continued its debate as to whether it would have any military role in the conflict' (Engberg, 2014: 159). It took the Council of the European Union three weeks to decide that it would establish a humanitarian mission to Libya, and the actual existence of that mission was made conditional on a request by the United Nations (UN) Office for the Coordination of Humanitarian Affairs (OCHA) (Koenig, 2014: 259). As no such request was ever made, the EU mission, which had been prematurely called EUFOR Libya, never came into existence. The EU's high degree of hesitation (lack of initiative and flip-flopping in the form of half-hearted measures combined with rhetoric condemnation)[10] was paired with a lack of full responsiveness to 'internal and external demands for [it] to act as a "comprehensive power"' (Koenig, 2014: 251; see also Engberg, 2014: 160–1). We can interpret the EU's policies and its inability to make a decision on the establishment of a Common Security and Defence Policy (CSDP) mission as very high hesitation and almost paralysis – a 'grey zone', given the potential for a transition from reluctance to consistent (and non-reluctant) rejection of any kind of engagement. Ultimately, however, the EU's policies shifted back from the grey zone to reluctance: hesitation was not so extreme as to lead to complete inaction since a decision on the mission was eventually made; moreover, the fact that EUFOR Libya never came into existence was ultimately not due to the EU's inaction, but rather to the lack of a request by the OCHA.

Another particular set of cases is those in which an actor is both highly recalcitrant (that is, rather openly hampering the initiatives promoted by others) and, at the same time, highly hesitant. In this case, we can expect the two dimensions of hesitation and recalcitrance to partially offset each other, so that the outcome will be a comparatively more moderate form of reluctance (as illustrated in the bottom right field in Table 2.1).

Summary

This chapter has aimed to develop a conceptualization of reluctance in international politics. The conceptualization built on (1) existing uses of the concept in the literature in order to identify the broad semantic field to which it relates; and (2) the concept's relationship to similar terms in the academic debate. Based on this concept reconstruction, reluctance was characterized as entailing the two constitutive dimensions of hesitation and recalcitrance. Corresponding indicators for empirical analyses were identified and the concept structure was outlined.

The discussion of under-aggression, under-balancing, isolationism, exceptionalism, free-riding and buck-passing has shown that the field of IR offers a range of conceptual tools related to reluctance, but that none of them is able to capture the essence of reluctance. The introduction of reluctance to the conceptual lexicon of IR has an added value in that it allows us to capture a particular way of doing foreign policy – one entailing hesitation and, at the same time, a recalcitrant attitude vis-à-vis the expectations articulated by others. This specific type of foreign policy seems to be rather widespread, but IR has so far failed to acknowledge its existence, usually assuming that states follow a clear and consistent

---

[10] See, for example, European Council (2011).

foreign policy path – or highlighting very specific forms of deviation from expected behaviour. In Chapter 3, I will proceed to outline a theoretical framework to explain the occurrence of reluctance and the variations in reluctant foreign policy that we can observe across different cases, issue areas and time periods.

3

Theorizing Reluctance
in World Politics

In order to explain why reluctance occurs, this chapter develops a theorization of reluctance in world politics. The conceptual discussion in Chapter 2 forms the basis of such theorization: as Goertz (2006: 5) argues in his seminal work, concept building is always strongly connected with theorizing because all social science concepts always inherently entail a causal dimension. In this chapter, I will therefore proceed by building on the two constitutive dimensions of reluctance – hesitation and recalcitrance – to develop a theoretical framework that helps explain why reluctance occurs in some cases but not in others, and why it occurs to different degrees. At the core of this theoretical framework is the very notion of foreign policy as a field that brings together domestic and international factors: on the one hand, foreign policies are clearly the result of a domestic process through which a range of actors within society aim to influence the government's approach to international affairs, and a number of domestic actors and institutions interact to reach foreign policy decisions. On the other hand, a country's foreign policy is always embedded in an international context, and subject to a range of constraints and expectations articulated by other actors.

This interplay of domestic and international factors will be the overarching framework to explain variations in the occurrence of reluctance. Those factors are clearly related to the two constitutive dimensions of reluctance: hesitation (with its elements of indecisiveness, flip-flopping and delaying) can be analysed in relation to domestic factors, and more specifically to the domestic process of preference formation, which can make it particularly difficult for a government to pursue a consistent and determined foreign policy (Destradi, 2018: 2224–5). As we will see, these difficulties in domestic preference formation can emerge for several reasons (political weakness, limited capacity, cognitive problems or normative struggles). Recalcitrance, which by definition refers to the idea of not conforming to others' expectations, is related to international factors, specifically to the expectations raised by international actors (Destradi, 2018: 2224–5). As we will see, these domestic and international explanatory factors are deeply interrelated.

The following sections will build on a diverse set of literatures from various theoretical traditions of International Relations (IR), Foreign Policy Analysis (FPA), Social Psychology and Psychology, to detail how different kinds of difficulties in domestic preference formation and competing international expectations will lead to reluctance. In a nutshell, I expect reluctance to occur if governments have difficulties in devising clear foreign policy preferences while facing competing international expectations addressed to them.

Difficulties in domestic preference formation

Foreign policy is always and inevitably the result of a domestic process through which a range of actors within a state compete for influence in shaping how the government will position itself vis-à-vis international actors. Liberal approaches to IR, most notably the work by Moravcsik (1997), focus on state preferences, arguing that they emerge as a result of interactions among societal actors striving to influence foreign policy. According to this understanding of international politics, 'The fundamental actors … are individuals and private groups, who are on the average rational and risk-averse and who organize exchange and collective action to promote differentiated interests under constraints imposed by material scarcity, conflicting values, and variations in societal influence' (Moravcsik, 1997: 516; emphasis removed). Ultimately, the interests of 'a subset of domestic society' (Moravcsik, 1997: 518; emphasis removed) will end up shaping state preferences on foreign policy, with institutions serving as a 'transmission belt' (Moravcsik, 1997: 518), and therefore selecting whose interests find greater resonance.

State preferences are therefore obviously not fixed, but vary across issues and can change over time (Moravcsik and Schimmelfennig, 2019: 66). Foreign Policy Analysis (FPA) as a subfield in IR has addressed in a much more systematic and specific manner how foreign policy comes about and which societal actors and institutional setups contribute to shaping foreign policy-making processes as well as foreign policy outcomes. The underlying assumption of FPA is that 'all that occurs between nations and across nations is grounded in human decision makers acting singly or in groups' (Hudson, 2005: 1). In the following sections, I will develop a theorization of reluctance in world politics that takes seriously the agent-oriented and actor-specific approach that is typical of FPA (Hudson, 2005: 2–3). In line with such theorizing, but also with liberal and constructivist IR, I start with the basic assumption that there is no such thing as a given 'national interest' but that, instead, foreign policy is always the result of complex processes and interactions among domestic actors.

My main contention is that the formation of foreign policy preferences or, broadly speaking, the identification of what a state (or, for that matter, any other collective actor involved in world politics) wants is not an easy and straightforward task. One of the reasons for the indecisive, muddling-through, non-committal behaviours that can be identified as 'reluctant' can therefore be found in the many hurdles that lie in such a process of foreign policy preference formation.[1] Difficulties in domestic preference formation can emerge for a number of reasons. I have grouped the most important ones under the labels 'political weakness', 'limited capacity', 'cognitive problems' and 'normative struggles'. In the following subsections, I will address how each of these factors can explain why governments might face difficulties in devising a clear preference on the course to follow in foreign policy in a specific case or on a specific issue or crisis. These explanations build on distinct theoretical traditions in IR and FPA. To some extent, they might reinforce each other: most prominently, for example, underlying normative struggles could contribute to the political weakness of a government. Nevertheless, they should be analytically disentangled given the distinct logics driving them. Importantly, the effects of each of these factors will likely be exacerbated by competing expectations articulated by international actors, which will put additional pressure on an already indecisive government.[2]

---

[1] Such a process is not necessarily identical with the process of foreign policy decision making, as preference formation (at least analytically speaking) will usually precede the actual process of decision making: before deciding how to behave, governments will normally need to know what they want. If this is not the case, they will end up pursuing exactly those hesitant policies I focus on in this book – with hesitation being one of the constitutive components of reluctance. This is where my theoretical approach deviates from the FPA literature on 'low-quality decision making' and on pathologies in the process of decision making such as groupthink (see, for example, Schafer and Crichlow, 2010), since that literature is mainly interested in problems in the foreign policy decision-making process, but does not explicitly focus on the underlying divergent interests and norms that might lead to hesitation. Moreover, my approach builds on the literature on foreign policy failure and 'fiascos' (see, for example, Oppermann and Spencer, 2016), but differs from it in a number of ways. In particular, I do not claim that reluctance is automatically a form of failure, but that it can even be a deliberately chosen policy, at least for a while. Moreover, I am not necessarily interested in goal attainment, but rather in reluctance as a peculiar type or way of doing foreign policy.

[2] In this chapter, I mainly refer to governments, as nation-states will be the focus of the empirical analysis in the following chapters, and as much of the literature focuses on foreign policy making by nation-states. However, the basic underlying idea of having competing external pressures and, at the same time, difficulties in devising a clear course of action due to competing internal pressures or different normative approaches by single groups or individuals can also be applied to all kinds of other collective actors engaging in world politics (from local governments to NGOs to multinational corporations, and so on). Both the concept and the theory of reluctance are, in other words, definitely

Political weakness

The first possible explanation for difficulties in preference formation relates to the political weakness of a government. The underlying idea is that stable and cohesive governments will find it easier to devise a clear course of action in foreign policy, and to formulate goals and priorities that are not immediately called into question and that do not lead to hesitation in foreign policy. In the case studies analysed in the following chapters, I have largely tried to exclude this potential explanatory factor for the emergence of hesitation by explicitly focusing on democratic governments during phases of political stability. For a more general theorization of reluctance, it is nevertheless important to keep in mind this explanatory factor.

The literature in the field of FPA has addressed the issue of whether governments' political weakness can have an impact on foreign policy mainly by focusing on coalition governments or, more generally, on 'coalition decision units' (Hagan et al, 2001). We can speak about a coalition decision unit if the authority to make decisions on foreign policy does not reside with a single actor or group but is, instead, dispersed among several political actors. In parliamentary democracies, these will be coalition governments. The literature on governing coalitions has highlighted that these 'face formidable problems of mutual oversight and control of the political executive' (Strøm et al, 2010: 531), and are generally less effective and efficient because of their, on average, shorter duration in power (Bejar et al, 2011).

Even more importantly, coalition governments are particularly likely to end up being deadlocked due to disagreements among coalition partners and to the very fragmentation of political authority (Hagan et al, 2001), which will induce them to 'produce very little coordinated policy' (Kaarbo and Beasley, 2008: 71) – something related (if not identical) to hesitation. Junior coalition partners might be particularly susceptible to pursue 'issue ownership' and to 'highjack' a coalition's foreign policy by threatening to withdraw from the coalition and therefore to bring the government down.[3] The power of small coalition partners will manifest itself most clearly if decisions require unanimity among the members of a coalition: reaching such unanimity might lead to long negotiations and potentially to delays and even paralysis of a government (Kaarbo, 2012: 33). Moreover, the result of lengthy negotiations among coalition partners could be an unconvincing and half-hearted minimum compromise reached after much back-and-forth

---

able to travel beyond the realm of international politics. This will be discussed in greater detail in Chapter 7.

[3] Kaarbo and Beasley (2008) have shown that coalition governments will pursue more extreme (either conflictive or peaceful) foreign policies due to the pressure exercised by small coalition partners.

negotiation to avoid the fall of the government, but clearly entailing the typical elements of hesitation, from a lack of initiative to flip-flopping.

Studies on Italian coalition governments, for example, have emphasized how governments' instability and related political weakness have hampered the emergence of a bipartisan consensus on foreign policy (Andreatta et al, 2002). According to Oppermann et al (2017), these weaknesses of coalition governments can be exacerbated by certain institutional constellations such as the issue of whether the senior or junior coalition partner holds the foreign ministry, or whether the foreign minister enjoys a high degree of discretion in policy making. Intra-coalition conflicts over foreign policy issues will be particularly likely to erupt if different parties hold the prime minister's office and the foreign ministry. Moreover, the likelihood of deadlock will increase in coalition governments where the junior coalition partner holds the foreign ministry but is constrained by a number of checks and balances that limit the foreign ministry's autonomy (Oppermann et al, 2017: 493–6). Still, some authors also highlight that coalition governments ultimately have the potential to produce more legitimate policies by allowing for the inclusion of minority viewpoints (see Kaarbo, 2012: 35–6).

Yet, the logic of coalition decision units not only applies to parliamentary democracies with multiparty cabinets. Hagan et al (2001) argue that we can find the same issues in presidential democracies in which the legislative and executive branches are controlled by competing parties,[4] and also in authoritarian regimes plagued by rivalries among competing factions and agencies. In defective democracies (Croissant and Merkel, 2019), for example, government instability can emerge because the de facto power lies with other actors in the state, such as the military, which might threaten to topple the government at any moment and may have already repeatedly done so in the past.

In authoritarian regimes, the government might also be weakened due to the de facto power of other institutional actors or due to strong tensions among competing factions. As Hagan et al (2001) point out, fragmentation can emerge in one-party regimes, monarchies or military juntas if there are several competing factions that are ultimately needed to uphold the government's authority. 'Fragmented action' will emerge in foreign policy if there are no clear rules on decision making and if no actor is powerful enough to unequivocally shape preferences (Hagan et al, 2001: 177–81). Moreover, in all kinds of regimes displaying coalition decision units, deadlock

---

[4] The French case, where cohabitation between a president and a prime minister of different parties can occur, reveals that clearly defined rules can mitigate the effect of this kind of coalition decision unit – even though political parties will still compete for attention, including on foreign policy issues (Pierce, 1991).

will emerge if decisions do not have to be unanimous (and therefore there are no veto players blocking them entirely), but if the actors that form part of the coalition decision unit are unwilling to bargain and are distrustful of each other (Hagan et al, 2001: 177–81).

We can therefore conclude by summarizing the findings of the literature on coalition governments in democracies and, more broadly, on coalition decision units in all kinds of regimes as follows: politically weak governments of all kinds will face huge problems in devising consistent preferences on foreign policy, even more so if the rules of decision making are not clear. If there is competition among multiple factions or actors who have different interests and are highly suspicious of each other and unwilling to compromise, a hesitant foreign policy will likely be the outcome. As we will see, we can expect these tensions to be reinforced by competing expectations and pressures from international actors. For example, international supporters or ideologically close patrons of single factions might compete over political influence on a country, thereby exacerbating political weakness and reinforcing hesitation in foreign policy. At the same time, in particularly severe crises, disagreement among coalition partners might be set aside for a while in the name of the 'national interest', leading to some consensus on foreign policy even in weak and divided governments (see Beasley et al, 2001: 221). As we will see, however, severe crises can lead to reluctance for other reasons.

While the case studies in this book focus on stable governments, thereby excluding government weakness as an explanation for hesitation, a few words on operationalization are in order here: if governments have slim majorities, if there is cohabitation in presidential systems, or if single coalition partners in a governing coalition are in a position to bring the government down, these may be indications of government weakness. The same applies for the presence of strong rivalries among different factions or agencies in authoritarian regimes. In these cases, it will be worthwhile exploring in greater detail through process tracing whether reluctance emerged because of difficulties in reaching common preferences among coalition partners on specific foreign policy issues.

Limited capacity

Another factor leading to hesitation in foreign policy is capacity problems. Here, the basic idea is that a government might have clarity on the goals it wants to achieve in its foreign policy, but that it will face huge difficulties in implementing its policies due to capacity problems. This does not imply that all small states and weak countries will automatically pursue a reluctant foreign policy. For one, the literature on small states has shown that even countries with limited resources can serve as norm entrepreneurs or adopt other creative ways to exercise influence in international affairs (see, for example, Benwell, 2011; Corbett et al, 2019). By contrast, small states might choose to pursue an approach of consistent non-engagement in foreign policy due to their limited capacities (see Chapter 7). As discussed in Chapter 2, a consistent policy of isolationism or neutrality, or a coherent refusal to become engaged in international crises would not count as reluctance: if they are implemented in a consistent manner, these policies are not hesitant and are therefore not reluctant. Instead, what we are interested in here are cases in which countries pursue hesitant and recalcitrant (and therefore reluctant) policies, which often manifest themselves in a mix of engagement and disengagement, or in half-hearted, muddling-through policies. These not only emerge due to government weakness, but also possibly due to weaknesses of another, more structural, kind: due to plain capacity problems in the country's foreign policy apparatus.[5] Decision makers, even if they centralize power in their own hands in a crisis situation, will always need to rely on the bureaucracies tasked with foreign policy-related issues: 'Governmental organizations still provide much of the information that decision-makers need to reach a decision' (Verbeek, 2017: 32). Foreign ministries' policy-making capacity (Amorim Neto and Malamud, 2019) is fundamental as bureaucracies play an important role in pre-selecting the alternative courses of action that are proposed to policy makers as well as in collecting evidence on the feasibility and chances of success of specific policies.

The FPA literature on foreign policy 'fiascos' or 'failures' does not generally put much emphasis on such structural capacity problems, which might plague a country's foreign policy apparatus, possibly because most case studies analysed in such literature are from great powers or more generally from the Global North (see, for example, t' Hart, 1990; Schafer and Crichlow, 2010; Verbeek, 2017; Kruck et al, 2018b). However, many countries in the Global South, even emerging powers striving for global status and recognition, might have difficulties in implementing a determined and responsive (that is, non-reluctant) foreign policy simply because their foreign ministries are helplessly understaffed or underfunded, or (relatedly) because their foreign policy is over-stretched (Marthoz, 2012). Even wealthy countries such as Israel are often mentioned as having an understaffed foreign ministry (Goren, 2020), and populist governments from the USA to Venezuela or the Philippines are well known for personalizing power and stripping the foreign policy bureaucracy of much-needed resources (Destradi and Plagemann, 2019; Drezner, 2019).

---

[5]   For an operationalization of policy capacity not explicitly focused on foreign policy, see Wu et al (2015).

A lack of foreign policy expertise due to underfunded universities or the absence of autonomous think tanks can contribute to difficulties for a government to formulate clear and independent foreign policy goals, possibly withstanding pressures from powerful allies or donors. Bureaucratic apparatuses can also suffer weaknesses after decades of corruption and nepotism, ultimately making it almost impossible for them to work efficiently. Similar problems can be found not only in states, but also in other international actors, most notably in international organizations. The World Health Organization (WHO) has often been studied as an example of an organization facing severe deficiencies in its procedures as well as 'poor coordination efforts [and] obstructive intra-organizational dynamics' (Kruck et al, 2018a: 15), which are considered to have led to its difficulties in managing pandemics such as 'Swine flu' in 2009 or the Ebola outbreak in 2014 (Kamradt-Scott, 2018).

Bureaucratic organizations not only play a crucial role in providing the necessary information for policy making, but also in actually implementing foreign policy (Verbeek, 2017: 33). In the field of foreign policy, the actors involved have traditionally been the foreign ministry, the defence ministry, and also the ministry of finance, the ministry of trade and the ministries or agencies tasked with development cooperation – and in recent decades, the number and scope of actors has increased enormously. As globalization has made a range of formerly domestic issue areas become transnational, the authority of foreign ministries has eroded and a number of new actors have come to play a role in shaping foreign policy, from additional departments and agencies (Jones and Hameiri, 2021: 36–7) to subnational units such as cities or states in federations, as actors of so-called 'paradiplomacy' (Sharma et al, 2020).

Given the proliferation of actors involved, it is little wonder that foreign policy frequently becomes an object in a struggle among different bureaucratic actors.[6] The FPA literature on bureaucratic politics has long addressed the issue of competing interests and goals of different government agencies, which end up shaping a country's foreign policy (Allison, 1971; Allison and Halperin, 1972). As Allison (1971: 146) puts it, government decisions are not the result of a single and consistent rational decision, but of 'politicking' among different government agencies. Foreign policy should therefore be characterized as 'a *resultant* of various bargaining games among players in the national government' (Allison, 1971: 6; original emphasis). In other words,

---

[6] Some of the mechanisms are similar to those in coalition governments, but the focus here is not on political weakness but rather on bureaucratic infighting. This can ultimately become a structural characteristic that is longer lived compared to political conflicts that might be resolved with a change in government.

there are no clear preferences at all to be formed – 'Governmental action does not presuppose government intention' (Allison, 1971: 175) – as it just emerges as a consequence of competition among the numerous bureaucratic actors involved with their distinct interests and goals.

In the best case, the outcome of such a struggle will be 'a compromise reflecting the power relations between the departments involved' (Verbeek, 2017: 33).The inclusion of a larger number of actors in foreign policy will also have a positive effect on the legitimacy of the policies adopted. However, the outcome could also be delays in the implementation of policies or a lack of initiative if bureaucratic infighting makes a compromise difficult to achieve, or flip-flopping if different agencies are able to prevail at different moments. While non-coordination (Bach and Wegrich, 2019) and bureaucratic infighting are widespread (and, to some extent, entirely normal) phenomena, if they go beyond a certain point they will hamper the work of ministries and agencies so as to ultimately weaken them. For this reason, extreme bureaucratic conflicts could ultimately be equated to capacity problems as they can undermine the bureaucracy's ability to support the government in the provision of information and the implementation of policies.

A related notion is that of fragmentation, which Jones and Hameiri (2021) put forward to explain why China's foreign policy is often contradictory and inconsistent. Here, the focus is primarily on different actors pursuing distinct policies on their own, with insufficient coordination among them – something that at first glance seems paradoxical in a country like China, which is often assumed to be strongly centralized. While phenomena related to such a lack of coordination do not fit neatly under the label of capacity problems, they certainly reflect idiosyncrasies in the process of preference formation that can lead to hesitation.

In order to assess capacity problems in the empirical analysis, I will discuss foreign ministries' policy-making capacities and look for instances of non-coordination or bureaucratic infighting, trying to reconstruct whether, for example, flip-flopping was a result of these processes at bureaucracy level. Expert interviews with individuals involved in the policy-making process or closely observing it will provide valuable additional insights into potential difficulties in preference formation that can be traced back to such capacity issues.

Cognitive problems

Another possible explanation for hesitation is related to cognitive and psychological factors. The literature in the field of FPA has long recognized that actors involved in foreign policy making might not act as rational decision makers seeking to maximize utility, but that their rationality may be 'bounded' (Simon, 1979). The main problem faced by decision makers is ultimately 'confusion' (Rathbun, 2007: 546) or uncertainty, which 'naturally allies with doubt, hesitation, [and] delay' (Steinbruner, 1974: 333).

An interdisciplinary strand of literature building on the insights of Psychology and Social Psychology has pointed out several ways in which bounded rationality and cognitive problems might play out in foreign policy. As Simon (1955: 101) puts it in his seminal work, '[b]ecause of the psychological limits of the organism (particularly with respect to computational and predictive ability), actual human rationality-striving can at best be an extremely crude and simplified approximation to the kind of global rationality that is implied, for example, by game-theoretical models'. The literature on bounded rationality therefore points to the need to consider the limits of human cognitive capacity for 'discovering alternatives, computing their consequences under certainty or uncertainty, and making comparisons among them' (Simon, 1979: 15). Faced with their own limitations, decision makers will develop strategies that enable them to still make acceptable decisions. Instead of reaching solutions that maximize their utility, they will adopt 'good-enough' solutions, for example 'stop[ping] searching for information once they have found a satisfactory alternative' (Redd and Mintz, 2013: S13) – what is called 'satisficing'.

How can we make sense of these heuristic strategies? Cybernetic theory argues that decision makers actually cope with uncertainty by 'understanding the decision as a simple one that does not require elaborate mental processing' (Mintz and DeRouen, 2010: 69) and by using information feedback loops – a highly simplified decision-making procedure that the proponents of the cybernetic model consider quite successful (Steinbruner, 1974: 13). Most other approaches to decision making under uncertainty, however, highlight the problems related to cognitive issues in decision making. Based on insights from Psychology, several studies share the assessment that decision makers will face huge problems in dealing with complex information and inextricably complicated situations. As Renshon and Renshon (2008: 511) put it, '[t]he enormous complexity of the real world, coupled with our inability to apprehend much less understand all its elements, leads to methods of complexity reduction'. Poliheuristic theory points out that individuals use cognitive shortcuts to simplify complex decision tasks – including false assumptions about correlations between factors, insensitivity to sample size, biases in choosing which pieces of information to consider, and so on, something that leads to 'systematic and predictable errors' (Tversky and Kahneman, 1974: 1131). Other analytical approaches highlight that decision makers will cope with uncertainty and complexity by resorting to analogical reasoning (that is, applying knowledge from past experiences to current decisions), by using standard operating procedures that might not fit the specific case, or by letting all kinds of biases shape their decisions (for an overview, see Redd and Mintz, 2013).[7]

While such cognitive phenomena are certainly important possible explanations for hesitation, they are extremely difficult to analyse empirically for political decision makers – actually, such cognitive processes are most reliably analysed in an experimental setting (see, for example, Jobe, 2003). As an alternative, it is more reasonable to focus on the factors that might have unleashed these cognitive mechanisms, assuming that they might lead to hesitation in foreign policy. I therefore argue that three interrelated factors play a central role in triggering hesitation in foreign policy: the severity of the crisis, time pressure and the novelty of a situation.

First of all, it is important to take into consideration whether actors involved in foreign policy making consider a crisis to be *particularly severe and threatening*. As the literature on crises has highlighted, actors' perceptions of a situation as a crisis are important (Bösch et al, 2020). Among many defining criteria, 'we speak of a crisis when policy makers experience "a serious threat to the basic structures or the fundamental values and norms of a system, which under time pressure and highly uncertain circumstances necessitates making vital decisions"' (Boin et al, 2005: 2). Making decisions in crisis situations can lead to decisional conflicts, that is, to 'situations producing the perception of a serious dilemma, that is, a choice between alternatives each of which would entail important losses' (Verbeek, 2017: 38). Decisional conflicts are therefore loss–loss situations, which can be expected to produce high emotional stress (Verbeek, 2017: 38; Sawatzky, 2022: 9).

---

[7] Another aspect sometimes mentioned in the literature is groupthink, which emerges when decision makers faced with stressful situations resort to 'excessive concurrence-seeking' (t' Hart, 1990: 7) in a group. Groupthink takes place if the decision-making group is highly cohesive, operates in an organizational context that displays some 'faults' and is faced with a stressful situation (t' Hart, 1990: 7–9): 'To preserve the clubby atmosphere, group members suppress personal doubts, silence dissenters and follow the group leader's suggestions. They have a strong belief in the inherent morality of the group, combined with a decidedly evil picture of the group's opponents' (t' Hart, 1990: 6). Groupthink produces 'overestimation of the group (illusion of invulnerability; belief in inherent morality)', close-mindedness and pressures towards uniformity (t' Hart, 1990: 10). But the 'fiascos' that are usually considered to emerge from groupthink are mostly not related to hesitation but to its contrary: to 'hasty and reckless policies' (t' Hart, 1990: 6). Decision-making groups will 'strive for a quick and painless unanimity on the issues that the group has to confront' (t' Hart, 1990: 6). Moreover, groupthink will lead decision makers to stick to previous policies, even getting entrapped in past commitments (t' Hart, 1990: 87–98), but this ultimately involves a high degree of consistency in foreign policy making. All this is quite the contrary of the indecisive and hesitant policies that are typical of reluctance.

Approaches from Psychology reach different conclusions about actors' ability to make decisions under stress: while some individuals might be able to focus better on their tasks under conditions of stress (Renshon and Renshon, 2008), others will be particularly likely to resort to shortcuts. Situations of crisis and high levels of stress might therefore induce decision makers to ignore relevant information or important alternative courses of action, to oversimplify, to rely on historical analogies, to overestimate the capabilities of the opponents and to adopt 'random behavior' (Mintz and DeRouen, 2010: 29) – something much in line with the flip-flopping that is typical of hesitation. In bureaucratic organizations, difficult decisions can lead to 'Defensive avoidance in the form of procrastination [and] buck passing' (Janis and Mann, 1979: 107), which will lead to another typical form of hesitation, namely delays.

Second, very much related to the issue of crisis is *time pressure*: if policy makers are under huge pressure and need to react quickly, this might make it particularly difficult for them to devise a consistent foreign policy course. In Psychology, the issue of decision making under time pressure has long been an object of study, leading to the insight that short or uncertain deadlines potentially requiring quick decisions usually increase stress levels (Renshon and Renshon, 2008: 513).

Third, the *novelty of the situation* is important: if decision makers are faced with a crisis or an issue that is entirely new and that they had never faced before, they will rather tend to adopt cognitive shortcuts (Mintz and DeRouen, 2010: 25) and to pursue indecisive policies. By contrast, 'seasoned experts are usually far more effective at maintaining performance under pressure' (Boin et al, 2005: 29). Here, it will matter how experienced decision makers are or how long governments have been in power, as we can expect these factors to mitigate the 'novelty' of some crisis situations because experienced actors and institutions may have already devised a set of best practices to adopt in situations of this kind.

All these cognitive problems are likely to be exacerbated if decision makers face strong external expectations and pressures. Studies from a range of fields, from Behavioural Economics and Psychology to Sports, have addressed the phenomenon of 'choking under pressure' (Gladstein and Reilly, 1985; Lewis and Linder, 1997; Yu, 2015).[8] This phenomenon describes a situation in which too much pressure and the prospect of high rewards in the case of success versus high punishments in the case of failure ultimately lead to under-performance and possibly to paralysis. While this phenomenon has not been systematically studied for foreign policy decision making, it relates well to the issue of competing external expectations, which I will go on to discuss.

---

[8]   I would like to thank Konrad Ringleb for suggesting that I address this issue.

To conclude, even if governments are strong and states do not face capacity problems, hesitation can emerge as a consequence of cognitive problems related to decision making. We can expect these problems to emerge in particularly severe crises, if time pressure is high and if governments need to step into uncharted territory. A lack of initiative, delays or flip-flopping – the typical indicators of hesitation – might emerge because of such cognitive problems faced by individual and collective actors while devising foreign policy preferences and implementing foreign policy. From this perspective, reluctance is an undesirable outcome of the decision-making process.

Normative struggles

Finally, there is one more pathway that can lead to hesitation in foreign policy: a struggle over the norms that should shape international conduct. Norms are defined in constructivist theories of IR as 'standard[s] of appropriate behavior for actors with a given identity' (Finnemore and Sikkink: 1998: 891), and they are considered to play a fundamental role in shaping actors' foreign policies. Hesitation can emerge as a result of the existence of competing norms prescribing different courses of action. One of the few empirical studies on 'reluctance', the analysis of US grand strategy by Dueck (2006), proposes a similar argument. Dueck (2006) explains reluctance with a tension between structural pressures and domestic strategic culture. And in particular, within strategic culture, he identifies two clashing 'cultural legacies' (Dueck, 2006: 5): on the one hand, liberal norms would imply an activist and expansive foreign policy; on the other hand, the tradition of 'limited liability' follows different norms and implies an unwillingness to carry the burden and costs of such policies.

The literature on role theory has also addressed the issue of competing norms, which it studies in terms of role contestation or role conflict. The notion of 'roles' and 'national role conceptions' was first applied to foreign policy issues by Holsti (1970), who defined national role conceptions as entailing 'policymakers' own definitions of the general kinds of decisions, commitments, rules and actions suitable to their state, and of the functions, if any, their state should perform on a continuing basis in the international system or in subordinate regional systems' (Holsti, 1970: 245–6). Against this backdrop, role conflict has been conceptualized as 'a disagreement between two roles towards the same situation and between role expectations from outside the country and role conceptions inside the country towards the same issue' (Kaarbo and Cantir, 2013: 466). These are obviously closely related to ideas about the ideational and normative foundations of a country's foreign policy, and therefore to normative struggles as they are addressed in this section.

As highlighted by Wiener (2014), norms are always contested and need to be so in order to be legitimate. Among the different modes of contestation, Wiener (2014: 2) identifies deliberation as a political mode, justification as a moral mode involving questioning of principles of justice, and contention as a societal practice critically questioning rules, procedures and regulations. While Wiener focuses on norms in global governance, contestation also plays an important role in domestic politics. A country's international engagement often touches on some of the key norms of a society, and foreign policy is often framed in highly moralistic terms (Rathbun and Pomeroy, 2021). Since these norms will naturally be contested, we can expect different actors and groups within society to potentially embrace competing norms and to struggle over which norms should prevail. In democracies, these actors can be opposition parties, civil society organizations, the media, public intellectuals, and so on.

By contrast, in autocratic regimes, the space for contestation of prevailing foreign policy norms will obviously be much more limited than in democracies. However, we can also expect normative arguments in this type of regime to be advanced by competing factions. While we might not observe actual arguing (Risse, 2000) over competing norms in the public sphere, since this would likely be interpreted as dissent and met with repression, we can expect competing factions – at least behind closed doors – to underscore their claims through references to specific norms such as sovereignty or justice in the face of perceived external oppression. In all kinds of regimes, normative struggles might emerge between governments and bureaucracies: the latter might have a long-established understanding of foreign policy and of the values that should guide it, leading to a substantial degree of path dependency in foreign policy. Such bureaucracy, however, might face a new government that is guided by a different set of norms, potentially clashing with the long-established normative foundations of foreign policy. Hesitation can therefore emerge as a result of these normative tensions between the executive and sections of the bureaucratic apparatus (Destradi, 2018: 2226).

Norm contestation can be expected to become particularly visible in crisis situations. In the aftermath of Russia's invasion of Ukraine in 2022, for example, a broad debate emerged within German society on the appropriateness of delivering heavy weapons to Ukraine – with proponents referring to norms of European solidarity and Germany's responsibility in Europe and vis-à-vis the victims of Russian aggression, and opponents emphasizing the dangers of nuclear war and the norms of restraint that have governed German foreign policy since 1945. In his speeches held in the months following Russia's invasion, Chancellor Scholz tried to strike a balance between these competing norms, ultimately resulting in an approach that was widely perceived as hesitant (see, for example, Kurbjuweit, 2022).

In emerging powers such as some of the countries analysed in this book, we can expect struggles over competing norms to emerge as a consequence of these countries' very process of 'rising'. Indeed, conforming to predominant international norms is usually considered to favour status gains, as complying with predominant international expectations, and therefore with prevalent normative standards, is usually part of a 'social mobility strategy' involving an increase in status (Larson and Shevchenko, 2010). However, these prevalent norms might be opposed to established domestic norms and unleash processes of contestation in the respective society. A contradictory, zig-zagging policy might emerge as a result of the government's attempts to balance the desire to conform to international normative standards while not alienating voters at home. Some of the incongruences in emerging powers' approach to the provision of global public goods in fields such as climate change mitigation are typical examples of these normative tensions (Hurrell and Sengupta, 2012). On the one hand, emerging powers are confronted with calls for the assumption of 'responsibility' commensurate with their increased power capabilities (Kenkel and Destradi, 2019); on the other hand, norms of fairness and justice lead these countries to call for the Global North to carry the burden of climate change mitigation given its historical responsibility for the emergence of this phenomenon (Hurrell and Sengupta, 2012: 465; Franchini and Viola, 2019: 5; Sengupta, 2020: 173).

Obviously, normative struggles frequently overlap with some of the other explanations mentioned, most notably government weakness and divisions in coalition governments. Difficulties in achieving compromises on what foreign policy course to follow are frequently related to different norms driving those actors' approach to foreign policy. Moreover, if those actors resort to such normative arguments to mobilize political support, reaching compromises might become even more difficult. While it is not always easy to disentangle the different paths that can lead to hesitation in empirical analyses, indications of normative struggles are given if domestic actors explicitly refer to such norms and motivate their positions with reference to them.

Competing international expectations

The second constitutive dimension of reluctance is recalcitrance, which, as mentioned, is closely related to the notion of disappointing the expectations articulated by others. All international actors continuously face some kind of expectation from their counterparts. These expectations will obviously vary depending on a range of factors. Powerful countries such as those analysed in this book will face greater expectations when it comes to problem solving or to the provision of public goods as compared to smaller states. In regional crisis management, such expectations will likely be raised in the first place by regional actors that ask a regional power for the provision of stability and crisis management. But some conflict parties or smaller states might also fear an intervention by a regional power they perceive as threatening, and therefore rather call for less engagement on its part. This means that expectations are not always calls for greater engagement, but can also be the opposite: requests not to interfere.

Moreover, the objects of expectations can vary: expectations can be very general and refer to an actor's broad approach to world politics, or entail calls for greater contributions to the key topics in world politics, such as world peace or the solution to global problems – think of regular calls by UN secretary-generals for states to maintain peace or of the Pope's calls for an end to global injustices and poverty. But expectations can also specifically refer to a certain situation and ask for very concretely defined measures – for concessions in negotiations over a free trade agreement, for an end to perceived meddling with a country's human rights record, for the support of a resolution in a multilateral setting, for the extradition of some alleged terrorists, and so on. Asking another government to do something is probably the most common form of diplomatic interaction, and all governments' foreign policy statements are full of exhortations, requests and calls for action on all kinds of issues.

Depending on the situation and the type of issue, such expectations can be articulated in very different ways. They can be formulated as mild appeals or even as threats. In situations of severe crisis, they can be expressed with particular urgency – think of the Ukrainian government's repeated calls for greater international support and arms provisions in the weeks following the Russian military invasion of February 2022, when President Zelensky virtually 'toured' European parliaments, urging governments to do more to save Ukraine and to protect its people by providing more weapons, imposing tougher sanctions and stopping doing business with Russia.

Expectations can therefore be analysed on a continuum entailing different intensities and, relatedly, different kinds of threatened consequences for non-compliance.[9] They can be articulated in a particularly demanding way, ultimately amounting to *coercion* if they are accompanied by threats in the case of non-compliance.[10] Coercion aims at inducing another actor to conform to one's expectations by threatening some kind of sanction or negative consequence if this does not happen (Byman and Waxman, 2002: 1). Such a coercive way of articulating expectations is a prerogative of powerful

---

[9] This discussion builds in part on a classification of foreign policy strategies developed in Destradi (2012b).

[10] On coercion, see, among many others, Cold War classics such as Schelling (1966) or Pennock and Chapman (1972).

countries that are ultimately in a position to implement such threats or of those actors who are in a position to withhold and deny something that is of value to the target of the expectation.

Other milder but still rather decisive ways of articulating expectations are *admonitions*, *exhortations* or *requests*, which have an 'imperative' character but do not entail the threat of sanctions in the case of non-compliance. They aim at changing the target's behaviour, but not necessarily its normative orientation as they mostly do not try to convince the target of the desirability of a policy change but rather refer to its need (Destradi, 2012b: 41–2). The softest way of expressing expectations is by trying to *persuade* a counterpart to accept one's demands. Persuasion can take place via verbal tools such as cajoling, by expressing hope and confidence that a problem will be addressed, but also, and most notably, through arguing. Here, actors will 'rely on a variety of techniques to persuade, including appeals to emotion, evoking symbols, as well as the use and extension of logical arguments' (Risse and Sikkink, 1999: 14). In other words, they will formulate an expectation outlining the inevitable consequences of non-compliance, but without formulating a threat, and will try to induce their counterpart not only to comply, but also to agree.

The significance of expectations in world politics has long been acknowledged as an important driver of foreign policy. Liberal approaches to IR have highlighted that state behaviour is, to a large extent, determined by what Moravcsik (1997: 520) called the 'configuration of interdependent state preferences', which implies that states always 'operate within the constraints imposed by the preferences of *other states*' (Moravcsik, 1997: 520: original emphasis). However, the theory does not further delve into the ways in which preferences are adapted and policy concessions are made in order to adapt to the preferences of other actors. Putnam's famous two-level game (Putnam, 1988) is another way of conceptualizing how governments ultimately have to navigate between domestic preferences and the preferences articulated by other actors. The underlying assumption remains one of rationality on the part of all actors involved, with leaders possibly playing actors from the two levels out against each other in complex bargaining settings.

While navigating two-level games is complicated enough, things get even more complex when international expectations are not homogeneous, but different actors articulate competing, opposed expectations. In fact, if expectations by different other actors diverge, it will become almost inevitable to disappoint at least one (and possibly multiple) of them. Competing expectations will therefore confront governments with substantial challenges and will likely exacerbate the effects of difficulties in domestic preference formation.

For politically weak governments with fragile coalitions, or in minority governments that need to rely on external supporters to stay in power, competing external expectations can be particularly dangerous. Indeed, these might come from international actors with close ties to single parties or specific domestic political actors, and might therefore contribute to an even greater polarization and to greater difficulties in achieving a compromise at the domestic level. Already unclear political preferences will become even less clear, thereby increasing not only recalcitrance but also amplifying hesitation and the muddling through that are so typical of reluctance.

Competing expectations will also likely put additional strain on governments that are already plagued by capacity problems, and may be an additional source of stress for decision makers facing cognitive problems in dealing with complex crises. The literature on choking under pressure highlights exactly these detrimental consequences of external expectations, which might seriously impair governments' ability to act. And, of course, competing expectations, especially by actors that are similarly valued partners to different groups within a country, might contribute to exacerbating existing normative struggles on the best way of doing foreign policy or solving a specific crisis. Sometimes, moreover, competing international expectations can also be the triggers of domestic divisions, leading to splits within governing coalitions or unleashing debates over norms that were long considered established and uncontested.

The interplay of difficulties in preference formation and competing expectations

Having outlined possible pathways to hesitation and to recalcitrance, these aspects need to be brought together in order to theorize reluctance in world politics. As discussed in Chapter 2, hesitation and recalcitrance are the two constitutive dimensions of reluctance. Both need to be in place in order to speak about reluctance because reluctance by definition involves a relationship between different actors. This means that reluctance will occur if governments face difficulties in devising clear preferences on foreign policy (due to political weakness, limited capacity, cognitive problems or normative struggles) and, at the same time, if they face competing expectations by international actors that are important to them. As mentioned in Chapter 2, hesitation and recalcitrance can occur in different intensities, and this will lead to different degrees of reluctance.

Looking at the various combinations and relating them to the theoretical discussion developed above, we need to think, first of all, about cases in which governments have very clear preferences on how to address a foreign policy issue. This will be the case if none of the discussed explanations for hesitation applies, that is, if governments are stable, do not face capacity limitations, do not have to address crises that are so severe and new that they put excessive strain on the cognitive capacities of decision makers, and do

Table 3.1: Explaining the occurrence of reluctance and its varying intensities

		Clear preferences ➜ No hesitation		Difficulties in preferences formation ➜ Hesitation	
			Low	Medium	High
No external expectations ➜ No recalcitrance		no reluctance	no reluctance	no reluctance	no reluctance
Competing external expectations ➜ Recalcitrance	Low	no reluctance	low reluctance	medium reluctance	high reluctance
	Medium	no reluctance	medium reluctance	medium reluctance	high reluctance
	High	no reluctance	high reluctance	high reluctance	medium reluctance

(the column between 'No hesitation' and the Low/Medium/High columns is labelled vertically: strategic reluctance)

not face particular normative struggles. In those cases, I expect governments to be able to devise clear and consistent preferences about the foreign policy they want to follow, that is, not to be hesitant. They can also be expected to be able to withstand external expectations, even competing ones by different important actors. In this case, recalcitrance will combine with decisiveness: these governments will be able to follow a clear and consistent foreign policy course, that is, they will not be reluctant.

If countries, by contrast, have weak and conflicted governments, if they face capacity problems, if they have to address extremely challenging crises under huge time pressures, or if they face struggles about the fundamental norms that should guide their foreign policy, we can expect them to be hesitant. We could think of very rare instances in which such hesitation is not met with any kind of external expectation: in that case, we would say that these governments would not be reluctant. Empirically, however, this will be an extremely unlikely constellation since most international actors face some kind of reaction and expectation concerning their international behaviour. For this reason, 'No reluctance' in the three upper-right boxes is marked in light grey in Table 3.1.

When it comes to the different combinations of hesitation and recalcitrance, we can expect the difficulties in devising clear foreign policy preferences to meet different intensities of competing external expectations, and therefore to lead to different intensities of reluctance. Importantly, as has become clear from the discussion in this chapter, difficulties in preference formation (that is, the factors driving hesitation) have greater explanatory power than external expectations when it comes to explaining why international actors are reluctant. Competing external expectations will usually exacerbate pre-existing problems with domestic preference formation by putting increased pressure on decision makers or by fostering rivalry among already competing domestic factions with distinct notions about what foreign policy goals to pursue.

To some extent, difficulties in preference formation might even be triggered by competing external expectations. Indeed, as mentioned, we can think of rare instances in which competing external pressures are so high that they put enormous strain on a government that, up to that point, had a clear preference on foreign policy. External pressures might end up dividing such a previously united government – not to the point of leading to its fall, but, for example, creating new fault lines within a governing coalition or empowering opposing factions, and thereby hampering the government's ability to formulate a consistent foreign policy. This would therefore be a case of an inability to resist competing pressures despite originally clear preferences. Moreover, competing expectations might increase pressure on a government, and thereby increase the stress level of decision makers to the point of triggering the cognitive problems discussed. Faced with a new crisis situation and with intense external pressure, a government might end up pursuing very hesitant policies involving flip–flopping or delaying important decisions or avoiding taking the initiative.

Finally, we can think of a different explanation for reluctance, in which causal primacy lies with international expectations: it involves governments that have very clear domestic preferences, but nevertheless pursue hesitant policies because they face competing expectations. In this case, the adoption of typical hesitant policies such as flip–flopping can be the result of an effort to conform to several of those expectations: the government will try to appease, at least for a while, all those actors that expect it to do different things, and this will inevitably lead to contradictory policies. Alternatively, inaction and delays might be employed as a way to 'buy time' instead of implementing what would be the preferred policy. Inevitably, these hesitant policies will be accompanied by recalcitrance because they de facto imply a lack of responsiveness vis-à-vis the expectations articulated by other actors. How can we explain this behaviour? I argue that in this case, since preferences are clear, hesitation is used in a strategic manner, in an effort to appease external actors and to buy time. The underlying assumption is a rationalist one, as I assume that a government will consciously pursue this kind of reluctant policy, for example to keep international criticism at bay while buying time to collect additional information or to wait for a crisis to unfold. In Table 3.1, this combination of hesitation and recalcitrance is labelled 'Strategic reluctance' and marked in grey. Obviously, this kind of policy will not work indefinitely, and relatively influential states in particular, such as emerging and regional powers, will need to take a clear stand at some point. Moreover, waiting too long might be a risky strategy as a crisis may develop in unexpected directions or this will alienate important international partners.

Alternative explanations

As discussed in Chapter 1, most conventional theoretical approaches in IR are ill equipped to study the very peculiar type of foreign policy addressed in this book, with its combination of hesitation and recalcitrance. Only a few existing studies are interested in similar empirical phenomena. Among them is the analysis of Indian foreign policy by Basrur (2023), which adopts neoclassical realism as a theoretical framework. The most prominent potential alternative explanation for reluctance, however, can be found in role theory (Holsti, 1970). Role theory has been adopted in IR and FPA by scholars dissatisfied with assumptions about states as unitary actors, and therefore interested in delving deeper into the agency side of the structure–agency debate (Cantir and Kaarbo, 2016: 2). Thereby, role theory is well suited to uncover domestic role contestation as well as the normative foundations of domestic debates over foreign policy. Indeed, role-theoretical analyses have sometimes been adopted to explain 'contradictory' behaviour, thereby sharing an interest with what is conceptualized as reluctance in this book (see, for example, Tewes, 2002). Moreover, role theory explicitly refers to the relationship between alter and ego, and acknowledges that external expectations can play a fundamental role in shaping foreign policy (Holsti, 1970; Tewes, 2002: 28; Harnisch, 2012: 52; Marthoz, 2012; Kaarbo and Cantir, 2013; Thies, 2017). In their analysis of Danish and Dutch decisions on participation in international military missions, Kaarbo and Cantir (2013) highlight the interplay between political differences among parties in coalition governments and their underlying roles, on the one hand, and external expectations, on the other. Especially in the analysis of the Dutch case, they show that external expectations can contribute to reshaping domestic preferences, something that 'ultimately ensured role performance according to alter expectations' (Kaarbo and Cantir, 2013: 477).

There are therefore many commonalities between the theorization of reluctance advanced in this book and role theory. At the same time, I consciously chose not to adopt a role-theoretical framework for a number of reasons. First of all, I opted for a more eclectic approach in order to build bridges to a broader set of debates and theoretical traditions in the fields of IR and FPA. Second, and more importantly, I wanted to develop a theoretical framework that identifies a broad range of possible drivers of reluctance, and particularly a set of different pathways to hesitation. This was important as I am interested in developing a theorization of reluctance that can be applied to a broad range of different cases. In particular, I wanted to develop a theoretical framework that does justice to the analysis of cases of the Global South, where the issue of capacity problems is of great relevance. Role theory does not seem to be well equipped to address the issue of governments that have very clearly defined national role conceptions but face substantial limitations in implementing such roles. In fact, the problem goes beyond mere inter- or intra-role conflicts or problems with role enactment (Tewes, 2002; Brummer and Thies, 2015; Thies, 2017), as it concerns a much more structural level of real 'physical' constraints to a state's agency. Also, the inclusion of cognitive approaches in explaining the emergence of hesitation goes beyond what role theory might be able to address: in cases of extreme and novel crises in which governments have to respond under time pressure, there are dynamics unfolding at the level of the individuals and institutions charged with crisis management, which cannot be captured by role theory. The problems in devising a way out of the crisis in most of these cases are not related to role conflicts, but to the plain impossibility of addressing a far too complex and challenging situation. Finally, I was interested in devising a theory of reluctance that can potentially travel beyond nation-states and be applied to other kinds of actors in world politics, and possibly even in contexts such as domestic or local politics. Working with national role conceptions would not fit well with this kind of setting, while political weakness, limited capacity, cognitive problems and normative struggles are explanations that fit all kinds of political actors at different levels of analysis.

How to study reluctance empirically

This section briefly describes how the theory of reluctance can be applied to the empirical analysis of the foreign policy of emerging and regional powers as it has been carried out for the chapters that follow. The first step of the analysis is the identification of reluctance and the determination of its intensity in each empirical case under consideration. To this end, I focused on specific crises, and I limited the time frame of analysis to the duration of each crisis, and more specifically to issues that were addressed continuously by the powerful country analysed, without longer interruptions in which decision makers turned their attention to other matters (see Chapter 2). This allowed me to isolate reluctance (with indicators such as flip-flopping) from longer-term policy shifts.

In each case, I looked for the indicators of reluctance described in Chapter 2 resorting to the secondary literature on the crisis as well as to primary sources such as government statements and speeches, but also original-language newspaper articles. I complemented available data with additional data generated for this project via 35 semi-structured expert interviews carried out with decision makers, observers, journalists and academics from India, Brazil and Germany. These interviews were carried out in a long time span, between 2013, when I did fieldwork in India on the subject of India–Afghanistan relations, 2015, when I carried out fieldwork in Germany on the issue of Germany's crisis management, up until 2022, when I did a set of additional online interviews on the cases of Brazil as well as India. All interviewees were anonymized (see the Appendix for a list of interviewees).

After assessing whether reluctance was in place in each of the cases, I moved on to apply the theoretical framework developed in this chapter in order to explain variations in the occurrence of reluctance. To this end, I applied the method of process tracing (Rohlfing, 2014: 150–67; Collier, 2011), trying to reconstruct whether political weakness, limited capacity, cognitive problems or normative struggles were in place in that specific case. In particular, I looked for the indicators that were developed for each of these pathways to hesitation in the previous sections of this chapter. In the empirical cases studied in this book, I chose governments during periods of political stability, which allowed me to exclude political weakness as an explanation.

For the analysis of capacity issues, I resorted to the secondary literature, but also, and most importantly, to decision makers' and experts' assessments as well as to information available on government websites and in the press. Since I conceptualized struggles within the bureaucracy as part of capacity problems, I also specifically explored interministerial tensions, and searched for detailed information about the departments and the actors involved in decision making in each of the crises analysed.

For the analysis of cognitive problems, as mentioned, I resorted to an assessment of the severity and urgency of the crisis as well as whether similar crises had occurred earlier. I complemented insights from the secondary literature and news reports with assessments by observers and decision makers. In these cases, interviews were particularly important in order to gain insights into whether the actors in charge of decision making did indeed feel overwhelmed by a crisis, or whether reluctance was perhaps used in a strategic manner, to buy time and appease external actors with their expectations. Of course, triangulation of sources was particularly important in this case, given the potential for self-apologetic statements on the part of government officials.

Finally, when it comes to normative struggles, for each case the analysis took into account a broad range of sources on the key norms guiding each country's foreign policy. Additionally, as mentioned, I analysed whether references to such key norms were present in the discourse by the government and the main opposition actors, aiming to find indications of contestation and of a struggle over which norms to follow in managing the crisis. Information gathered through interviews complemented these insights.

Concerning international expectations, I collected information on relevant international actors' positions on each crisis, and on whether these actors expressed some expectations directed at the governments of India, Germany or Brazil as a crisis manager. I also assessed the different intensities of such expectations, focusing on the notions outlined earlier in this chapter (coercion, admonitions, exhortations, requests, persuasion). I used the policy makers' and experts' assessments in the interviews to further try to reconstruct how these expectations were received by the government, and to what extent they played a role in possibly exacerbating existing problems with domestic preference formation.

4

India's Reluctant Crisis Management in South Asia

Since the early 2000s, it has become commonplace to consider India an 'emerging' or 'rising' power, or actually one of the most important countries in an emerging multipolar world (see, among many others, Cohen, 2002; Pant, 2008; Narlikar, 2010; Kahler, 2013; Pardesi, 2015; Basrur and Sullivan de Estrada, 2017; Plagemann et al, 2020). With its stunning economic growth, India gained increasing international visibility and attention. This was paired with an active foreign policy on the part of New Delhi, with India improving its relations with the USA, expanding its engagement in South–South cooperation, and becoming active in a number of minilateral and multilateral forums such as BRICS (Brazil, Russia, India, China, South Africa) and IBSA (India, Brazil, South Africa), but also in the G20.

At the same time, with its population of almost 1.4 billion inhabitants (in 2021; see The World Bank, 2022), India is now an indispensable actor for solving all kinds of global problems, from climate change mitigation to global health or disarmament. In global affairs, successive Indian governments have long pursued a surprisingly consistent and coherent foreign policy aimed at increasing India's international status – much in line with the goal outlined by India's founding father Jawaharlal Nehru on the night of the country's independence: that India *attain her rightful place in the world* (Schaffer and Schaffer, 2016: 1; original emphasis). The preferred means for such status-seeking policy had always been that of pursuing an 'independent' or 'autonomous' foreign policy. During the Cold War, this policy manifested itself in the guise of non-alignment, while in the following decades it was variously labelled by decision makers or observers as 'strategic autonomy', 'non-alignment 2.0' (Khilnani et al, 2012), 'multialignment' (Hall, 2016a) or 'all-alignment' (Haidar, 2022a). Regardless of the label used, what the foreign policies of successive Indian governments had in common over the decades was the effort to pursue an independent approach, which did not bind India to one specific alliance (partner) but instead gave it greater flexibility in international politics. Despite the broad ideological differences of successive Indian governments (Destradi and Plagemann, 2023), this approach can be considered a guiding thread in India's foreign policy, which was pursued very consistently.

However, if we look at India's foreign policy in its region, South Asia, things are different. In this region, conventionally considered to comprise India, Bangladesh, Sri Lanka, the Maldives, Nepal, Bhutan, Pakistan and Afghanistan, India is clearly the 'regional power' (Destradi, 2010; Nolte, 2010; Prys, 2010). In geopolitical terms, it even has a hub-and-spokes position in the region, with several of its smaller neighbours bordering India but not sharing borders with each other. Still, despite its clear predominance in terms of power capabilities, India has not managed to play a leading role in the region (Destradi, 2012b).

Things are obviously complicated by the fact that Pakistan, India's arch-enemy since the bloody partition of British India in 1947, is a nuclear-armed rival with whom India has a painful and unresolved territorial dispute over Kashmir (Ganguly, 2002; Kapur and Ganguly, 2010). But India has also not been willing to actively engage in the South Asian Association for Regional Cooperation (SAARC) (Michael, 2013), an organisation that has not de facto played any relevant role in the region over the past decades. Furthermore, India has long had the 'fear that SAARC would constrain India's own strategic space'.[1] Indeed, the region is barely integrated, including in economic terms: only 5.6 per cent of South Asia's overall trade volume is intra-regional (as compared, for example, to 22.4 per cent in Southeast Asia; see Asian Development Bank, 2021: 18).

Indian governments have repeatedly tried to improve India's relations with its South Asian neighbours, but most initiatives have not moved beyond simple rhetoric. For example, in the 1990s, India's Foreign Minister Inder Kumar Gujral announced a series of principles, which, for the first time, involved the notion of non-reciprocity in India's approach to its neighbours (the 'Gujral doctrine'), but ultimately did not lead to substantial improvements or to anything close to India taking over a leadership role in the region. Similarly, Prime Minister Modi's 'Neighbourhood First' initiative has not led to major changes, and observers argue that India has been losing influence to China in its neighbourhood over the past two decades (Kaura and Rani, 2020).[2]

---

[1] Interview I6, former high-ranking government official, New Delhi, 14 November, 2013.

[2] In 2013, an interviewee had already pointed out that 'keeping this area as an area of Indian influence – this is getting increasing challenging for us' (Interview I4, Indian scholar, New Delhi, 12 November 2013).

Overall, it is not surprising that India's approach to the region has been termed 'reluctant' (see, for example, Mitra, 2003). In this chapter, I will apply the concept and theory of reluctance developed in Chapters 2 and 3 to analyse India's approach to two crises in its regional neighbourhood. My focus is on a period of domestic political stability in India: on the years of the government of Prime Minister Narendra Modi of the Hindu nationalist Bharatiya Janata Party (BJP, Indian People's Party). The BJP-led National Democratic Alliance (NDA) won 336 out of 545 seats in India's Lok Sabha (lower house of Parliament) at the 2014 general elections. This allowed Modi to govern with a comfortable majority during his first term in office. Faced with an increasingly weak and divided opposition, at the 2019 general election, the NDA won a landslide, securing 352 seats in the Lok Sabha, 303 of which were held by the BJP.

Modi's BJP-led government was also stable during its second term, with no substantial challenge coming from the opposition. Despite poor performance in several policy fields, including dismal management of the COVID-19 pandemic, approval ratings for Modi remained extremely high (*The Times of India*, 2022). The years of the BJP-led governments in India saw the increasing spread of Hindu nationalist ideology and a gradual transformation of India into a majoritarian state (Chatterji et al, 2020; Jaffrelot, 2021). The notion of *Hindutva* (Hinduness), which constitutes the core of the BJP's Hindu nationalist ideology, ultimately equates India's nationhood with the cultural-religious traditions of Hinduism, and claims that Hinduism is superior to other civilizations. It goes hand in hand with the notion of Hindus as a victimized majority, and with discrimination of Muslims and other minorities. At the same time, it calls into question the secular character of the Indian state.

Combined with Modi's populism (Plagemann and Destradi, 2019), this has led to a weakening of India's democratic institutions in the years of the BJP-led governments. In 2021, Freedom House classified India as 'partly free' for the first time, 'due to a multiyear pattern in which the Hindu nationalist government and its allies have presided over rising violence and discriminatory policies affecting the Muslim population and pursued a crackdown on expressions of dissent by the media, academics, civil society groups, and protesters' (Freedom House, 2022). Similarly, V-Dem classified India as an 'electoral autocracy' for the first time in 2021 (Alizada et al, 2022). Importantly, these obvious instances of democratic backsliding and fundamental changes to the secular order enshrined in India's constitution did not lead to widespread resistance to Modi or the BJP,[3] ultimately confirming the stability of the government.

---

[3] Even episodes such as the huge farmer protests in 2020/21 did not substantially challenge the government's stability.

The analysis in this chapter will focus on two very different types of crisis in India's regional neighbourhood of South Asia: on the conflict in Afghanistan between the formation of Modi's BJP-led government in 2014 and the period immediately following the fall of Kabul to the Taliban on 15 August 2021; and on a serious domestic political crisis related to the introduction of a new constitution in Nepal (2015–17). As we will see, India's approach to these two very different crises was reluctant.

In the case of Afghanistan, India's reluctant policies were mainly driven by the massive pressure resulting from competing expectations vis-à-vis India, with Western actors and to some extent the Afghan government calling for greater Indian involvement, while Pakistan was strongly opposed to greater Indian engagement. These competing expectations were accompanied by capacity problems and domestic normative debates in India, which led to difficulties in developing a clear preference on how to deal with the situation. In the case of Nepal, reluctance was first and foremost a consequence of capacity problems resulting from a lack of coordination among Indian actors and institutions dealing with the crisis, which were accompanied by competing expectations articulated by different Nepalese actors.

India and crisis management in Afghanistan

Among the countries of South Asia, Afghanistan has obviously been the most conflict-ridden over the past decades. After the terrorist attacks of 11 September 2001 and the Taliban government's refusal to extradite Osama Bin Laden to the United States, the USA and an international coalition launched Operation Enduring Freedom and invaded Afghanistan. While the Taliban regime was quickly ousted and Hamid Karzai was elected as head of the Afghan Interim Administration, the situation in the country remained volatile. What followed were two decades of conflict and instability, as the UN-mandated International Security Assistance Force (ISAF), involving over 40 countries, tried to consolidate democracy and promote state building in Afghanistan while preventing a return to power of the Taliban and the emergence of other extremist forces.

The year 2014, which marks the starting point of the analysis in this chapter, was also a turning point for the situation on the ground in Afghanistan. In fact, on 28 December 2014, ISAF operations were formally concluded, and the responsibility for the country's security was handed over to the Afghan National Security Forces (ANSF). The years that followed were characterized by a gradual worsening of the security situation on the ground (see, for example, Murtazashvili, 2016; Fair, 2018), with an increase in the Taliban's presence in ever larger parts of the country and the emergence of new groups such as the Islamic State-Khorasan (IS-K) threatening to further destabilize the country. While the USA and a number of Western countries kept a military presence in the country, they started emphasizing the need to find a diplomatic solution. In particular, under President Donald Trump, the urge to put an end to US engagement in Afghanistan increased, leading to the search for negotiated solutions.

A flurry of diplomatic activities ultimately led to the signing of the Doha Agreement between the USA and the Taliban in February 2020 – notably, with no involvement of the Afghan government. The Doha Agreement envisaged the withdrawal of all US troops from Afghanistan by April 2021, in exchange for the Taliban's promise to prevent extremist groups from using the territory of Afghanistan to carry out attacks against the USA and its allies (US Department of State, 2020). While the date for the withdrawal of American troops was later shifted to 31 August 2021, the Taliban used the summer of 2021 to launch a remarkable military offensive. This allowed them to capture province after province within a few weeks, as Afghan troops deserted or were unable to stop the Taliban's advance. On 15 August 2021, the Taliban captured Kabul as President Ashraf Ghani fled abroad. As the Taliban declared victory and the last US troops left the country on 30 August (Gaouette et al, 2021), the phase of the conflict in Afghanistan analysed in this chapter ends.

India's approach to the conflict in Afghanistan

India has a long history of engagement with Afghanistan, and a very obvious interest in the country's stability. The story of *Kabuliwala*, about an Afghan merchant based in Calcutta, famously narrated by Bengali poet Rabindranath Tagore, is often mentioned in India to exemplify the deep historical and cultural roots of Indian–Afghan relations. Over the past decades of Afghanistan's tormented history, India has played a changing role, from the challenge of dealing with the Soviet occupation of the country to the adoption of a 'proxy-war format vis-à-vis Pakistan in Afghanistan during the 1990s and early years of the twenty-first century' (Paliwal, 2017: 23) via the open support of the anti-Taliban Northern Alliance, up to the acceptance of the Karzai presidency and the realization of the need to negotiate with the Taliban in the face of the withdrawal of Western troops (for a detailed reconstruction of Indian–Afghan relations and India's policies vis-à-vis Afghanistan, see Paliwal, 2017). Throughout such a history, having a stable and possibly India-friendly Afghanistan in the face of hostile relations with Pakistan has always been India's primary goal. As one interviewee put it, 'India has a strong interest in making sure that Afghanistan does not descend into a fractured political situation, leaving room to forces that have targeted India'.[4]

---

[4]   Interview I6, former high-ranking government official, New Delhi, 14 November 2013.

Over time, the details and modalities on how to achieve such a goal have changed, but successive Indian governments have pursued the following set of objectives: to prevent Pakistan from destabilizing Afghanistan, to reduce Afghanistan's dependence on Pakistan, and – relatedly – to promote a possibly Afghan-owned and Afghan-driven political process in Kabul (see Paliwal, 2017: 287). At the core of India's objectives in Afghanistan was the need to prevent the country from becoming a base for terrorists able to harm India (Chaudhuri and Shende, 2020: 20), as well as the desire to make Afghanistan a bridge towards Central Asia – even though the latter objective became increasingly unrealistic against the backdrop of growing instability in Afghanistan. Despite these very clear goals and a vital interest in having a stable and friendly Afghanistan,[5] India has faced huge challenges in achieving these goals to date. All this has induced some observers to claim that Afghanistan was, to some extent, a 'test case' (Pant, 2010) for India as a rising power. Instead of addressing India's policies vis-à-vis Afghanistan in terms of success or failure, however, this chapter focuses on the very nature of such policies and on whether they were reluctant – that is, hesitant and recalcitrant.

Overall, during the years of the BJP-led governments of Prime Minister Modi (2014–21), India's approach towards Afghanistan was reluctant. Even though the situation on the ground was different, given growing instability and the withdrawal of Western troops, and even though the Afghan government was putting less pressure on India, overall we can argue that the Modi government carried on with the policies that had been adopted by the preceding UPA (United Progressive Alliance) I and UPA II governments of Manmohan Singh. During those years, New Delhi had pursued a hesitant policy, signing a Strategic Partnership Agreement in 2011, which was not fully implemented, however, and displaying a high degree of flip-flopping and indecision over the provision of equipment and training to Afghan troops. India's policies had also been recalcitrant, since what New Delhi provided remained far below the levels and amounts requested by the Afghan government (Destradi, 2014; see also Destradi, 2018).

Under Prime Minister Modi's two terms in office, India's policies continued to be hesitant, albeit less so than in the past because the Afghan government simply did not request as much support from India as President Karzai had previously requested. In fact, an important shift was represented by the changing government in Kabul, where Ashraf Ghani became president (flanked by 'chief executive' Abdullah Abdullah) in September 2014. Initially, Afghan–Indian relations deteriorated, primarily given Ghani's intention to

---

[5]   According to an Indian expert, however, stability was never a major interest on the part of New Delhi. Interview I1, Indian expert, New Delhi, 18 October 2013.

improve relations with Pakistan (Mullen, 2016: 107), but they improved again from December 2015 onwards.[6]

In the following, I will address India's policies, asking to what extent they were reluctant, with a focus on (1) security issues, and especially the delivery of weapons and military equipment to Afghanistan; (2) development cooperation; (3) India's approach to the political situation in Afghanistan, and especially to the issue of whether and how to negotiate with the Taliban; and finally, (4) I will briefly address India's approach to Afghanistan during the turbulent weeks around the Taliban's takeover in August 2021.

On the important issue of the delivery of weapons and military equipment, New Delhi remained hesitant, as during the years of the UPA I and UPA II governments. Three unarmed Cheetal helicopters, which were supposed to be delivered to Kabul in 2014, were made available with one year of delay and after letting two deadlines expire – reportedly because the governments of India and Afghanistan were looking for some special occasion to celebrate the handover – but ultimately the transfer happened quietly in April 2015 (Pubby, 2015). New Delhi, to some extent, shed its previous recalcitrance on the delivery of offensive weapons, which it had previously refused to provide. The first such delivery was an Mi-25 attack helicopter, which India donated to Afghanistan in December 2015 (Maass, 2015). Three more helicopters of this type, which India had promised to Kabul, were delivered in 2016 (Gady, 2019).

According to one of the Indian scholars I interviewed, the delivery of helicopters was 'an important symbol of political intent' on the part of New Delhi, which should not be under-estimated, especially given India's own limitations in terms of its air defence capacity.[7] At the same time, the helicopters were reportedly grounded and unable to operate for long periods due to lack of spare parts. Ultimately, there are reports about the Afghan government being disappointed by India's support, with Afghanistan's ambassador to India stating that 'at times requests have been delayed for too long' (Haidar and Peri, 2016). In 2019, New Delhi provided the Afghan Air Force with four Mi-24V attack helicopters as a replacement (Gady, 2019), based on an agreement with Belarus, where the helicopters (paid by India) came from.

Deals of this kind were also supported by the USA, which, after Russia's annexation of Crimea and the imposition of sanctions on Moscow, could not buy Russian-made military equipment or spare parts, and therefore reportedly encouraged India to do so instead (Gady, 2019). Indeed, there was also a shift in India's approach: the Indian government had previously

---

[6]   Interview I9, Indian scholar, online, 8 November 2022.
[7]   Interview I9, Indian scholar, online, 8 November 2022.

declared that it was not upgrading Soviet-era military equipment in Afghanistan (Ministry of Defence, 2015), but it ultimately moved in that direction. Interestingly, however, according to the Stockholm International Peace Research Institute (SIPRI) Arms Transfers Database (SIPRI, 2022), India's deliveries of weapons only took place in 2015 and 2016, and there were transfers from Belarus in 2019, but no other deliveries took place in the other years between 2014 and 2021, further underscoring India's hesitation.

Concerning the training of troops, India continued to support Afghanistan by providing training on Indian territory to Afghan troops as well as to the Afghan police force. Around 700–800 Afghan soldiers attended 'short-duration "tailor-made" courses [for them]' every year (Pandit, 2021). Moreover, by 2021, New Delhi had supplied, among other things, 285 military vehicles to Afghanistan. At the same time, the Strategic Partnership Agreement , which the two countries had signed in 2011, saw no further action in the following years. The agreement included the following points:

- Establishment of a mechanism for regular bilateral political and foreign office consultations. Political consultations to be led by foreign ministries of both countries and to include summit-level consultations convened at least once a year.
- Consultation and cooperation at the UN and in international fora.
- Establishment of a 'Strategic Dialogue to provide a framework for cooperation in the area of national security. The Dialogue will be led by NSAs [National Security Advisers] and involve regular consultations with the aim of intensifying mutual efforts towards strengthening regional peace and security' (MEA, 2011).
- Assistance on the part of India 'as mutually determined, in the training, equipping and capacity building programmes for Afghan National Security Forces' (MEA, 2011).

Moreover, the agreement included a series of provisions aimed at increasing bilateral trade and economic ties, capacity building, education and cultural relations (MEA, 2011). While in the latter domains India was certainly engaged in Afghanistan, the vaguely formulated provisions concerning the delivery of equipment to the ANSF were only implemented to a limited extent, and the implementation of other provisions was delayed: it was only in December 2015, during Modi's first visit to Afghanistan, that it was decided to hold a first Strategic Partnership Council meeting headed by the foreign ministers in early 2016 – a delay of five years (Kaura, 2017: 34). A second meeting was held in 2017 (MEA, 2017; Embassy of India, 2020), but there are no reports of further meetings taking place in the following years. At the same time, one of the experts I interviewed pointed out that such a failure in implementation should not be overestimated: the Strategic Partnership

Agreement should be considered first and foremost 'an outcome' of the Indo–Afghan rapprochement under Karzai – and one that mattered greatly to Afghanistan since it was the first agreement of this kind that Afghanistan had signed.[8]

Overall, therefore, during the period analysed the Indian government became somewhat less hesitant compared to the years before 2014 (see Destradi, 2014). However, its readiness to provide weapons and equipment must be put into perspective: those were the years after the formal transfer of responsibility for the security of Afghanistan to the ANSF in 2014, and those were years marked by a clear deterioration of the security situation on the ground. After the difficult phase in bilateral relations between 2014 and the end of 2015, Afghan government officials started asking New Delhi again for more help and for more substantial amounts of military aid, but faced a high degree of recalcitrance on India's part:

> Kabul had long been requesting India for offensive military hardware and has several times presented a wish list of urgent military hardware. A revised list was handed over to India in August [2016] during the visit of the Chief of Afghan National Army General Qadam Shah Shaheem and was discussed at the highest level during Ghani's visit in September. (TOLOnews, 2016)

Similar requests for 'training equipment, air and ground mobility assets, engineering infrastructure and light infantry weapon[s]' (Swami, 2015) had already been posed, for example, in 2015 by Afghanistan's national security adviser, Mohammad Hanif Atmar (Swami, 2015). The USA also reportedly put pressure on India in 2016 concerning the delivery of combat helicopters (Gady, 2016). While India, with the delivery of such helicopters, proved to be responsive to Kabul, such a shift to a policy of 'incremental gift giving' (Joshi, 2016) was not long-lived, as there are no reports of an ongoing provision of weapons during the following years, despite a further worsening of the situation on the ground (see Kuimova and Wezeman, 2021).

In 2019, a report by the US Congressional Research Service (CRS) summarized India's approach as follows: 'New Delhi has not shown an inclination to pursue a deeper defense relationship with Kabul' (CRS, 2019). As an Afghan expert put it, especially during the years of the Ghani presidency,

> ... there was nothing serious going on with India. The understanding under Ghani was ... that India is a great friend that absolutely does

---

[8] Interview I9, Indian scholar, online, 8 November 2022.

not do anything that goes against the wishes of the Americans. There were talks in 2014 that if the US leaves and the Army is only trained to do war on terror and not to defend the country, there was talk about whether India might step in. But then India disappeared from this discussion. [India and Afghanistan at that time were like] two lovers who said I love you, you love me, but let's not go to bed.[9]

But military support was not the only way for India to engage in Afghanistan. As an Indian scholar I interviewed put it, 'Strategically, India had no role in Afghanistan except for being in contact with various groups. It was forced to remain confined to the developmental sector'.[10] Indeed, development aid in many ways represented the most important component of New Delhi's engagement. India had become Afghanistan's fifth-largest bilateral donor, carrying out a diverse range of projects in the country – from large and prestigious infrastructure projects such as the Salma Dam or the Parliament building to huge numbers of highly successful small-scale development projects, including in remote rural areas (for an overview, see, for example, MEA, nd).

Under Prime Minister Modi, the Indian government repeatedly reassured Afghanistan about India's continued commitment to the development of the country. In 2016 Modi famously promised, 'India will not forget you or turn away. ... Your friendship is our honour; your dreams are our duty' (quoted in Kaura, 2017: 35). In 2017, the Indian and Afghan governments created a so-called 'New Development Partnership' that would envisage the creation of '116 High Impact Community Development Projects' to be implemented in 31 provinces (MEA, 2017). And in 2021 the Indian external affairs minister, speaking to the UNSC, claimed: 'India will continue to provide all support to the Government and people of Afghanistan in realizing their aspirations for a peaceful, democratic and prosperous future, free of terror, so as to protect and promote the rights and interests of all sections of Afghan society' (MEA, 2021b). Interestingly, however, despite this increased rhetorical commitment, during Prime Minister Modi's two terms in office, Afghanistan became a less and less relevant recipient of Indian aid. As shown in Table 4.1, while in the fiscal year 2007–08 Afghanistan was the recipient of as much as a quarter of India's total technical cooperation, and in the following years under the Congress-led government it regularly benefited from around 10 per cent of India's total aid, this share clearly declined under Prime Minister Modi. In 2020–21, Afghanistan only received 5 per cent of India's aid, which, over the years, was gradually redirected towards countries

---

[9]   Interview I11, Afghan scholar, online, 16 November 2022.
[10] Interview I10, Indian scholar, online, 15 November 2022.

Table 4.1: Share in India's total aid and loan budget targeted at Afghanistan

Year	Share in India's total aid and loan budget (%)
2007–08	25.47
2008–09	15.82
2009–10	12.17
2010–11	10.63
2011–12	8.47
2012–13	15.19
2013–14	9.70
2014–15	10.78
2015–16	7.42
2016–17	6.58
2017–18	5.08
2018–19	6.42
2019–20	4.89
2020–21	5.37

Source: Author's own composition based on MEA annual reports (disaggregated data for Afghanistan was not available before 2007)

such as Nepal (7.2 per cent in 2014 to 10 per cent in 2020), Mauritius (5.1 per cent in 2017 to 13.8 per cent in 2020) or the Maldives (0.4 per cent in 2014 to 4 per cent in 2020).

This decline in India's aid to Afghanistan might be related to the difficult situation on the ground and to problems with the implementation of development projects. However, it stands in strong contrast to the official positions by the Indian government, with its claims of continued commitment to Afghanistan. Indeed, there are some reports about Afghan recipients being dissatisfied with India's development projects. According to a study published by the Friedrich Ebert Foundation on India's role in the economic stabilization of Afghanistan, 'delays and the inability to deliver on promises lead to dissatisfaction and negatively affect the image of the donor country. The proposed investment by a consortium led by state-run Steel Authority of India (SAIL) of up to US$6 billion in the Hajigak mines in Bamyan province is one such example' (D'Souza, nd: 16).

Concerning the political future of Afghanistan, the Indian government pursued a more consistent approach, gradually changing its position, but without much flip-flopping. One of the most important questions in the period analysed was the issue of negotiations with the Taliban, and of how to possibly bring them into the political mainstream. India had long adopted the position that there should be no talks with the Taliban, and that there could not be a distinction between 'good' and 'bad' Taliban. However, after a series of attacks against Indian workers, India had itself had backdoor contact with the Taliban (Paliwal, 2017; Pant and Paliwal, 2019; Chaudhuri and Shende, 2020: 17).

As the situation in Afghanistan worsened, the Indian government was forced to gradually abandon its intransigent stance about dialogue with the Taliban. At the end of the UPA II government, the Indian minister of external affairs stated that India supported 'an Afghan led, Afghan owned, and Afghan controlled process that will help reconcile and mainstream members of armed opposition groups who are willing to give up terror and accept the Afghan constitution and who will be willing to participate as equal citizens' (MEA, 2014). A similar position was adopted by the BJP-led government of Prime Minister Modi, as India officially kept the position of supporting an 'Afghan-owned, Afghan-led reconciliation process' (Pant and Paliwal, 2019), but was extremely sceptical about involvement of the Taliban due to their close ties to Pakistan. However, in 2019, India reportedly reached out to the Taliban and started declaring that it would 'participate in all format of talks that could bring about peace and security the region [sic]' (Pant and Paliwal, 2019).

The Doha negotiations, which were held between the USA and the Taliban without including the Afghan government, were observed with scepticism by India. Nevertheless, the Indian government signalled its acceptance of the agreement by sending its ambassador to Qatar to attend the signing ceremony (see Haidar, 2020):

> ... the first time that a serving Indian official has attended an event with the presence of the Taliban or even been in physical proximity since the Atal Bihari Vajpayee government sent the then external affairs minister, Jaswant Singh, to deliver three terrorists (including Masood Azhar) into Taliban 'custody' at Kandahar airport in December 1999 as part of the deal to release hostages on board a hijacked Indian airliner. (*The Wire*, 2020)

Notably, the official statement on the agreement by a spokesperson of India's Ministry of External Affairs (MEA) avoided welcoming the deal, merely taking 'note that the entire political spectrum in Afghanistan, including the Government, the democratic polity and civil society, has welcomed the opportunity and hope for peace and stability generated by these agreements' (MEA, 2020b). Later on, as intra-Afghan talks started in Doha, the Indian government sent a high-ranking representative – 'a significant move, given India's reticence in acknowledging power-sharing arrangements in Kabul' (Roy, 2020) – and in March 2021, India's external affairs minister, Subrahmanyam

Jaishankar, declared India's support for such intra-Afghan negotiations (Haidar, 2021). According to Chaudhuri and Shende (2020), India's approach to the peace process was perceived as hesitant in Afghanistan: 'Afghan insiders like Khenjani, who have historically been well disposed toward India, argue that "New Delhi waited too long on the peace process" and that despite its "enormous leverage and capital" in Kabul, it consciously pushed itself to "irrelevance"'. As the Taliban were regaining control of larger parts of territory in Afghanistan, the Indian government acknowledged that it had been in touch with various factions and leaders of the Taliban (Basit, 2021).

Overall, therefore, India's assistance to Afghanistan in matters of security as well as, to some extent, its development policy were characterized by inconsistency and flip-flopping. On the matter of Afghanistan's political future, by contrast, India's position evolved gradually, without too many contradictions, except for the obvious discrepancy between its declared refusal to negotiate with the Taliban and, de facto, the existence of backchannel contacts with them. Yet those actors inside Afghanistan who were positively inclined towards India were reportedly dissatisfied with what they perceived as New Delhi lagging behind on developments on the ground. Generally speaking, India's hesitation vis-à-vis Afghanistan was also accompanied by recalcitrance, especially when it came to the Afghan government's requests for more substantial provision of military support.

The takeover by the Taliban on 15 August 2021 obviously changed the situation dramatically. This critical moment caught all international actors involved in Afghanistan entirely unprepared. India was no different: in the chaotic days preceding the fall of Kabul, the Indian government hastily decided to close the Indian Embassy and to evacuate its personnel. An extremely reluctant approach could be observed on the issue of providing visas to Afghans, with a series of sudden shifts in India's policy. In fact, on 17 August, the Indian government announced the introduction of a new emergency e-visa category for Afghans of all faiths (Mitra, 2021a). What initially looked like a generous policy, however, ended in chaos. On 25 August, the Ministry of Home Affairs announced that all visas already issued to Afghan citizens would be invalidated due to security concerns (MHA, 2021). Within a few days, as many as 40,000 applications were made for the new emergency visa programme, but in the end the Indian government issued only some 200 visas. By extending the provisions of its Citizenship (Amendment) Act of 2019, India ended up facilitating the so-called repatriation for persecuted Hindus and Sikhs from Afghanistan, but not for Afghan Muslims (Mitra, 2021a; *The Wire*, 2021). This obviously reflected the preference of the Hindu nationalist BJP in government, and the religious polarization reigning within India.[11] All

---

[11] Interview I10, Indian scholar, online, 15 November 2022.

these developments were seen very critically by Afghan citizens hoping to find refuge in India.[12] The Afghan ambassador still based in Delhi expressed his disappointment: 'At the time of crisis, we don't look at other nations but at India. We don't look at Bangladesh or Sri Lanka or Nepal or Pakistan or China with whom we share a border. ... And then the "cold feet" response [by India] was disheartening. It disheartened us' (Mitra, 2021a).

Finally, in another turnabout, in June 2022 India reopened its diplomatic representation in Kabul. Since it did not officially recognize the Taliban government, it sent only a 'technical team' of officials (Haidar, 2022b). Still, of the countries that had closed their embassies in Afghanistan, India was the first to reopen. As opposed to all the previous reluctance and indecisiveness, this was, in many ways, a bold, non-reluctant policy. According to one of the experts I interviewed, 'this is ... the behaviour ... of a country that is serious about its regional interests. And is willing to open its embassy despite attacks on Gurudwaras [carried out in June 2022 and obviously targeted against India]' (see Kermani, 2022).[13] At the time of writing this book (November 2022), however, it seems too early to assess whether this shift should be interpreted as a longer-term move towards a more determined, non-reluctant Indian policy vis-à-vis Afghanistan.

Explaining India's reluctance in crisis management in Afghanistan

How can we explain India's continued reluctance in crisis management in Afghanistan during the years 2014–21 – under a prime minister who was highly engaged and active in foreign policy, and whose ideology of Hindu nationalism called for a more 'muscular' engagement of India in international affairs, all the more vis-à-vis its arch-enemy Pakistan (Destradi and Plagemann, 2023)? Certainly, we need to take into account important changes in the situation on the ground in Afghanistan.

First of all, as mentioned, Afghan–Indian relations were initially tense under President Ghani, primarily given his declared intention to improve relations with Pakistan.[14] Second, and more importantly, the security situation in Afghanistan worsened after the formal transfer of responsibility for the security of the country to the ANSF in 2014, with dramatic increases in fatalities in the following years (see UCDP, 2022a). These were factors

---

12 Interview I11, Afghan scholar, online, 16 November 2022.
13 Interview I9, Indian scholar, online, 8 November 2022.
14 According to an Afghan scholar, Ghani's rapprochement towards Pakistan took place 'out of desperation, but Delhi interpreted it as Afghanistan changing side' (Interview I11, Afghan scholar, online, 16 November 2022).

71

that obviously made the implementation of development aid projects more difficult. However, it could have been expected that the Indian government would then become more actively engaged in providing weapons and military supplies, given India's vital interest in the stability of Afghanistan, but this did not happen.

As outlined in Chapter 3, reluctance can best be explained by a combination of difficulties in domestic preference formation and competing expectations. In the following, I will discuss the four possible alternative pathways that might lead to problems in devising clear foreign policy preferences, before moving on to discussing competing expectations.

The first possible reason for difficulties in achieving clear foreign policy preferences at the domestic level is the government's political weakness. As discussed, the case studies chosen in this book deliberately refer to periods of domestic political stability in order to exclude this potential explanation. In the case of India under Modi, political stability is evident. In both its terms in office, Modi's BJP had a comfortable majority in the Lok Sabha (lower house of Parliament) and the NDA coalition was stable – and after the BJP's landslide victory of 2019, even more so. In other words, Modi could govern without fearing any kind of blackmailing by smaller coalition partners. The opposition was so weak that it had no means to challenge the government's policies in any way. All this points to the fact that political weakness cannot count as an explanation for India's continued reluctance in dealing with the situation in Afghanistan.

A possible alternative explanation is represented by the limited capacity of a government to devise clear preferences on foreign policy or to implement certain policies. As discussed in Chapter 3, this can be related to two factors. On the one hand, it can derive from structural capacity problems in a country's foreign policy apparatus, which might be understaffed or underfunded, or perhaps faced with an over-stretched foreign policy; it can also be reinforced by a lack of foreign policy expertise. On the other hand, capacity problems can derive from 'politicking' among different government agencies, with bureaucratic infighting ultimately leading to flip-flopping, delays and other manifestations of hesitation. In the case of India, some of these factors were certainly in place. India's MEA is notoriously understaffed (see, for example, Marlow, 2018), with a diplomatic corps of only 850 officers in 2022 (MEA, 2022), comparable to the size of Singapore's. Yet, Indian diplomats are usually considered to be well trained and highly professional, and many high-ranking bureaucrats are well informed about Afghanistan.[15]

Given that India had four consulates in Afghanistan, and that the Indian secret services reportedly regularly used those consulates to gather intelligence

---

[15] Interview 19, Indian scholar, online, 8 November 2022.

about the situation in the country (as well as about Pakistan's activities there; see Paliwal, 2017), we cannot conclude that India's reluctance was due to a lack of information about the situation in the country. Still, one of the interviewees pointed out that 'Indians have good information, but not knowledge' of Afghanistan, as the Indian foreign policy community still sees Afghanistan through a Cold War lens, failing to understand the profound social and political transformations that the country has experienced since the 1990s.[16]

At the same time, under the populist government of Prime Minister Modi, we have seen increasing efforts at centralizing and personalizing foreign policy decision making, which contributed to a weakening of the MEA in the processes of foreign policy making (Plagemann and Destradi, 2019). Such a process was not without friction among the different agencies involved. In the case of relations with Afghanistan, it would probably be an exaggeration to claim that bureaucratic infighting between different agencies was a driver of the government's reluctance. However, tensions among different agencies certainly reflected and reinforced existing normative struggles. In particular, the Indian foreign policy bureaucracy during the period analysed largely continued to embrace a strategic culture and an approach to international affairs focused on 'Nehruvian' ideals, that is, on notions shaped by the thinking of India's founding father and first foreign minister Jawaharlal Nehru. With his belief in the notion of India being a force for good in world politics and his *Panchsheel* (Five Principles of Peaceful Coexistence) (respect for territorial integrity and sovereignty, non-aggression, non-interference in internal affairs, equality, and peaceful co-existence), Nehru shaped India's strategic culture for decades. The MEA is the institution that most clearly embraced those principles, which remained in place for a long time, implying a high degree of path dependency (Hall, 2016b). At the same time, it was exactly this kind of Nehruvian discourse that Modi and his government tried to eradicate after coming to power, seeking to replace it with notions of India pursuing a more 'muscular' foreign policy in line with Hindu nationalist ideology – and indeed, there is research that shows how even the Indian diplomatic corps started to embrace some aspects of such an ideology and to translate it into its diplomatic practice (Huju, 2022). Still, especially in the first years after the formation of the BJP-led government, normative disagreements about the issues of non-interference and sovereignty, as well as about the need to pursue a more or less confrontational policy vis-à-vis Pakistan, certainly played a role in reinforcing existing tensions among the bureaucracy as well as among 'conciliators' and 'partisans' in the Indian foreign and security policy establishment (Paliwal, 2017).

---

[16] Interview I11, Afghan scholar, online, 16 November 2022.

Moreover, there are reports about disagreements between the MEA, the National Security Council and the prime minister around the issue of whether to appoint a special envoy for Afghanistan around 2020. According to Chaudhuri and Shende (2020: 17), 'The idea of a special envoy has been "floating around for a long time"', but 'There is, according to former senior Indian officials, "a strange resistance" to the appointment of a special envoy. Bureaucratic turf protection is cited as the most common reason for the objection' (Chaudhuri and Shende, 2020: 18). During the dramatic days and weeks after the Taliban takeover of Afghanistan in August 2021, the issue of the emergency visa also became a bone of contention between different Indian ministries.[17] An explanation along the line of capacity problems therefore seems to have a rather substantial explanatory power, especially in combination with the issues of normative struggles and competing external expectations and pressures.

Cognitive problems, by contrast, do not seem to play a major role in explaining India's reluctance, except for the tense phase of the Taliban takeover of Kabul in 2021. For one, India had been involved in Afghanistan for decades. Obviously, the announcement of the handover of formal responsibility for the security of the country to the ANSF from 2014 created a great amount of uncertainty in New Delhi. Also, the shifting stances of successive US administrations, with their alternating announcements of troop withdrawals and successive prorogations of US presence in the country (Laub, 2017), contributed to make the situation less predictable for Indian policy makers. However, there are no indications that would lead us to assume that the long crisis in Afghanistan put Indian decision makers under severe pressure to act, or that the novelty of the situation induced them to adopt all sorts of cognitive shortcuts, which might explain hesitation.

Things are different, of course, when it comes to the dramatic weeks after the Taliban takeover of Kabul in August 2021. In that situation, decision making was extremely difficult for all international actors involved – the Indian government was certainly not an exception, and indeed, most other countries closed their embassies and evacuated their personnel. The chaotic policies on the emergency visa, and especially the decision to nullify all visas already issued to Afghans, can, in part, be explained as a short-term reaction to genuine security concerns: according to some reports and to one of my interviewees, the agency tasked with issuing Indian visas in Kabul was raided immediately after the Taliban takeover (Mitra, 2021b), generating fears in India that the Taliban, or members of other groups, might misuse such stolen visas to enter India amidst the general chaos.[18] Still, the later

---

[17] Interview I9, Indian scholar, online, 8 November 2022.
[18] Interview I11, Afghan scholar, online, 16 November 2022.

decision to issue only some 200 visas for Afghans, and to mainly let Sikhs and Hindus enter the country but to exclude Muslims, cannot be explained by cognitive problems of decision makers acting under extreme pressure – instead, normative and ideological issues played a major role.

Finally, the fourth possible explanation for hesitation developed in Chapter 3 focused on normative struggles. The underlying idea is that different groups within society might refer to competing norms related to how the country should behave in international affairs or in a specific issue area or crisis. The very process of arguing and of trying to devise a common line to follow that reconciles possibly competing norms is what might lead to the zig-zagging and muddling through that are typical of hesitation. In emerging powers, as discussed in Chapter 3, these tensions might even be exacerbated by the very process of 'rise' (and therefore of efforts at increasing the country's international status), in which established domestic norms might come to clash with the normative standards promoted by the higher status group that the government of the rising power aims to join. In the case of India, the crisis in Afghanistan had long been debated in the Indian strategic and foreign policy community, revealing the existence of clearly competing norms in different strands of the debate. In the following, I will discuss competing norms with regards to India's (1) development assistance; (2) crisis management and security policies; and (3) approach to the political settlement to be achieved in Afghanistan, and the issue of whom to talk to and thereby whom to legitimize as a political actor.

The first debate concerns in very concrete terms the question of what India should (or should not) do in Afghanistan. Development assistance and capacity building were areas that were never really called into question in the Indian debate. Quite to the contrary, the notion of supporting South Asian countries in their development, and serving as a role model in the process, has long been an important element in India's foreign policy. India was active as a donor from the 1950s onwards and launched the Indian Technical and Economic Cooperation Programme (ITEC) in 1962 (Chaturvedi, 2012: 562; Fuchs and Vadlamannati, 2013: 111), and South Asia had long been the primary focus of India's development programme. Norms of solidarity with developing countries of the Global South had long played a role in Indian foreign policy. And indeed, also in the years of Modi's BJP-led government, the government emphasized the norm of solidarity in its approach to Afghanistan (see, for example, *Afghanistan Times*, 2019; MEA, 2021a). The notion of helping Afghanistan and the Afghan people was therefore in line with well-established principles in India's foreign policy, and it was not really an object of contestation in the domestic debate.

By contrast, India's security engagement in Afghanistan had been a much-debated issue in the years after 2001, and all the more so as it became clear that war-weary Western countries would sooner or later withdraw their troops. As the Obama administration took over in the USA, fears of a 'zero-option', which would have left Afghanistan to its own fate, unleashed a heated debate in New Delhi on the desirable extent of India's security engagement.

Practically all relevant actors in New Delhi agreed that 'boots on the ground' was not an option for India (Destradi, 2014: 109).[19] India had had a short but painful experience with its failed peace mission to Sri Lanka in the late 1980s (Biswas, 2006; Rajagopalan, 2008), and there was a high degree of aversion towards military intervention in neighbouring countries across the political spectrum. In normative terms, this dovetailed with India's long-standing commitment to non-intervention, which had its origins in Nehru's *Panchsheel*. Importantly, during the years under Prime Minister Modi, the Indian government quite explicitly tried to distance itself from anything related to 'Nehruvianism' as several key elements of Nehruvian ideology contrasted starkly with the ideological tenets of Hindu nationalism – first and foremost the idea of India being a secular state, which has been challenged by the BJP and its notion of *Hindutva*, which basically equates India's nationhood with Hindu cultural-religious traditions (Jaffrelot, 2010; Palshikar, 2015: 720).

When it comes to foreign policy, the shift to a BJP-led government led to a growing and interesting tension between sections of the foreign policy establishment, most notably the diplomats of the MEA, who still strongly embraced Nehruvian norms in their thinking about India's foreign policy (Hall, 2016b), and a government ever more willing to adopt a foreign policy driven by norms inspired by Hindu nationalism. However, in the case of Afghanistan, the desire to be perceived as a more decisive actor pursuing a 'muscular' foreign policy clashed with the danger of provoking Pakistan. As Paliwal (2017) discusses extensively, India's Afghanistan policy over the decades has been strongly driven by the tension between, on the one hand, India's desire to support friendly actors in Afghanistan in order to create a counterweight to Pakistan's influence and, on the other hand, awareness of the risks of going too far with such policy, possibly provoking Pakistan.[20]

It is exactly this kind of dilemma that the BJP-led government of Modi faced in the years 2014–21. The government tried to leave behind the normative baggage of Nehruvianism, but could certainly not depart from the norm of non-interventionism, as this would have unleashed a dangerous reaction by Pakistan. The Indian government also tried to show that it was acting independently from Western pressures, thereby not following up on the calls

---

[19] Interview I7, former high-ranking government official, New Delhi, 22 November 2013.

[20] As an Indian scholar interviewee put it in 2013, 'Both [India and Pakistan] tend to look at Afghanistan through the prism of their relations' (Interview I8, Indian scholar, New Delhi, 26 November 2013).

for greater engagement issued, for example, by the Trump administration. In fact, as Donald Trump publicly mocked the Indian government for not doing enough in Afghanistan, both the Indian government and the opposition Indian National Congress reacted with an outcry, emphasizing that India did not need 'sermons' from the USA on what to do in Afghanistan (Das, 2019). In other words, the norm of independence in foreign policy was also part of the debate on the best approach to adopt vis-à-vis Afghanistan. The reluctance displayed by India in its approach towards Afghanistan can therefore be well explained as a result of such struggles over which norms should shape Indian foreign policy more broadly.

When it comes to the third issue analysed, the question of the political future of Afghanistan, debates in India mostly addressed the issue of how to deal with the Taliban. At least since the hijacking of Indian Airlines Flight 814 in 1999, the Taliban had been India's nemesis. Indeed, the Indian position had long been that there should be no political dialogue with the Taliban, and that no distinction between 'good' and 'bad' Taliban could be made. As Paliwal (2017) points out, the Indian establishment had long been divided between what he calls 'partisans' and 'conciliators'. The former were actors who strongly viewed the situation in Afghanistan through the prism of the India–Pakistan rivalry and, as a consequence, claimed that India should develop close relations with all Afghan political actors who were opposed to Pakistan or at least independent of Pakistan's influence, and that it should actively support such actors. Relatedly, negotiations with the Taliban were considered unacceptable. By contrast, the so-called conciliators were actors who believed that India should adopt a more pragmatic approach vis-à-vis the internal political situation in Afghanistan, politically engaging with (almost) all relevant actors, including the Taliban and their factions. Importantly, according to Paliwal (2017: 12), partisans and conciliators could be found across the political spectrum in India.

In this regard, the years 2014–21 entailed both continuity and change: while partisans and conciliators continued to exist in New Delhi, and while India had started quietly building ties to various Afghan insurgent groups, 'ranging from Hekmatyar to various Taliban figures linked to the Quetta Shura' (Paliwal, 2017: 228), starting from 2015 the conciliators clearly prevailed (Paliwal, 2017: 214), mainly driven by developments on the ground and by the need for India not to become irrelevant to Afghanistan. All this became particularly prominent when the USA, under President Trump, started direct negotiations with Taliban representatives in Doha, something that forced the Indian government to position itself on this matter. In that context, as discussed, there was a high degree of scepticism in India about the USA, not only negotiating with the Taliban, but doing so without including the Afghan government (Chaudhuri and Shende, 2020). Still, there was a tension between India's desire to be recognized as a cooperative member of the international community and therefore accept the course of events, and the norms of sovereignty and non-interference, which the Indian government considered crucial for the political settlement in Afghanistan. In fact, India was interested in 'dilut[ing] the so-called "Western model" of reconciliation, and to make it an Afghan-owned enterprise, however difficult it may be' (Paliwal, 2017: 252). Over the years, the Indian government stuck to its formulation of calling for an 'Afghan-led, Afghan-owned' settlement, or, as it was called in 2020, an 'Afghan-led, Afghan-owned and Afghan-controlled' peace process (MEA, 2020a). At the same time as this goal seemed increasingly unrealistic to achieve, the Indian government ultimately came to accept the Doha Agreement and the need to support the intra-Afghan dialogue process. Moreover, after the Doha Agreement, the Indian government called for 'a leading role of the United Nations, since that would help improve the odds for a lasting and durable outcome' (MEA, 2021b).

In sum, normative struggles within the Indian foreign and security policy establishment were certainly a relevant factor in explaining New Delhi's hesitant Afghanistan policy during the years 2014–21. Competing norms were at play in India's approach to development and security, and to the issue of political reconciliation. Paliwal (2017: 13) also acknowledges that the existence of these normative debates on Afghanistan led to a confusing (and therefore hesitant) policy on the part of India: 'Simultaneous activism of these seemingly disparate advocacies generates dynamics that imparts nuance (but also confusion) to the way India behaves in Afghanistan'. These normative struggles, as well as the frictions among different agencies and sections of the foreign and security policy community, were further reinforced – and, to some extent, even determined – by competing international expectations. At the same time, the decision to re-open the embassy in June 2022 can be interpreted as an at least temporary resolution of such a normative struggle to the advantage of what Paliwal would call the conciliators. As one interviewee put it, 'according to a survey [carried out] in India, only 27 per cent of the people [in India] are in favour of dealing with the Taliban. But the bureaucracy sees that this needs to be done',[21] and therefore pushed through this rather unpopular policy.

As discussed in Chapter 3, competing international expectations can be a major factor that contributes to explain reluctance. In the case of Afghanistan, India was indeed subject to opposite expectations, with substantial possible consequences, which put the government under a high degree of pressure. On the one hand, successive governments of Pakistan expressed the clear expectation that India should stay out of Afghanistan and not influence it. Pakistan has long pursued an approach labelled 'strategic depth' vis-à-vis

---

[21] Interview I9, Indian scholar, online, 8 November 2022.

Afghanistan – a notion involving the idea of Afghanistan being a territory available for the retreat of Pakistani troops in the case of an attack from India – something that obviously entailed the need to have Pakistan-friendly actors in power in Afghanistan (Parkes, 2019). It is therefore not surprising that the Pakistani government wanted the country's arch-enemy, India, to limit its influence in Kabul as far as possible.

Replying to a question concerning what role Pakistan thought India should have in Afghanistan, in 2017 Pakistan's Prime Minister Shahid Khaqan Abbasi replied:

> Zero. [Laughter.] India – we don't foresee any political or military role for India in Afghanistan. I think it will just complicate the situation and it will not resolve anything. So if they want to do economic assistance, that's their prerogative, but there's no – we don't accept or see any role politically or militarily for India in Afghanistan. (Council on Foreign Relations, 2017)

Pakistani government officials reiterated this position in the following years. For example, in 2019 in a weekly press briefing by the government, the spokesperson repeated: 'India has no role in Afghanistan' (MFA, 2019). Moreover, Pakistan regularly accused India of using its consulates in Afghanistan to spy on Pakistan, and more generally to use its presence in Afghanistan to destabilize Pakistan's provinces of Khyber Pakhtunkhwa, Federally Administered Tribal Areas (FATA) and Baluchistan (Paliwal, 2017: 9–10).

The USA and a number of Western countries were other influential actors articulating expectations vis-à-vis India, which were clearly related to their own gradual disengagement from Afghanistan. Since 2009, when President Barack Obama had announced a withdrawal of ISAF troops, the issue of the USA and its allies gradually withdrawing from Afghanistan was one of the major developments in the country. Under the Trump administration, the desire to leave Afghanistan became increasingly acute. In that context, Trump repeatedly asked India to increase its engagement in Afghanistan, be it in terms of economic support (*The Economic Times*, 2019) or of military aid (Raj, 2019). In 2019, he mocked India for having built a library in Afghanistan, implying that the Indian effort had been minimal and that New Delhi should do more: '"I get along very well with India, Prime Minister Modi. But … he is constantly telling me he built a library in Afghanistan. … That's like … five hours of what we spent [in Afghanistan]. … I don't know who is using it"' (quoted in BBC News, 2019).

By calling for greater Indian engagement, the US administration was pursuing a very different course compared to that of past administrations, which had deliberately excluded India from playing a more prominent role in Afghanistan, mainly in order not to provoke Pakistan. As Kaura (2017: 38) puts it,

> Trump's policy has been viewed as a remarkable turnaround for the US that earlier wanted to keep India out of its Afghanistan for fear of offending Pakistan. India was viewed as part of the problem till the Obama administration, and now Trump has argued that India should be viewed as part of a solution to the Afghan conflict.

As the reduction of Western troops was being planned and proceeded, other Western countries also called for greater Indian involvement. The UK started 'pushing India for a larger economic, but primarily military role' (Taneja, 2017), and in 2019 the German special envoy for Afghanistan, Markus Potzel, stated: 'We would like to see India play a bigger role in Afghanistan' (TOLOnews, 2019). Finally, calls for greater Indian support were regularly issued by successive Afghan governments (with the exception of the first months of the presidency of Ashraf Ghani, when relations with India were rather tense; see Katju, 2015). Successive Afghan governments had presented 'wish lists' of weapons and military supplies to decision makers in New Delhi, asking for help (see, for example, Swami, 2015). For example, after India had donated four attack helicopters to Afghanistan, the Afghan ambassador to India stated: 'We are grateful for the four helicopters. But we need more, we need much more. Today we are heading into a situation that is worrisome for everyone in the region including India' (Miglani, 2016). More generally, the Afghan experts interviewed reported that in Afghanistan the perception prevailed that India was 'bandwagoning' with the USA[22] and was 'engaged, but unable to give anything'.[23] By contrast, in India, Afghanistan was perceived as asking for too much: 'The Afghans want so much, we will never be able to fulfill it'.[24] These clearly divergent expectations – with Afghanistan and the West calling for greater Indian engagement and Pakistan being very clear about its rejection of a more extensive Indian role – certainly contributed to increase the pressure on decision makers in New Delhi concerning India's engagement in Afghanistan.

To conclude, India's continued reluctance vis-à-vis Afghanistan in the years 2014–21 can best be explained by a combination of competing external expectations and normative struggles. Ultimately, India was faced with a very challenging situation in Afghanistan, torn apart between, on the one hand, the desire to contribute to the stabilization of the country and to respond

---

[22] Interview I3, Afghan academic, New Delhi, 31 October 2013.
[23] Interview I11, Afghan scholar, online, 16 November 2022.
[24] Interview I7, former high-ranking government official, New Delhi, 22 November 2013.

to the requests to do so by the Afghan government and Western powers; and on the other hand, the need not to provoke and antagonize Pakistan beyond a certain point in order to avoid an escalation of the India–Pakistan conflict, and thereby to stick to its declared commitment to non-interference.

India and crisis management in Nepal

The second case analysed in this chapter is a crisis that differs in many ways from the major and long-standing security crisis in Afghanistan. In fact, in this section, I focus on India's approach to a domestic political crisis that unfolded in Nepal, one of India's smaller neighbouring countries. The crisis took place between 2015 and 2017, and it revolved around the issue of the introduction of a new constitution in Nepal.

Nepal had recently undergone a momentous political transition. After 10 years, the civil war between the government and the rebels of the Communist Party of Nepal (Maoist) (CPN-M) had come to an end in 2006. As a result of a peace agreement between the rebels and the political parties of the Seven Party Alliance (SPA), an interim constitution had been introduced in 2007 (Gellner, 2007: 85).[25] Moreover, in May 2008, the new constituent assembly in its first session had proclaimed the Republic, thereby putting an end to monarchy. In August 2008, a new power-sharing government had been formed. These were substantial changes: 'An extreme Left-wing guerrilla force had earned the right to head the government through democratic means, fulfilling the mandate of the ten-year-long people's war to write a new constitution and declare Nepal a republic, dismantling the 240-year-old monarchy' (Mehta, 2020: 130).

In the following years, the development of a new constitution, which was supposed to replace the interim one, proceeded only slowly and with multiple extensions of the originally envisaged timeline (see ICG, 2012a). Ultimately, after a devastating earthquake that hit Nepal in April 2015, the main political parties represented in the Constituent Assembly decided to fast-track the long-delayed constitutional process, adopting a new constitution on 20 September 2015. The constitution transformed Nepal into a federal, democratic and secular republic. However, this process was accompanied by massive protests by disadvantaged groups dissatisfied with several of the provisions entailed in the new constitution (see Strasheim and Bogati, 2016). Disagreements concerned, among other things, the issue of the boundaries of new states within Nepal's new federal system, electoral representation and affirmative action, the delineation of constituencies and

---

[25] For an overview of Nepal's history, see Whelpton (2005). For analysis of the role of India in Nepal's complex democratic transition, see Destradi (2012b).

citizenship clauses restricting women's ability to pass full citizenship rights to their children (ICG, 2016: 2). In particular, the Madhesis and Tharus, ethnic groups living in the southern part of the country, were worried that the constitution would perpetuate the traditional dominance of Nepal's upper caste hill elites, which had shaped the country's political fate for centuries. But Janajatis, Dalits,[26] women's groups and religious minorities also expressed their dissatisfaction with what they considered insufficient efforts at addressing their marginalization and historical injustices.[27] The protest in the southern region of Nepal went on for months, repeatedly turning violent and leading to over 50 casualties (Human Rights Watch, 2015; The Asia Foundation, 2017), with the police even resorting to firing into the crowds.

Protests started as a reaction to the plans by the established political parties to fast-track the constitutional process after the earthquake, and became particularly virulent after the adoption of the constitution on 20 September 2015. Three days later, the United Madhesi Democratic Front (UMDF), an organization that brought together several Madhesi parties, declared that it would impose a blockade on all customs points at the border with India (ICG, 2016: 19).[28] This measure was supposed to put pressure on the elite in Kathmandu because the largest part of Nepal's trade crossed such customs points: Nepal imported practically all its fuel, kerosene, cooking gas, and so on from India, and was dependent on a steady flow of such supplies due to its limited storage capacities (ICG, 2016: 19). Building materials, fertilizers and pesticides also came from India across such border posts. Indeed, India and Nepal share an open border (a rarity in South Asia), and the very geopolitical situation of Nepal had made the country highly dependent on India for centuries.

The blockade continued for 135 days, seriously harming Nepal's economy and almost leading to a humanitarian crisis. As Dixit (2015) described the

---

[26] The term 'Madhesi' refers to 'a population of caste-based Hindus and Muslims residing in the Tarai region, who speak plains languages such as Maithali and Bhojpuri, and have extensive economic, social and family ties across the border in northern India. "Tharu" refers to the indigenous populations of the Tarai plains, some communities of which are concentrated in large numbers in the far-western plains and the districts of Kanchanpur and Kailali. "Janajati" refers to the umbrella term for a large number of ethnic groups, most but not all from the hills, who are outside the Hindu caste system and claim distinct languages, cultures and, often, historical homelands' (ICG, 2016: 1). Dalits are low-caste Hindus, formerly discriminated as 'untouchables'.

[27] Interview I12, Indian scholar, online, 18 November 2022.

[28] A Nepalese scholar interviewee pointed to the fact that protesters retired to the no-man's land between India and Nepal in order to escape persecution by the Nepalese security forces, and this is how the blockade emerged in the first place. Interview I13, Nepalese scholar, online, 20 November 2022.

situation at the time, '[a] country of 28 million people has ground to a halt, schools are closing, hospitals are turning away patients, public transport is limited, industries have shut, tourist arrivals have plummeted'. The blockade seriously damaged the entire country. Ultimately, the blockade was revoked on 8 February 2016. This was due to government repression of protests and to a general fatigue among all actors, but also happened because the black market was thriving,[29] and the government was able to increase its imports from China (Jha, 2016a).[30] According to one interviewee who highlighted the role of India in the blockade, 'After the Indian policy makers realized it [was] not working ... they started pulling back on it, and this is where they alienated the Tarai'.[31]

Unsurprisingly, the political crisis in Nepal continued, with high levels of political instability in the following months. In this chapter, I will also include in the analysis the period between the end of the blockade and the parliamentary elections of November–December 2017, which were the first elections held in the country since 1999, and the first under the new federal state structure. While political instability in Nepal did not end in 2017, the elections and the subsequent formation of a Leftist alliance government in many ways marked the conclusion of the turbulent phase associated with the adoption of the new constitution.

The months that followed the lifting of the blockade were characterized by continued political infighting among the main political parties of Nepal.[32] In July 2016, the government of Prime Minister Khadga Prasad Sharma Oli of the Communist Party of Nepal (Unified Marxist-Leninist) (CPN-UML) resigned after a no-confidence motion filed by its coalition partner CPN (Maoist Centre), the party that had emerged from the previous rebel group. Its head (and former rebel leader) Pushpa Kamal Dahal ('Prachanda') took over the government in a coalition with the Nepali Congress (NC), one of the country's established parties. He handed over government leadership to NC President Sher Bahadur Deuba on 24 May 2017, as per their coalition agreement. In the following months, the new government approved some constitutional amendments that addressed a number of Madhesi grievances, such as the creation of two provinces (instead of one) that included exclusively districts from the southern Tarai plains, or the

---

[29] According to a Nepalese scholar, 'the Madhesis [themselves] got involved in smuggling. So they used to smuggle gas, all sorts of goods from India to Nepal. So it were those people who launched the movement that got engaged in this smuggling [and thereby ultimately undermined the blockade itself]' (Interview I13, Nepalese scholar, online, 20 November 2022).

[30] Interview I12, Indian scholar, online, 18 November 2022.

[31] Interview I10, Indian scholar, online, 15 November 2022.

[32] The following discussion of political developments in Nepal builds on ICG (2022).

introduction of naturalized citizenship for non-Nepali (usually Indian) women who marry Nepali men.

In the second half of 2017, local elections were held in Nepal, and finally, federal parliamentary and provincial elections took place in two phases, on 26 November and 7 December 2017. They were won by the 'Leftist alliance' composed of the CPN (Maoist Center) and the CPN-UML. In February 2018, the two parties merged to form the Communist Party of Nepal, and their leaders Oli and Dahal agreed to share the post of prime minister during the newly elected Parliament's five-year term.

India's reluctant approach to the crisis in Nepal

India's approach to the protracted crisis in Nepal was characterized by a high degree of reluctance, as revealed in particular by the ambivalence and continuous flip-flopping of the Indian government in its approach to the blockade and to various Nepalese political actors. India has a long history of close relations with Nepal, which is also, however, a long history of continuous meddling with the smaller country's domestic affairs. Ever since India's independence, successive Indian governments considered Nepal to be part of India's sphere of influence, and induced Nepal to try to cope with its 'sandwiched' position between China and India by attempting to play the two neighbours off against each other.

The Indo–Nepal Treaty of Peace and Friendship of 1950, which is still in force, included an obligation of mutual consultation in case of tensions with neighbouring countries, while Articles 6 and 7 extended reciprocal rights to citizens of both countries in matters of residence, trade, ownership of property, and so on. As a consequence, the border between India and Nepal is entirely open (Hachhethu and Gellner, 2010: 136–7). Among the many episodes of Indian meddling with Nepal's internal developments over the past decades was a (so-called 'de facto') blockade imposed by India in 1989 after Nepal had introduced restrictive measures against Indian citizens concerning immigration and work permits, and had tried to emancipate itself from New Delhi's hegemony by buying weapons from China without informing India – both violations of the 1950 treaty, according to New Delhi (Whelpton, 2005: 113). As Parajulee (2000: 191) put it, 'the trade and transit dispute … was the culmination point of a growing uneasiness with the structure of the bilateral relationship, characterized by Nepal's desire for "independence" and India's desire for "control"'. Moreover, India had played a highly ambivalent role in Nepal's democratization process in the years 2005–08, supporting King Gyanendra's authoritarian regime as long as it could and providing it with weapons and training against the Maoist rebels, but at the same time quietly serving as a facilitator of a political dialogue between the Maoist rebels and the democratic parties, which ultimately was crucial to Nepal's peace process and democratic transition (Destradi, 2012a).

In the years 2015–17, New Delhi pursued an approach that can certainly be defined as reluctant – with reluctance understood as a mix of hesitation and recalcitrance (see Chapter 2). In particular, New Delhi's approach to crisis management in Nepal entailed many inconsistencies and contradictions. As aptly summarized by Jha (2017a), India's policy was characterized by 'inconsistency, ad-hoc policy making, multiplicity of power centres, conflicting messages, and absence of will'. Moreover, it entailed some degree of recalcitrance when it came to (competing and contradictory) requests made by different political actors from inside Nepal.

As protests started to erupt in the Tarai region in the context of the fast-tracking of constitutional reform in 2015, New Delhi was initially supportive of the concerns of the Madhesis. Prime Minister Modi's government had put some effort into improving relations with Nepal and other South Asian countries in the context of its 'Neighbourhood First' initiative, and India had helped Nepal with reconstruction efforts and aid after the 2015 earthquake (Muni, 2015a: 18). Moreover, the Indian government supported the idea of having a more inclusive constitution in Nepal.[33] However, in the period that followed, and during the drafting of the new constitution, the Indian government repeatedly changed its policies.

Muni (2015b: 18) identifies three contrasting phases in this process: initially, India pursued a 'hands-off' approach, appearing 'assured and somewhat complacent in letting the process evolve in the hope that suggestions for an inclusive constitution offered by the Indian leadership, including by Prime Minister Modi, in his engagements with the Nepali public and leaders at various levels, would prove sufficient'. In a second phase, the Indian government took the approach that ' "any constitution is better than no constitution" (an expression used informally by the senior Indian foreign service officials)'. In this phase, 'Many of the prominent Nepali leaders like Sher Bahadur Deuba of the NC, and Prachanda of the Maoists, were invited to India for consultations where all of them promised to take Madhes and other groups on board' (Muni, 2015b: 18). Finally, in September 2015, the 'third and what may be called as the panic stage was reached when New Delhi realized that Nepal's constitutional process had slipped out of their reach' (Muni, 2015b: 18).

At this point, only a few days before adopting the new constitution, India's then-foreign secretary, Subrahmanyam Jaishankar, was sent to Kathmandu to pressurize the Nepalese government in order to induce it to give more time to the constitutional process (Jacob, 2022). The Indian foreign secretary

---

[33] Interview I12, Indian scholar, online, 18 November 2022.

also tried to convince the Nepalese government to abide by the protesters' demands and to make the constitution more inclusive (Majumder, 2015), but this obviously came too late and was perceived as meddling with Nepal's internal affairs. As one of the interviewees put it, 'That was a stupid move'.[34] But the Indian government continued to try to pressurize Nepal up to the very last minute: just a few hours before the ceremony for the introduction of the constitution, India's ambassador reportedly met Nepal's Prime Minister Sushil Koirala 'to express Delhi's disappointment at the process going through' (Majumder, 2015). Moreover, in its official statement after the adoption of the constitution, the Indian government pointedly only 'noted' that the constitution had been introduced – a clear signal of its disappointment.[35] After all those unsuccessful attempts at influencing things at the last minute, the Indian government reportedly started lobbying for the introduction of amendments to the constitution (Roy, 2015) and, most importantly, tacitly supported the blockade (*The Times of India*, 2015a; Jha, 2017c).

There are different interpretations about India's role in the blockade. The Indian government firmly denied any role in it: 'Let me take this opportunity to also clarify to Hon'ble Members that contrary to some canards on this issue, there is no blockade by India, which we have repeatedly clarified, of supplies going to Nepal. Obstructions are by the Nepalese population on the Nepalese side, in which GoI [Government of India] cannot interfere' (MEA, 2015). Instead, according to the International Crisis Group (ICG, 2016: 19), the blockade 'appears to have been instigated by New Delhi, unhappy that its cautions about the constitution-writing process were unheeded and concerned about instability along the open border. However, Madhesi parties and activist groups quickly claimed responsibility'. The ICG (2016: 20) then adds, 'even if the blockade was indigenous, the major parties and Kathmandu establishment were correct that India was in concert with Madhesi parties. ... Madhesi protestors' efforts were bolstered from the Indian side by bureaucratic foot dragging, new complications for transit and customs procedures and suddenly absent officials'. The latter interpretation was also seconded by some of the interviewees, who put it this way: 'India acted by omission, not commission. On its side of the border, it did not push for the blockade to be lifted. It looked the other way, it was implicitly supportive of the uprising on the Madhesi side'[36] and 'There is an impression that India instigated blockade. But my impression is that it was not instigated by India, but that it was internal. It was [a] fully internal movement'.[37] Regardless of the issue of whether India instigated the imposition of the

---

[34] Interview I10, Indian scholar, online, 15 November 2022.
[35] Interview I12, Indian scholar, online, 18 November 2022.
[36] Interview I12, Indian scholar, online, 18 November 2022.
[37] Interview I13, Nepalese scholar, online, 22 November 2022.

blockade or not, through its role in the blockade, India clearly alienated the local population in large parts of Nepal, as pointed out by Indian opposition politician Shashi Tharoor:

The problem was not just that this came across as overbearing, but that it had all the subtlety of a blunderbuss: instead of sending a message to the elite in the hills, we hurt people we didn't want to hurt – the aam aadmi [common man] of Nepalis [sic]. An ordinary worker in Kathmandu who can't get an auto-rickshaw to take his pregnant wife to a hospital because there's no petrol in the pumps isn't going to worry about the niceties of constitutional inclusiveness. He is just going to curse India for doing this to him. We made enemies of the very people we have always claimed are our brothers. (Tharoor, 2017)

In the following months, however, India's approach changed. As the Nepalese government under Oli started to move closer to China, New Delhi feared that it might lose its traditional influence over Nepal.[38] Against this backdrop, India reportedly started to 'prod ... the Madhesis to withdraw the blockade' (Jha, 2017a). In July 2016, in a new policy turn, the Indian government persuaded Prachanda of the CPN-M to withdraw from the governing coalition and thereby to sideline Prime Minister Oli, who had come to be seen as excessively friendly vis-à-vis China (Jha, 2016b). It was reportedly India that 'brokered an agreement between Prachanda and Deuba' (Jha, 2017d) of the NC, thereby promoting the creation of a new coalition government. This government, initially under the leadership of Prachanda, introduced a series of changes to the new constitution that were in line with the demands of protesters from the Tarai, and it enjoyed better relations with New Delhi. Reportedly, Prachanda had promised to Indian Prime Minister Modi to amend the constitution during a visit to Delhi and a meeting on the sidelines of the BRICS summit in October 2016 (Jha, 2017b).

Importantly, however, in May 2017, India's approach towards Nepal took another turn: Indian diplomats in Kathmandu reportedly told the leaders of the Madhesi movement to drop their demands related to the constitution – 'a move seen as a dramatic U-turn on a policy crafted over two years' (Jha, 2017b). This shift came after Manjeev Singh Puri was appointed ambassador to Nepal in March 2017 (Jha, 2017b). The Indian Embassy also conveyed to the leaders from the Tarai that they should participate in the upcoming local elections 'or face marginalisation' (Jha, 2017b). Ultimately, this meant that India suddenly was 'almost making a two year policy exercise futile'

---

[38]   See also Interview I12, Indian scholar, online, 18 November 2022.

(Jha, 2017a), and understandably creating much disappointment among the Madhesis.

When Shah Bahadur Deuba of the NC took over the prime ministership from Prachanda in June 2017, the Indian government was reportedly very satisfied, given that the NC had traditionally been close to India, and that New Delhi had even supported Deuba in internal party elections (Jha, 2017d). Ultimately, however, the electoral success of the leftist coalition of CPN-UML and CPN-M meant a loss of influence for India, as the new government was interested in strengthening ties with China, and India–Nepal relations reached an all-time low. According to Prashant Jha, one of the most attentive observers of India–Nepal relations, India acted as an 'ineffective and incompetent manager of Nepal's domestic politics and put off everyone' (Jha, 2017a). Upreti (2016: 112) argues: 'There is no doubt that India lacks clarity and consistency in its approach towards Nepal'. Overall, the multiple twists and turns in the policies of the Indian government vis-à-vis the issue of constitutional reform in Nepal amounted to a clear case of strong hesitation.

To some extent, New Delhi's approach was also recalcitrant, as India ignored or rejected the requests of various political actors in Nepal. In particular, its initial support for the Madhesis was at a certain point replaced by a dismissive attitude, something that created a huge disappointment among the representatives of the Madhesis and all those fighting for a more inclusive constitution (Tewari, 2017). The *Hindustan Times* quotes a senior leader of a Madhesi party, as saying 'For over a year and a half, India agreed with us on the need for an amendment and the impossibility of accepting elections under this constitutional framework as it exists. But ever since a new ambassador has come in, we are being told to give up the agenda' (quoted in Jha, 2017b).

Explaining India's reluctant approach to Nepal

How can we explain India's reluctance in dealing with the crisis in Nepal, and ultimately India's failure to devise a consistent policy able to guarantee continued leverage for New Delhi in the face of growing Chinese influence? Given India's clear interest in keeping close relations with Nepal and its worries about 'losing' Nepal to China (see, for example, Khobragade, 2016; Singh, 2016), the reluctant policies adopted by New Delhi are particularly surprising. In fact, India–China competition in South Asia has been a matter of major concern to Indian policy makers over the past decades.

Of the explanations discussed in Chapter 3, and as mentioned, political weakness and instability of the government were not in place in the Indian case. The second explanation, labelled 'limited capacity', by contrast seems to yield a substantial amount of explanatory power. In the literature on foreign policy, capacity problems are usually mentioned to refer to weaknesses in the bureaucracy. However, this is an aspect that does not seem to be relevant in Nepal's case. In fact, many of India's most accomplished diplomats have served in Nepal, revealing the comparatively high prioritization of this bilateral relationship on the part of New Delhi. While India's bureaucratic corps is tiny and understaffed, it therefore seems difficult to argue that India's diplomats were not able to adequately deal with Nepal, also given the huge cultural affinity between the two countries (Upreti, 2016: 109). Somewhat paradoxically, it rather seems that the closeness between India and Nepal and their respective political elites might have led to an excessive uncoordinated meddling by various actors from India. This lack of coordination can contribute to explain some of the inconsistencies in India's policies, and can therefore count as a sort of variant of the capacity problems discussed in Chapter 3. In fact, over the decades, a range of Indian actors exercised influence over Nepalese politics with different aims. Already at the time of the transition to democracy, India had played an ambivalent role because of 'the divergent priorities of the different Indian agencies involved in shaping New Delhi's Nepal policy' (Destradi, 2012a: 297). These comprised the Indian security establishment, which had long cultivated close ties with the Royal Nepalese Army and had an interest in the survival of the monarchy. Within the Indian National Congress there were figures close to the Nepalese royal family, such as Karan Singh, a former minister and diplomat, who had been sent by then-Prime Minister Manmohan Singh to negotiate with the Nepalese king. By contrast, Indian leftist parties had connections to the Nepalese Maoist rebels, and indeed Baburam Bhattarai, one of the leading figures at the beginning of the Maoist rebellion, had earned a PhD at the renowned Jawaharlal Nehru University in New Delhi.

As Varadarajan (2010) put it, the high number of different Indian interlocutors being in touch with different actors within Nepal contributed to 'amplify the existing policy dissonance in Delhi and [to] create maximum confusion'. During the period analysed, this trend continued. According to India's former foreign secretary Vijay Gokhale (2021), 'India appeared to be micro-managing Nepal's politics in pursuit of its core interests and acting tactically with local political actors'. S.D. Muni, one of India's experts with the deepest knowledge of Nepalese politics, argues that, in 2015, during the phase preceding the adoption of the new constitution,

> ... [c]onflicting and confusing messages from the formal policymaking establishments and from the diverse constituencies of the BJP's ideological affiliates were going to Nepal. It was not clear as to what were India's priorities: an inclusive constitution addressing Madhesi concerns or an accommodation of Hindutva and monarchical preferences, or perhaps both. Lapses on the part of Indian diplomacy now pushed it in the

company of Nepali Hindu fanatics and left extremists on the one hand and marginalized forces on the other. (Muni, 2015b: 18–19)

Indeed, members of the BJP and of other Hindu nationalist organizations were connected to the established Nepalese elites close to the former Hindu monarchy. There is ample evidence about close relations between Indian Hindu nationalist organizations and Nepalese royalists. Nepal's king Birendra, who was in power between 1972 and 2001, was declared emperor of all Hindus by the Vishwa Hindu Mahasangh, an organization forming part of the Indian family of Hindu nationalist organizations called Vishwa Hindu Parishad (Rae, 2021). It is therefore not surprising that one of the most contentious issues for Indian political actors was the question of whether Nepal would become a secular state or not. According to an interviewee, 'When the constitution was being made, India's leadership was trying to see if the "secular" word could be removed from the constitution. [They had] an issue with Christian conversions [which were spreading in Nepal]'.[39] Among the Indian actors who tried to push for the removal of secularism from the Nepalese constitution was Yogi Adityanath, a hardline Hindu nationalist and chief minister of the Indian state of Uttar Pradesh, which borders the Tarai region (see Chaudhury, 2017). But also BJP President Rajnath Singh claimed that making Nepal a secular state was an error (Jha, 2015). Ultimately, however, 'Nepal's new constitution has only accommodated them to the extent of making the cow a national animal, discouraging cow slaughter and adding a definition of "secularism" that covers respect and protection of all religion, including Hinduism' (Muni, 2015a).

Other actors from India, meanwhile, pushed for a greater inclusion of Madhesi demands in the constitution. Among those was Lalu Prasad Yadav, leader of the Rashtriya Janata Dal (RJD, National People's Party) in the state of Bihar, the other Indian state that shares a long border with the Tarai region (*Business Standard*, 2016). The RJD in fact tried to use the fate of the Madhesis, which have strong ties to the people in Bihar, as a tool for political mobilisation during the October–November 2015 elections in the state – something that the BJP-led Indian government also reportedly did through its support for the blockade (see Bose, 2015; Jaleel, 2015). According to an expert from Nepal, the BJP during that phase mainly supported the demands of the Madhesis, while politicians of the Indian National Congress and communist parties from India rather sided with the people in the north of Nepal, reflecting the deep political polarization characterizing both India and Nepal.[40]

---

[39] Interview I10, Indian scholar, online, 15 November 2022.
[40] Interview I13, Nepalese scholar, online, 20 November 2022.

In sum, therefore, different political actors from India had close connections with some counterparts in Nepal and were trying to pursue distinct, and at times changing, agendas in shaping the future of the neighbouring country. India's hesitant policies can therefore be traced back to the difficulties in preference formation related to having, plainly speaking, too many cooks spoil the broth of India's Nepal policy. Different actors from India, deeply enmeshed with internal politics in Nepal, had multiple strategic objectives, which led to conflicting policy approaches. As an interviewee put it, 'Then you have all this mumbo jumbo getting together. There are different channels of communication'.[41]

Moreover, there are indications that some of the twists by New Delhi were simply the result of negligence or personalized politics. For one, Tharoor (2017) claims that, during the final phases of the drafting of the constitution,

> ... our embassy, which was led by Ambassador Ranjit Rae ... read the warning signs in time and sent urgent messages to New Delhi calling for early diplomatic intervention. These were ignored. As I have mentioned earlier, one astute observer told me privately that the 'PMO took its eyes off the ball'. That was the Modi government's first mistake. By the time it woke up to the impending crisis and dispatched the foreign secretary to Kathmandu, it was already too late.

Moreover, one of the interviewees interpreted the Indian government's decision to send Jaishankar to Nepal at the last minute as a result of Prime Minister Modi being offended by the Nepalese government:

> Modi's visit to Nepal in 2014 was a success, when he went to the constituent assembly there. What happened after 2014, there were two issues: Modi wanted to have direct access to [the] Tarai people and to address a gathering. There were efforts to give bicycles, goodies to [the] Tarai people to establish a rapport [with India]. The Nepalese government did not allow it, they did not want the Tarai constituency to be strengthened. [That was a] personal affront to Modi.[42]

Cognitive problems, the third possible explanation for reluctance discussed in Chapter 3, seem to have a more limited explanatory power as the crisis in Nepal was not a sudden and acute phenomenon. Indeed, given India's elites' good knowledge of the situation in Nepal, the disaffection of the Madhesis and other minorities should have been well known for decades. And at least the long duration of the constitutional process that followed

---

[41]   Interview I10, Indian scholar, online, 15 November 2022.
[42]   Interview I10, Indian scholar, online, 15 November 2022.

the adoption of the interim constitution should have revealed to Indian decision makers that there were some very serious grievances building up in the country. It does not therefore seem appropriate to claim that Indian policy makers were caught by surprise by the unfolding of events in Nepal, and were therefore turning to hesitant policies out of a cognitive inability to cope with the situation. Rather, India's reactive approach seems a result of neglect on the part of the central government, combined with multiple uncoordinated efforts at influencing Nepal's politics on the part of various political actors from India.

Finally, normative struggles should be taken into account as a possible explanation for India's reluctance in Nepal. To some extent, this explanation is a useful complement to the competing approaches by different domestic actors, and it is also related to the issue of expectations targeted at India. The main problem with Indian engagement in Nepal was the widespread perception among Nepalese elites and the broader Nepalese society about Indian meddling with their country's domestic politics. Given India's track record of repeated interference ever since independence, it is little wonder that the Nepalese public was very sceptical of India. In his memoir, India's former ambassador to Nepal Ranjit Rae (2021) vividly describes the outrage at India that was widespread among the population, with massive protests breaking out over some remarks by Bollywood actors or quarrels about the origins of Yoga and Buddhism. Representatives of Nepalese civil society and the Nepalese elite therefore again and again expressed the expectation that India not meddle with Nepal's domestic affairs and finally respect Nepal as a sovereign country with a distinct identity (see, for example, Ghimire, 2009; Arora, 2015; *The Hindu*, 2016). At the same time, quite paradoxically, most sections of Nepal's political elite repeatedly turned to India to get support for their domestic political struggles, expecting the Indian government to support their cause – be it the continuation of privileges for the hill elites, or the promulgation of a genuinely inclusive constitution, or New Delhi's support in battling competing parties and factions.

These competing expectations articulated by various political players from Nepal put the Indian government under considerable pressure. They dovetailed with existing differences among the Indian political elite about whether to support the demands of the Madhesis or rather the hill elites of Nepal.[43] They also related to normative struggles within the Indian foreign policy establishment on how to deal with Nepal, which mainly revolved around the contradiction between the well-established norm of non-interference versus the promotion of India's national interests in the face of growing Chinese influence. In this sense, India's approach towards

---

[43] Interview I13, Nepalese scholar, 20 November 2022.

Nepal in the years 2015–17 did not differ much from previous phases, in which New Delhi had already faced the danger of 'losing' Nepal to China. However, especially under Nepal's Prime Minister Oli, the threat of growing Chinese influence become ever more tangible. The merger between the CPN-UML and CPN-M was reportedly strongly influenced by China (Gokhale, 2021), and China became an important economic player in Nepal (see, for example, Bhatia et al, 2016). In March 2016, Oli visited Beijing and signed a bilateral transit transport agreement that granted Nepal access to China's ports (CrisisWatch Database, 2022). China became engaged in infrastructure projects in Nepal, and it opened a number of border transit points and started exploring the feasibility of a cross-border railway connection (Gokhale, 2021). All this was a cause of concern in India and was seen as running against India's national interests. This obviously stood in contrast with the traditional notion of non-interference, to which Indian policy makers frequently referred, mentioning the sovereignty of Nepal, despite India's long history of interference in the country (see, for example, *Hindustan Times*, 2017).

While competing domestic expectations played an important role in increasing pressure on the Indian government and in bolstering various Indian political actors' sometimes competing approaches towards Nepal, international expectations were not a major factor in the case of India's crisis management in Nepal. While the international community was long involved in development assistance activities in the country and had supported the peace process, its reaction to Madhesi protests and to the blockade was 'largely muted' (ICG, 2016: 16), apart from an exhortation by UN Secretary-General Ban Ki Moon in November 2015 for 'all sides' to lift the blockade (*The Times of India*, 2015b). As the ICG (2016: 16) puts it:

> Western donors have felt hobbled in recent years by criticism that they promoted culturally inappropriate liberal values and muddied the waters in the first CA [Constitutional Assembly]. They have also been under pressure to channel development funds through the government and to show results via spending, so are loath to give further offence. There is fatigue with the seemingly endless post-conflict transition, feckless politicians and the global proliferation of far more deadly conflicts. Most donor countries and the UN welcomed the sixteen-point agreement, despite clear signs there was no buy-in from Madhesi and other marginalised groups.

In this context, it is not surprising that international donors or Western countries did not express any strong expectation vis-à-vis India. The Nepalese diaspora in countries like the USA, moreover, was itself deeply divided between supporters of the Madhesis and of the hill elites, thereby sending contradictory signals to their host countries.[44] And the Indian government was not making any major efforts at explaining the situation in Nepal to international actors, according to an interviewee.[45]

To conclude, the case of Nepal constitutes another case of reluctance in regional crisis management on the part of India. Despite its obvious interest in a stabilization of the situation, the Indian government failed to pursue a policy that would have contributed to it. Quite to the contrary, New Delhi's approach was highly contradictory, with a series of about-turns that left the Nepalese people and elites deeply disconcerted. Besides hesitation, India was recalcitrant as it was not able to find clear responses to the various expectations and requests articulated by different political actors in Nepal.

Given this specific situation, in this case reluctance can best be explained by focusing on the weaknesses and limitations of India's policy making, which displayed a total lack of coordination among different political actors close to specific sections of Nepalese society. The competing initiatives and interests of those actors led to flip-flopping policies, while the central government neglected the issue for a long time. New Delhi's difficulties in decision making were reinforced by competing expectations by Nepalese actors as well as by broader underlying normative debates about the key norms driving India's foreign policy. In particular, the desire to take seriously the norm of non-intervention obviously clashed with the need to keep India's influence in Nepal vis-à-vis China's growing presence in the country.

---

[44] Interview I13, Nepalese scholar, online, 20 November 2022.
[45] Interview I12, Indian scholar, online, 18 November 2022.

5

Germany's Mixed Approach: Not Always a Reluctant Hegemon

With the outbreak of the Eurozone crisis in 2009, Germany came back centre stage in European politics, and continued to play a central role in the 2010s, for example through its initially leading role in the so-called 'refugee crisis' of 2015–16.[1] Overall, therefore, the 2010s clearly saw the increased political weight of Berlin in Europe, sparking debates about what kind of power Germany had become. Several of those debates were explicitly framed around the notion of 'reluctance':[2] for example, Paterson (2011) famously argued that Germany was a 'reluctant hegemon' in Europe, and *The Economist* took over this notion on one of its covers in 2013, calling for a more active engagement of Germany in Europe, arguing that 'Germany's current foot-dragging poses larger dangers' (*The Economist*, 2013).

The notion of reluctance was often used with reference to Germany's unwillingness to engage militarily (Maull, 2000a: 57; Breuer, 2006: 211; Dyson, 2011: 244). Moreover, several authors depicted the German government as indecisive and erratic in its foreign policy, highlighting that, particularly during the Eurozone crisis, 'Leadership from Berlin has been hesitant' and plagued by a 'capacity-expectations gap' (Bulmer, 2014: 1245). Quite the opposite of these assessments, a range of other observers maintained that Germany was not 'reluctant' at all. The more apologetic ones argued that German policies actually reflected a careful approach to policy making (Münkler, 2015: 162), and that Germany had a long tradition of quiet, low-key leadership and engagement in European affairs and global governance (see, for example, Mützenich, 2015: 276–7). Critical observers argued

---

[1] Some sections of this chapter were published in an earlier version as a working paper; see Destradi (2015).

[2] As discussed in Chapter 2, the term was mostly used in an unspecified manner, not corresponding exactly to the conceptualization of 'reluctance' used in this book.

instead that Germany was only ostensibly hesitant since it consistently pursued its policy of austerity throughout the Eurozone crisis, imposing its will on the rest of Europe (Beck, 2012). This assessment reflected a more general criticism of German policies coming from Anglo-Saxon economists and Southern European publics and politicians (*Spiegel Online International*, 2015), and a widespread uneasiness about a revival of German power and assertiveness related to fears of a re-emergence of the 'German question' in geo-economic and geo-political terms (Kundnani, 2014; Hellmann, 2016; Fix, 2018).

Similar discussions about indecisiveness and muddling through in German foreign policy characterized the months after Russia's invasion of Ukraine in February 2022 (Dempsey, 2022a; *The Economist*, 2022). Chancellor Olaf Scholz' announcement of a *Zeitenwende*, a sea change in German foreign policy involving substantive increases in military spending and the promise to deliver weapons to Ukraine (Bundestag, 2022), were followed by what many criticized as a non-committal approach, in which the German government adopted a wait-and-see attitude, clearly disappointing not only the Ukrainian government but also many of its international partners. As it was put in *Spiegel Online* in May 2022, Chancellor Scholz:

> ... walked a tightrope, always doing only what is necessary in order not to anger [Gemany's] allies, yet not enough: pulling the brake on weapons deliveries and adamantly refusing to travel to Kyiv. The rejection of a leadership role in Europe comes from the very same nation that took the greatest advantage from cheap Russian energy imports and whose political establishment cultivated the closest ties to Moscow. (von Rohr, 2022)

While discussions about German 'reluctance' were therefore at the core of analyses and commentaries on German foreign policy throughout the first two decades of the new millennium, the analysis in this chapter focuses on the 2010s, mostly because at the time of this writing (July 2022), events in Ukraine were still unfolding. The empirical analysis therefore addresses crisis management in Germany's extended neighbourhood with a focus on Germany's role in the Libya crisis (2011) and the Ukraine crisis of 2014–15. Those were times of political stability in Germany, albeit with different governing constellations under Chancellor Angela Merkel.

Between 2009 and 2013, Merkel was at the helm of a 'black-yellow' coalition of her centre-right Christian Democratic Union (CDU) and its sister party Christian Social Union in Bavaria (CSU) with the liberal Free Democratic Party (FDP). With the 2009 election, the CDU and CSU had gained 239 seats in the Bundestag (the German federal Parliament) and the FDP had 93 seats, which means that the coalition enjoyed a comfortable majority of 332 mandates out of 622 in total (Bundeswahlleiter, 2009). At the 2013 election, Merkel's CDU/CSU achieved a remarkable result of 311 mandates out of 631, but her previous coalition partner FDP failed to achieve the 5 per cent of votes required to enter the Bundestag (Bundeswahlleiter, 2013). Therefore Merkel ultimately entered a 'grand coalition' with the Social Democratic Party (SPD, Social Democratic Party), which had gained 193 mandates (Helms et al, 2019). The 2010s was therefore a phase of political stability in Germany – indeed, a further Merkel chancellorship at the helm of a 'grand coalition' with SPD followed after the 2017 elections.

As we will see, Germany was clearly reluctant concerning military intervention in Libya, and this reluctance was mainly driven by difficulties in domestic preference formation related to normative tensions. In the case of the Ukraine crisis of 2014–15, the German government displayed a very different approach, showing an entirely new determination and willingness to shed its foreign policy reluctance. It was able to do so because the government articulated clear domestic preferences and could overcome competing international expectations by crafting a common European position on sanctions against Russia – an approach that was remarkably different from Germany's highly reluctant policies after the start of Russia's war of aggression in 2022.

The analysis in this chapter is based on a range of primary sources, including speeches, parliamentary debates and news reports, as well as secondary sources. Furthermore, it is informed by 14 face-to-face or telephone interviews with German government officials, academics and other experts, which were carried out in April and May 2015.

Germany's reluctant approach to intervention in Libya

In the field of security, the 2011 intervention in Libya on the basis of UNSC Resolution 1973 (UNSC, 2011b) and the Responsibility to Protect (R2P) principle has been one of the salient cases of crisis management in the European neighbourhood in recent years. The crisis developed in the context of the Arab Spring, as Libya's authoritarian leader Muammar al-Gaddafi's violently repressed protests against his regime. In February 2011, those protests became particularly virulent in the city of Benghazi, which had become a stronghold of armed resistance by rebel groups (Payandeh, 2011: 373). Protests in Tripoli, for example, were violently crushed by security forces and mercenaries, backed by air attacks from warplanes and helicopters shooting on protesters (Kirkpatrick and El-Naggar, 2011). According to estimates, as many as 1,000–2,000 people died in the months preceding the international intervention (Milne, 2011).

In response to such increasing violence, on 26 February 2011, the UNSC approved Resolution 1970 (UNSC, 2011a), which condemned violence, imposed sanctions and referred the matter to the International Criminal Court (ICC). However, violent suppression of dissent continued, and in February 2011 Gaddafi threatened to unleash a bloodbath in rebel-held Benghazi. He told the public to 'capture the rats' and 'cockroaches', otherwise there would be a 'slaughter', and threatened to hunt anti-government groups 'house by house' and 'inch by inch' (Barker, 2011), asking his supporters, 'come out of your homes, attack them in their dens' (BBC News, 2011). As a consequence, at the beginning of March 2011, the idea of establishing a no-fly zone to prevent Gaddafi's air force further targeting civilians became increasingly concrete.

Pressure for intervention was particularly strong from France and the UK, while the USA under the Obama administration was initially more cautious. Indeed, Secretary of Defense Robert Gates expressed his worry that, since 'a no-fly zone would need to begin with strikes against Libya's air defense systems, [this] could easily be perceived as a further US attack against a Muslim country' (quoted in Chivvis, 2015: 15). However, calls for a no-fly zone became more widespread, as they came from the National Transitional Council (NTC), an organization speaking for the Libyan rebels, from the Gulf Cooperation Council (GCC), and on 12 March even from the Arab League (Payandeh, 2011: 376; Chivvis, 2015: 15; Vaughn and Dunne, 2014).

Ultimately, on 17 March the UNSC passed Resolution 1973, which demanded an immediate ceasefire and authorized the international community to establish a no-fly zone and to use all necessary means – short of foreign occupation – to protect civilians in Libya (UNSC, 2011b). The core argument used in the resolution was based on the R2P principle, according to which the international community is responsible for protecting civilians from genocide, war crimes, ethnic cleansing and crimes against humanity, if necessary by employing coercive measures under Chapter VII of the UN Charter (UN, 2005; Bellamy, 2010; Thakur, 2016). Yet it is important to note that, even though Gaddafi's suppression of protests had already been massive, 'In essence, the international community mobilised to prevent mass atrocities primarily on the basis of speech-acts which were treated as if they were reality' (Vaughn and Dunne, 2014: 39), basically taking Gaddafi at his word.

The draft of Resolution 1973 was submitted by France, Lebanon, the UK and the USA. It was adopted with 10 votes in favour, none against and five abstentions. Those abstentions came from China and Russia as well as the non-permanent members Brazil, India and Germany (UNSC, 2011b) – and it is precisely this German abstention and Germany's policies in the following phase of the Libyan crisis that are the object of analysis in this chapter.

When it comes to the implementation of Resolution 1973, this initially involved military operations by the French, British and Canadian air forces as well as the US and British naval forces, which launched air strikes against Gaddafi's army. Military operations in the early stages were mostly led by France and the UK, sharing command with the USA. From 31 March onwards, the intervention became a NATO operation named Unified Protector. A number of additional NATO and non-NATO members were involved in the operations, including Belgium, Denmark, Italy, the Netherlands, Norway, Spain, Qatar and the United Arab Emirates (UAE) (Chivvis, 2015: 23), mostly enforcing the naval blockade and no-fly zone and providing logistical support.

Military operations soon went beyond the original mandate of protecting civilians, as the international coalition ultimately supported Libyan rebels fighting the regime. Indeed, within and among coalition partners, there was no clarity on the ultimate objective of the military mission. French President Nicolas Sarkozy, British Prime Minister David Cameron and US President Barack Obama had called for the ousting of Gaddafi. German Foreign Minister Guido Westerwelle had taken the same stand: 'A ruling family that wages such a brutal war against its own people is at an end. The dictator cannot stay' (quoted in FAZ, 2011). However, the UN mandate only referred to the protection of civilians, thereby leading to a high degree of ambiguity in the goals of the operation. In mid-April, at a meeting of NATO foreign ministers, '… the striker group also decided that Qaddafi's forces were fair game anywhere in Libya as long as attacks against civilians were occurring somewhere because those attacks posed an intrinsic threat to the Libyan populace' (Chivvis, 2015: 30). In the following months, rebel forces gradually gained control of large parts of the country, seizing the capital Tripoli in August with the support of heavy NATO bombing, and leading Gaddafi to flee. Yet, despite such progress, the UK and other members of the alliance claimed that the operation should continue since, as long as Gaddafi was at large, a potential threat to civilians continued to exist (Chivvis, 2015: 40). Ultimately, Gaddafi was killed in an attempt to flee from the siege of Sirte and Bani Walid on 20 October. One week later, the UNSC voted to conclude the operation by 31 October.

In its aftermath, the military intervention in Libya was much criticized as it had obviously overstretched its mandate, ultimately using the argument of the protection of civilians to pursue regime change (see, for example, Thakur, 2013). In reviewing British policies, an investigation report by the Foreign Affairs Committee of the House of Commons highlighted a number of mistakes, criticizing, in particular, that threats to civilians were not adequately verified, that the British government (and, by extension, the international community) 'selectively took elements of Muammar Gaddafi's rhetoric at face value; and [that] it failed to identify the Islamist elements in the rebellion' (House of Commons, 2016: 39).

Germany and its approach to the crisis in Libya

Much has been written in the past decade about Germany's approach to the Libya crisis and particularly on its decision to abstain, which was very surprising as it broke with Germany's traditional, decades-long commitment to a broad alignment with Western partners on important foreign policy issues. Indeed, this abstention is frequently taken as an example of Berlin's 'reluctance' or 'unwillingness to play a leadership role' (Bulmer and Paterson, 2013: 1400). According to some authors, the decision stood in the tradition of Germany's *Kultur der Zurückhaltung* (culture of restraint) and of its 'civilian power' approach to the use of military force (Maull, 2012). According to others, it was an indication of a new, more openly interest-driven foreign policy approach on the part of Berlin (Miskimmon, 2012).

Several studies have tried to make sense of Germany's decision, in some cases adopting a role-theoretical approach (Oppermann, 2012; Harnisch, 2015; Matzner, 2018) or addressing more generally domestic debates on the legitimacy of the intervention (Bucher et al, 2013) as well as discussing the issue of electoral incentives (Hansel and Oppermann, 2016). The analysis in this section builds on such work as well as on a range of primary sources and expert interviews. It focuses on two related but distinct aspects of crisis management: on the one hand, on the decision to abstain on Resolution 1973, and on the other hand, on the decision not to join the military mission (albeit later supporting it indirectly in various ways). Again, the previously outlined concept of reluctance can prove helpful to assess German policies. In fact, a coherent and consistent implementation of a policy of *Zurückhaltung* would not amount to reluctance. But in the decision on Libya, the German government was far from coherent in its approach.

Indeed, Berlin's policies in the Libya crisis involved both hesitation and recalcitrance. The German government's recalcitrance initially mainly manifested itself vis-à-vis requests by France and Britain. In fact, Sarkozy and Cameron had pushed most explicitly for military intervention in Libya right from the beginning, while the Obama administration had long been sceptical and itself hesitant and reluctant (Chivvis, 2015: 14; see also Chapter 7). At a meeting of NATO defence ministers on 10 March 2011, Germany opposed proposals on a no-fly zone, with Defence Minister Thomas de Maizière stating that 'the situation in Libya was "not the basis for any kind of military intervention by NATO"' (quoted in Mackenzie and Pawlak, 2011). On the following day, at an extraordinary session of the European Council on the developments in Libya, Sarkozy and Cameron tried to convince European partners of the need to impose a no-fly zone over Libya, but Germany reportedly rejected such initiative, 'with Angela Merkel leading a campaign to block talk of air strikes and no-fly zones' (Traynor and Watt, 2011), and the issue ultimately not being mentioned in the outcome declaration (European Commission, 2011). Similarly, at a G8 meeting on 14–15 March 2011, Germany acted as a 'brakesman' (Rinke, 2011: 48) vis-à-vis French and British requests, blocking the inclusion of a mention of a no-fly zone in the meeting's communiqué (Tisdall, 2011). On that occasion Westerwelle stated that 'Germany did not want "to get sucked into a war in north Africa"' (quoted in Tisdall, 2011). Up to that point, however, Germany's recalcitrance was paralleled by that of the USA, which had similarly not declared its approval for French and British plans.

After the USA ultimately committed itself to support a draft resolution referring to the use of 'all necessary means' on 16 March 2011, pressure on Germany to come to a rapid decision grew immensely. British Prime Minister Cameron and Foreign Minister William Hague reportedly telephoned Berlin to convince Merkel, Westerwelle and de Maizière to support the resolution (Miskimmon, 2012: 398). But Germany did not comply with such expectations of its international partners. Its recalcitrance did not go so far as to impede the adoption of Resolution 1973, as Germany abstained but did not vote against the resolution. Indeed, Berlin took care that it would not be responsible for making the resolution fail: 'in a call with Cameron shortly before the vote, Merkel assured her counterpart that if passing the resolution ultimately depended on German support, Germany would vote "yes"' (Brockmeier, 2013: 79). Therefore, German recalcitrance did not reach the level of 'blocking others' initiatives'. Still, the German abstention – along with countries like Russia, China, India and Brazil – provoked a wave of discontent among Germany's traditional partners and harsh criticism from the USA and NATO (Niedermeier, 2011).

As US Undersecretary of State Nicholas Burns put it in an interview, 'Even if Germany had decided not to contribute military forces one would hoped [sic] for much greater political support from Germany for this mission. And the fact that Germany held out and abstained, I think, really puts into question German leadership at NATO' (quoted in Deutsche Welle, 2011). French Foreign Minister Alain Juppé drew the conclusion that Germany was destroying European unity: 'The common security and defence policy of Europe? It is dead' (quoted in Ash, 2011). In sum, Germany's policies were perceived by its allies as 'disconcerting and half-hearted' (Maull, 2012: 36), and led observers to accuse Germany of having not only impeded common European action but also possibly having contributed to a worse outcome of the Libyan crisis (Münkler, 2015: 149).

During the phase of the implementation of Resolution 1973 and the military operations, the German government was similarly recalcitrant, as it did not fulfil its allies' expectations, which would have wanted a more extensive engagement on the part of Germany in support of the mission. NATO Secretary-General Anders Fogh Rasmussen criticized Germany's decision as 'absurd', arguing that not providing its military capabilities to the benefit of the alliance essentially amounted to a withdrawal of support (*Spiegel Online*, 2011a). As Burns put it, '... if Germany cannot support the operation militarily at least it should take a leading role on the humanitarian side' (Ash, 2011), and in July 2011 President Obama called for German engagement in rebuilding the country: 'There is going to be a lot of work to do when Gaddafi does step down, in terms of getting the Libyan people back on their feet. ... And my expectation is going to be that there will be full and robust German support' (quoted in Schneider, 2011). On 23 March 2011 the German cabinet decided to indirectly provide support to the mission by increasing its role in surveillance flights in Afghanistan, thereby freeing NATO Airborne Warning and Control System (AWACS) capacities for Libya – something de Maizière termed a 'political sign of our solidarity with the alliance' (*Spiegel Online*, 2011b), thereby revealing the ambiguity inherent in Germany's position. In mid-May 2011, Germany also reportedly provided flare ammunition for the enforcement of the no-fly zone in Libya, and declared its readiness to support NATO with the provision of weapons components (*Spiegel Online*, 2011d). Moreover, large parts of the military operations in Libya were led from the Ramstein Air Base, a US Air Force base in southern Germany, and the United States Africa Command (AFRICOM) in Stuttgart (Bundestag, 2011e: 11195; *Spiegel Online*, 2011f; Torres, 2011). In the following months, the German government announced that it would provide loans to the Transitional National Council, including a loan of €100 million in July 2011 (CNN, 2011), as well as an offer to provide post-conflict police trainers (Chivvis, 2015: 29).

Overall, therefore a high degree of recalcitrance characterized Germany's approach to the Libya crisis. Germany's recalcitrance, however, did not lead to a consistent policy, which would have been the exact opposite of reluctance. Interestingly, some representatives of Germany's governing parties (CDU/CSU and FDP) claimed that the German approach was actually one of continuity with previous policies of military restraint, and that this approach allowed Germany to be perceived as a coherent and reliable partner (Matzner, 2018: 149). Moreover, government representatives and members of the governing parties claimed that the decision not to participate in military operations naturally derived from abstention on Resolution 1973 and was therefore a further sign of coherence. As Rainer Stinner of the FDP put it in the debate in the Bundestag on 18 March,

> I believe that the federal government has followed a very stringent line of argumentation ...: First, it was decided that Germany would not take part in military actions in Libya for reasons that the foreign minister outlined extensively; that was the first point. This was consequentially followed by the decision to abstain in the related vote at the UN Security Council. This is a consistent and stringent line of argumentation. (Bundestag, 2011d: 11147)

Yet, despite these assertions, Berlin's approach to the crisis was characterized by a high degree of hesitation and many inconsistencies.

Flip-flopping manifested itself through rapidly changing and contradictory statements and policies on the part of the German government. During the process of drafting UNSC Resolution 1970, which condemned Gaddafi's use of force against civilians and imposed sanctions on members of his regime, German diplomats were '"supportive" and even "pushy"' (Brockmeier, 2013: 66), and Berlin 'criticised its fellow European countries for not having condemned Gadhafi earlier and with clearer language' (Brockmeier, 2013: 66). Westerwelle apparently 'initially [offered] no opposition to a no-fly zone' (Brockmeier, 2013: 67), but started criticizing it in early March 2011. Germany's contradictory approach also manifested itself in the shifting requirements for the involvement of Arab states articulated by Westerwelle: he first argued that a no-fly-zone mandate would need the 'approval' of Arab states, later set their 'active participation' in the implementation as a condition, and ultimately argued that their 'leadership' would be necessary (Brockmeier, 2013: 67, 76). Moreover, as Joffe (2011) points out,

> At the begin of the Libya crisis, no-one cried louder than Guido Westerwelle 'Qaddafi must go'! But no one turned away more quickly than our Foreign Minister. This calls into question another principle of which Berlin is so proud: predictability. Saying one thing in the morning and a different one in the evening manifests either insecurity of judgement – or unreliability.

In the aftermath of Germany's abstention on Resolution 1973, German government representatives similarly took an ambivalent position concerning the military intervention. While a large part of the German government's argument had focused on the dangers and potential legitimacy problems of the military mission, in June 2011 Chancellor Angela Merkel 'said ... that her country shares the hope "that this NATO mission is successful."'(quoted in CNN, 2011). Similarly, in May 2011, Merkel was quoted as saying 'Even though Germany abstained, for me, it was clear that as soon as the UN resolution on Libya was passed, it was also our resolution. It is our resolution and we are just as interested to see it carried out successfully as, say, Britain, France and the USA' (NPR, 2011). Such efforts at discursively walking a tightrope between the rejection and support of military intervention was noted very critically by observers (Joffe, 2011).

Moreover, other policies by Germany reinforced the contradiction with Merkel's statements of political support. In particular, on 22 March 2011, the German government withdrew German warships from the NATO fleet in the Mediterranean, where they had been engaged in patrols and counter-terrorism in the context of operation Active Endeavour since 2001 (Sperling, 2022: 581). One of the reasons they gave for this was the potential risk of having to use force given the imposition of a weapons embargo in the Libya crisis. The same happened for the withdrawal of personnel from AWACS aircraft monitoring North Africa so as not to have them involved in Libya, which would have required a parliamentary mandate (Bundestag, 2011f; *Spiegel Online*, 2012a). But then, surprisingly, and revealing the high degree of hesitation of the German government, in April 2011, Berlin even offered to participate in the military mission by sending troops to secure the transportation of aid in the context of a potential EUFOR (European Union Force) Libya mission, which ultimately did not materialize (Bundestag, 2011b; *Zeit Online*, 2011).

In August, the government promised that it would 'constructively check' the option of sending troops to a potential stabilization mission (*Spiegel Online*, 2011g). Germany also provided various forms of more indirect support to the military mission. Ultimately, by September 2011, as many as 103 members of the German armed forces were reportedly involved in the identification of targets and the transmission of commands to AWACS planes (*Spiegel Online*, 2011c).

To conclude, Germany's approach to the issue of intervention in Libya was characterized by both a high degree of recalcitrance and of hesitation. In the following section, I will discuss possible alternative explanations for this high degree of reluctance on the part of the German government.

Explaining German reluctance in the Libya crisis

Among the possible explanations of reluctance, political weakness does not seem to be a convincing one. Germany had a coalition government, but the coalition was stable and there were no signs of the FDP, as the junior coalition partner holding the foreign ministry, trying to blackmail the CDU/CSU or leading to deadlock, as expected by some sections of the FPA literature (see Chapter 3). The decision to abstain was strongly driven by Foreign Minister Westerwelle of the FDP (Miskimmon, 2012: 396), and some studies argue that a possible explanation for Germany's abstention might have been electoral considerations of the FDP ahead of two regional elections to be held on 27 March 2011, given that the German public was broadly opposed to a NATO mission in Libya, and even more so to German participation in such a mission (see, for example, Maull, 2011: 112–13). Indeed, Westerwelle, who at that time was also party chairman, was largely unpopular, and opinion polls gave the FDP reasons to worry about not reaching the 5 per cent threshold in those regional elections (Hansel and Oppermann, 2016: 115–16). However, most analyses concur in arguing that debates on the intervention in Libya did not feature obvious cleavages along the lines of political parties or competing political ideologies. Indeed, the CDU/CSU and the FDP broadly shared the goal of reducing military expenditure (*Zeit Online*, 2010) and downsizing the Bundeswehr, and they suspended conscription in July 2011 (*Zeit Online*, 2010; Bundestag, 2011a). Moreover, Merkel was mainly focused on the management of the Eurozone crisis and the consequences of her decision to abolish nuclear energy in the wake of the Fukushima accident, so she largely left decision making on the Libya issue to Westerwelle (Hansel and Oppermann, 2016: 120). Overall, therefore, the governing coalition emphasized unity and 'there was no substantial conflict within Berlin concerning what course of action Germany should take on the UN vote' (Miskimmon, 2012: 401).[3]

Interestingly, by contrast, intra-party divisions were widespread: with the exception of the Left, which has traditionally been staunchly opposed to any kind of military engagement, the other political parties displayed internal divisions on Resolution 1973 (Miskimmon, 2012: 398; see also Brockmeier, 2013: 82). In the governing CDU, some voices were critical of Germany's abstention: for example, Ruprecht Polenz, chair of the Foreign Relations Committee in the Bundestag, called for other forms of engagement and solidarity with alliance partners (Atlantic Council, 2011), foreign policy spokesperson Philipp Mißfelder would have preferred a vote in favour, and security policy expert Roderich Kiesewetter expressed his belief that the Bundestag would have approved some limited form of mandate (see Brockmeier, 2013: 82). And at a later stage, while the military operation was ongoing and Gaddafi's troops were being pushed back at growing speed, within the FDP different party members also provided divergent assessments of such success: Westerwelle claimed that the positive developments in Libya could be traced back to the successful imposition of sanctions (and, by extension, that his position on Germany's abstention had proved to be right), while FDP leader Philipp Rösler explicitly thanked Germany's allies, thereby openly calling into question the wisdom of his party colleague at the helm of the foreign ministry (*Spiegel Online*, 2011e).[4] To conclude, therefore, political weakness unleashed by disagreement within the governing coalition is not a suitable explanation for Germany's highly reluctant policy in the Libya crisis.

---

[3]   Brockmeier (2013: 79) argues that Westerwelle had actually even planned to vote 'no' on Resolution 1973, and that abstention might have been a coalition compromise. She also suggests that Chancellor Merkel might have agreed on abstention at the UNSC out of fear that her government might fall apart, but there is no evidence to confirm this assessment since, indeed, most studies highlight the existing unity among coalition partners and ministries.

[4]   To some extent, this calls into question unity within the FDP on the matter of military interventions, which is, for example, described by Hansel and Oppermann (2016: 120).

The second possible explanation refers to limited capacity, which can be understood in terms of a weakness of the bureaucratic apparatus in charge of foreign policy, and possibly also in terms of bureaucratic infighting, which might hamper the formation of domestic preferences and the adoption of a coherent and responsive foreign policy line. Such competition among ministries is not infrequent in German foreign policy, especially among the Federal Foreign Office, the Chancellery, the Federal Ministry for Economic Cooperation and Development and the Federal Ministry for Defence. In the case of Libya, however, the conventional bureaucratic politics model does not seem to apply for Germany. As Miskimmon (2012: 401–2) points out, there was no obvious competition between the Federal Foreign Office, the Chancellery and the Federal Ministry of Defence: 'Foreign Minister Westerwelle has been criticized for his handling of his brief, but on the issue of Libya there was widespread support within the government for his decision' (Miskimmon, 2012: 402), and 'Westerwelle, Merkel and de Maizière all agreed that German involvement was out of the question' (Miskimmon, 2012: 401). While one of the interviewees pointed out that there were divergences of opinion between the Federal Chancellery and the Federal Foreign Office (and that large parts of the bureaucracy in the Federal Foreign Office did not agree with the line chosen by the foreign minister),[5] another interviewee highlighted that Merkel ultimately stuck with her foreign minister's course.[6]

Indeed, as discussed, intra-party differences seemed to be more explicit than inter-party ones. Concerning material capacities, these were not limited to the extent of making it impossible for Germany to pursue a consistent policy: even if the Bundeswehr was in bad shape, voting in favour of Resolution 1973 would not have automatically forced Berlin to participate in the military mission, as it is actually common for states to support resolutions in the UNSC but then not to participate in the mandated missions. Moreover, Germany had already engaged in a series of missions before, most notably in Afghanistan, where it was operating under tight constraints but nevertheless engaging with its allies. Interestingly, on 26 February 2011, as the situation in Libya was already escalating, the German Air Force had rescued 134 employees of the company Wintershall AG from Libya and flown them to Crete. As Miskimmon (2012: 395) puts it, this 'demonstrates swift and decisive action of the part of the German government to intervene' in the case of Libya – something that was not observable later on. Moreover, Germany had no problems concerning its diplomatic capacity, and indeed its mission at the UN was well staffed (Brockmeier, 2013: 75).

---

[5] Interview G11, German academic, Hamburg, 27 April 2015.
[6] Interview G12, German academic, Hamburg, 27 April 2015.

The third explanation discussed in Chapter 3 focuses on cognitive problems and addresses the issues faced by decision makers who have to make tough choices in difficult situations. In particular, the severity of the crisis, time pressure and the novelty of a situation play a role here. Some of these factors were in play in the case of Libya, and can certainly contribute to explain German reluctance, at least concerning the country's abstention in the UNSC (but less the continued inconsistencies in Germany's approach in the months following the vote).

In the decision on the position to take at the UNSC, time pressure played a crucial role. In particular, the German government was taken by surprise by the speed with which its international partners came up with a resolution (Matzner, 2018: 140). Moreover, Germany was surprised by the sudden shift in the USA's position on the imposition of a no-fly zone. In fact, the Obama administration had long been sceptical of the proposals by Sarkozy and Cameron (Blomdahl, 2016: 147–8). The disastrous aftermath of US interventions in Iraq and Afghanistan, combined with uncertainties about both the Libyan rebels' capacities and political orientations as well as about the potential economic consequences of another operation, contributed to a high degree of war-weariness in the Obama administration (Mann, 2013; Blomdahl, 2016: 148). On 2 March 2011, Secretary of Defense Gates had declared in Congress that such a no-fly zone would have to begin with air strikes against Libya's air defence systems, 'which could easily be perceived as further US attacks against a Muslim country' (Chivvis, 2015: 15). Shortly thereafter, NATO Secretary-General Rasmussen had stated that NATO had 'no intention to intervene in Libya' (Chivvis, 2015: 16). It was only after the Arab League endorsed the idea of a no-fly zone on 12 March 2011, and Secretary of State Hillary Clinton was assured by Arab leaders that they would support such a mission, that the approach of the Obama administration changed (Bilefsky and Landler, 2011; Chivvis, 2015: 17). Ultimately, the USA's decision to support a resolution endorsing a no-fly zone and 'all necessary means' was made on 15 March, when Obama convened a meeting of the National Security Council, and a new draft resolution including these changes was introduced on the following day (Chivvis, 2015: 19). This course of events can contribute to explain Germany's reluctant approach to the issue of the vote on UNSC Resolution 1973. In fact, German foreign policy has traditionally closely followed that of its international partners, with a particular role of the USA. As long as the US administration was reluctant itself, the German government was in a somehow comfortable position, probably not feeling the need to take urgent action despite the pressures by France and the UK. With the sudden turn in Washington, however, Germany was isolated.

One of the main problems was that Germany did 'not [have] enough time for a decision, Germany knew about Washington's decision only 36 hours in advance'.[7] As a consequence, the issue of intervention in Libya was debated in the Bundestag on 16 March, but its members were not informed about the shift in the USA's position in time. In fact, the Obama administration informed the German ambassador about Washington's new course and about the new draft resolution envisaging 'all necessary means' only on 16 March, when in Berlin it was already afternoon (Brockmeier, 2013: 71–2). Ultimately, this meant that the parliamentary debate was carried out based on outdated assumptions (Brockmeier, 2013: 65), something highly problematic given the importance of a parliamentary mandate in all decisions regarding the use of force. Moreover, the decision on intervention in Libya was obviously a high-risk one, in which German government officials feared the potential unknown consequences of an international intervention (Brockmeier, 2013: 67–8). Westerwelle publicly stated: 'I do not want German soldiers to be drawn into a Libyan war, nor will I take part in a war being waged with German soldiers in Libya. We should have learned from recent history that this is not a solution' (Deutschlandfunk, 2011). Merkel added that, compared to Germany's allies, 'we have a different opinion concerning the chances of success of the mission' (*Tagesspiegel*, 2011).

Ultimately, the decision to abstain on Resolution 1973 was characterized by a series of mishaps in the decision-making process, with Westerwelle acting 'without a decision paper ..., via telephone conference. None of the advisors could slide in [to stop him]'.[8] Moreover, Westerwelle was reportedly not aware of the fact that supporting a resolution would not automatically imply participation in military operations (Brockmeier, 2013: 78). Possibly due to time pressure, here we have a case of decision making in which the foreign minister resorted to cognitive shortcuts, reverting to his party's traditional rejection of military interventionism (Hansel and Oppermann, 2016: 117) almost by default. The literature on decision making under pressure also tells us that the novelty of a situation can play a role in inducing leaders to resort to cognitive shortcuts (Mintz and DeRouen, 2010: 25), and that this will happen more likely to inexperienced decision makers as compared to seasoned experts (Boin et al, 2005: 29). According to Bucher et al (2013: 525), 'Since events moved very quickly, it is well conceivable that the German elite were caught by surprise and had difficulty formulating policy responses. This is supported by the ... finding that the arguments in favour and against intervention changed in the German newspapers from week-to-week'. Moreover, Westerwelle was 'a weak foreign minister',[9] and was not experienced in foreign policy matters. He had been in office since

---

[7] Interview G5, German government official, Federal Chancellery, Berlin, 23 April 2015.
[8] Interview G8, German expert, Berlin, 24 April 2015.
[9] Interview G12, German academic, Hamburg, 27 April 2015.

October 2009 and had not shown any particular initiative (Schlieben, 2011; *Spiegel Online*, 2016). Concerning the specific case of Libya, he reportedly was most likely not aware of what the R2P principle was (Brockmeier, 2013: 68), nor did he know that it would have been possible for Germany to vote in favour of Resolution 1973 and still not to participate in the military mission mandated with such a resolution.[10]

While reluctance in the context of the vote on Resolution 1973 can therefore to some extent be explained by focusing on cognitive problems in a situation full of uncertainty and time constraints, this explanation does not work as well when it comes to explaining Germany's continued reluctance in the following weeks and months, while the military operations in Libya were going on. The elements of urgency were no longer in place, and there was much more information available to decision makers.

One possible reason for Germany's continued reluctance can be found in the fourth explanation identified in this book, normative struggles.[11] The issue of interventions abroad and, more generally, of the use of military force, had been a major topic in domestic political debates in Germany for decades, and had gained increased relevance from the 1990s onwards. The question of whether Germany should support its allies in a military intervention in Libya aimed at protecting civilians from their own murderous regime therefore touched on a number of important norms driving German post-war foreign policy, which, however, contradicted each other. The issue of whether to support military intervention or not therefore led to debates that uncovered deeper normative struggles in German foreign policy, which help explain the flip-flopping and muddling-through approach taken by the government.

Among the norms most frequently mentioned by those who were sceptical about military intervention in Libya was the norm of the rejection of military violence and the peaceful resolution of disputes. Restraint in the use of military force was a crucial component in Germany's self-understanding as a 'civilian power' in the post-war era (Kirste and Maull, 1996). The notion

---

[10] Other scholars argue that Germany's decision to abstain was driven by rational cost-benefit calculations (see, for example, Miskimmon, 2012). However, this assessment does not take into account the reluctance that surrounded the UNSC vote and that also characterized the German position in the following months. A rationalist account of Germany's approach ultimately fails to explain all the muddling through and flip-flopping by the German government; in other words, it fails to explain the reluctance that characterized Germany's approach to crisis management in Libya.

[11] Matzner (2018: 142) frames her similar analysis in terms of domestic role contestation. As discussed in Chapter 3, my theoretical approach is compatible in many respects with role theory, but it also includes other explanatory factors that go beyond national role conceptions, for example the issue of capabilities.

of the peaceful resolution of disputes was especially mentioned by Foreign Minister Westerwelle and representatives of the FDP, who referred to the principles of *Genscherism* – after former German Foreign Minister Genscher of the FDP, who was an advocate of negotiated settlements to international disputes and had promoted a policy of compromise between East and West during the Cold War. Building on such tradition, Westerwelle claimed that Gaddafi should be deposed using non-military means, including sanctions and criminal prosecution (Deutschlandfunk, 2011). In his government declaration in the Bundestag on the day following Germany's abstention in the UNSC, Westerwelle declared: 'So-called surgical interventions don't exist. Every military operation will also claim civilian lives. We know that from painful past experience' (Bundestag, 2011d: 11138). And in the months following the start of the international mission, he kept emphasizing his preference for a peaceful resolution of disputes (Auswärtiges Amt, 2011).

Positions emphasizing the norm of the rejection of military violence could be found across the political spectrum. These were, not surprisingly, promoted by the traditionally pacifist Left party ('No war for oil! No military support, neither for one nor for the other side!'; Bundestag, 2011c: 10822) and, to a lesser extent, by representatives of the Greens: 'The use of military force is ... the ultima ratio and for us necessarily requires a UN mandate. Beyond that, on this matter I share the scepticism of the federal government concerning the implementation and the effect of a no-fly zone ...' (Bundestag, 2011c: 10825).

The norm of the rejection of military violence also related to the norm of autonomy in decision making, which was sometimes mentioned in political discussions, mostly by representatives of the CDU. As Ruprecht Polenz of the CDU put it in the debate held in the Bundestag on 18 March 2011,

> I believe that restraint [*Zurückhaltung*] is the right approach. Being part of an alliance does not mean that Germany has to be part of everything that NATO does. If this was the case, we would not need parliamentary approval [of military missions] anymore and could just say: NATO decides on everything in Brussels, and we join. (Bundestag, 2011d: 11145)

Speaking in the name of the CDU/CSU parliamentary group, Philipp Mißfelder claimed 'I don't think that Gaddafi and his henchmen will be impressed by the actions of the European Union of the past weeks. ... Instead, I believe that we need to set priorities of our own' (Bundestag, 2011c: 10826).

Opposed to these were the norms of solidarity with allies and commitment to multilateralism, which had been at the core of German post-war foreign policy. Being loyal to its alliance partners and to NATO was a core tenet in

German foreign policy, which had also been used as a major justification for Germany's participation in the intervention in Kosovo (without a UN mandate) along with its NATO allies. At that time, the government had forcefully pushed for the principle of 'never alone', highlighting that Germany did not want to deviate from the approach taken by its international partners (Maull, 2000b: 11). In the Bundestag debate carried out on 18 March 2011, in the aftermath of Germany's abstention on Resolution 1973, members of the opposition in particular pointed out that Germany was risking alienating its allies and splitting Europe. As Ralf Mützenich of the SPD put it, 'Our problem, the problem of Germany now is that there is no common European position anymore' (Bundestag, 2011d: 11140).[12] But also government representatives and members of the governing parties tried to reassure the opposition and the country that Germany remained committed to its allies and to multilateralism. Merkel emphasized the norm of solidarity when referring to Germany's increased support for AWACS operations in Afghanistan (Bundestag, 2011f: 11252), and Westerwelle declared in the Bundestag: 'The international engagement of the Germans is appreciated. It is not as if Germany was not ready to take on international responsibility, for example by deploying 7,000 soldiers in the Bundeswehr's missions abroad' (Bundestag, 2011d: 11139). In the same parliamentary debate, an FDP representative claimed:

> Yes, we would have preferred to find a common line with our European partners. This was not the case. We are sorry about it, but this is how things are. Nevertheless, we will support our partners in Europe, in NATO, and in the world wherever we can to help them carry out their difficult task. (Bundestag, 2011d: 11149)

In the months following the vote at the UNSC, the norm of solidarity with allies was also very much present in the German debate, with criticism also coming from members of the governing parties. For example, CDU politician Günther Oettinger criticized the German government's policy, claiming that 'Our boycott hasn't even reached Gaddafi, it were the weapons or our NATO partners, it was not German reticence [*Zurückhaltung*]', and he thanked Germany's NATO partners, earning the applause of some 200 members of the CDU (*Süddeutsche Zeitung*, 2011). And quite paradoxically, in August 2011 even Westerwelle expressed his 'respect for what [Germany's] partners have done for the implementation of Resolution 1973' (*Süddeutsche Zeitung*, 2011).

---

[12] For an interesting discussion of different interpretations and nuances in different parties' understanding of the 'alliance partner role', see Matzner (2018: 149–53).

At the same time, another norm driving the debate was the notion of solidarity with the people of Libya fighting for democracy and against an oppressive regime – again, something that was mentioned across the political spectrum. In the parliamentary debates around the decision on intervention, members of the FDP put much emphasis on the notion of the freedom of the Libyan people, very much in line with their party ideology. As the operations went on, Westerwelle emphasized Germany's solidarity with the Libyan people, promising help in the reconstruction of their country (*Spiegel Online*, 2011g), and after Gaddafi's death, Merkel expressed Germany's readiness to support Libya on its way towards democracy, the establishment of the rule of law and national reconciliation (Merkur.de, 2011). Interestingly, however, the Responsibility to Protect was not mentioned prominently as a norm in German domestic political debates on Libya. Indeed, only Renate Künast of the Greens and Heidemarie Wieczorek-Zeul of the SDP referred to R2P in the parliamentary debate of 18 March (Miskimmon, 2012: 399; see also Brockmeier, 2013: 68).

Overall, to conclude, the German government was torn apart between different normative commitments and traditions, which, interestingly, cut across party lines, reflecting intra-party divisions. Those competing norms certainly contributed to the difficulties in achieving a clear preference on the course to follow on Libya and, correspondingly, to zig-zagging and highly contradictory policies. In the case of crisis management in Libya, reluctance can therefore be explained with cognitive problems related to time pressure when it comes to the very specific decision of how to vote on Resolution 1973. Normative struggles certainly also played a role in shaping and reinforcing such cognitive problems and difficulties in decision making. When it comes to the German government's reluctance in the following months, while the NATO mission was ongoing, normative struggles seem to have the greatest explanatory power, as the German government hoped to be seen as loyal to its allies but continued to be constrained by its more general aversion towards the use of military force.

Germany and the Ukraine crisis of 2014–15

An interesting shift in Germany's approach to the management of security crises in Europe's neighbourhood came about with the Ukraine crisis of 2014–15, in which Germany displayed a higher degree of determination and a willingness to at least partially shed its reluctance in foreign and security policy as compared to the Libya crisis. The crisis in Ukraine broke out shortly after the German president, foreign minister and defence minister had held a series of coordinated speeches at the Munich Security Conference 2014, arguing for 'faster, more decisive and more substantial' foreign policy decisions on Germany's part (Gauck, 2014; Hellmann et al, 2015).

The Eurozone crisis had revived debates about Germany's role in the world and criticism about German 'reluctance'. The speeches of 2014 were part of an effort by the German government to promote public support for a greater engagement of Germany in foreign affairs. They were followed by a broad academic and public debate on Germany's role in Europe and the world, as well as by some initiatives aimed at critically reviewing Germany's diplomatic capacities, most notably the 'Review 2014' process initiated by the Federal Foreign Office (Federal Foreign Office, 2015; Opitz et al, 2022). Against this backdrop, the crisis in Ukraine offered an unexpectedly timely testing ground for Germany's new ambitions.

In the following, I will focus on Germany's role in the Ukraine crisis between November 2013 and February 2015, which, for the sake of clarity, I divide into four phases: (1) the Euromaidan protests (November 2013–February 2014); (2) the annexation of Crimea (February–March 2014); (3) the outbreak of conflict in eastern Ukraine and the downing of flight MH17 (April–September 2014); and (4) the negotiations about the Minsk I and II agreements (September 2014–February 2015). The analysis will show that Germany's approach displayed only a low degree of reluctance, which was initially due to the outgoing government's weakness and later to cognitive problems, but was gradually replaced by a more determined approach. Leaving reluctance behind was possible mainly because the German government decided to pursue a crisis management approach based on a combination of negotiations and sanctions. This approach was acceptable to most German political actors because it bridged normative divides between those who called for a peaceful solution to the crisis and those who argued for a tougher approach towards Russia in light of its blatant violation of international law. With the benefit of hindsight, we know that such a non-reluctant approach was relatively short lived, and that, after the start of Russia's war of aggression against Ukraine in February 2022, Germany reverted back to highly reluctant policies.

In November 2013, the Ukrainian government, as a consequence of Russian pressure, announced that it would indefinitely postpone the signature of a planned Association Agreement and a Deep and Comprehensive Free Trade Area agreement with the EU. As a consequence, massive protests broke out in Kyiv (Herszenhorn, 2013), also calling for an end to corruption, abuses of power and human rights violations, and ultimately for the resignation of President Viktor Yanukovych. They came to be known as the Euromaidan protests, and escalated sharply on 18–20 February 2014, when dozens of protesters were killed, some by snipers from the roofs of the surrounding buildings. Ultimately, on 21 February 2014, an agreement was signed between Yanukovych and leaders of the parliamentary opposition, envisaging, among other things, the restoration of the 2004 Constitution, the formation of an interim government including members of the opposition, and presidential elections to be held before the end of 2014. The foreign ministers of Poland, Germany and France, who had served as mediators, witnessed the signing of the agreement (Larsen, 2014: 9). On the following day, Yanukovych fled to Russia, and an interim government was formed. However, in the following months, protests continued in various forms (Carnegie Europe, 2019), with people in western and central Ukraine displaying a clear preference for joining the EU (Center for Insights in Survey Research, 2015).

These developments ultimately induced the Russian government to increase pressure on Ukraine, fearing a loss of influence on the country. Shortly after Yanukovych fled, pro-Russian protests emerged in Crimea, and by the end of February it became clear that Russia was covertly preparing a territorial annexation of the peninsula (*The Guardian*, 2014). Initially, this was carried out by unidentified Russian troops ('little green men'), who occupied strategic locations such as airports and military bases (BBC News, 2014b). On 27 February, Russian forces took over the Supreme Council, the Crimean parliament, dissolved the existing Council of Ministers and installed a pro-Russian prime minister (Flikke, 2015). A referendum was held on 16 March, which, unsurprisingly, had the result of over 96 per cent of voters asking for Crimea's integration into the Russian Federation. On 18 March, Russian President Vladimir Putin signed a treaty that formally declared Crimea's annexation to Russia.

Another important phase of the Ukraine crisis was the months of April–September 2014, which were marked by a gradual escalation of the situation in eastern Ukraine, where pro-Russian separatists were fighting against the Ukrainian government – with the active support of Russian armed forces, as later emerged. This period was marked by debates on the imposition of sanctions on Russia. A turning point was the downing of a civilian plane (Malaysian Airlines flight MH17) on east Ukrainian territory on 17 July, which led to 298 civilian deaths. Investigations revealed that the plane had been shot down by a Russian surface-to-air missile launched from a pro-Russian separatist-controlled area in Ukraine (Dutch Safety Board, 2015; BBC News, 2018). As a consequence, the first economic (that is, 'third stage') sanctions targeting Russian banks, energy companies and weapons manufacturers were agreed on 29 July 2014 (European Council, 2014a).

Finally, the fourth phase analysed in this section concerns the search for negotiated solutions, in which Germany played an active role. It started with the signing of an agreement between representatives of the Russian and Ukrainian governments as well as of the eastern Ukrainian separatists in Minsk on 19 September 2014. The agreement envisaged a ceasefire, the establishment of a demilitarized zone and the expulsion of all foreign fighters from Ukraine (BPB, 2014; Flikke, 2015: 4; Fischer, 2019). However, none of these elements were implemented, and fighting continued.

After a period of relative calm in late 2014, a new phase of escalation began in January 2015 with attacks on the cities of Mariupol and Debaltseve (Standish, 2015). Ultimately, on 12 February, long negotiations took place in Minsk between German Chancellor Merkel, French President Hollande, Russian President Putin, Ukrainian President Poroshenko, and the leaders of the self-proclaimed 'People's Republics' of Donetsk and Luhansk, resulting in a 'Package of measures for the Implementation of the Minsk agreements', commonly known as the Minsk II agreement (UN Peacemaker, 2015). The accord detailed the implementation of the Minsk I agreement and envisaged an 'immediate and full' ceasefire in particular areas of the Donetsk and Luhansk districts, the creation of a buffer zone, monitoring on the part of the Organization for Security and Co-operation in Europe (OSCE), the release and exchange of hostages, and constitutional reforms in Ukraine entailing decentralization. The issue of local elections and local self-government was left for the Trilateral Contact Group to discuss (UN Peacemaker, 2015). The Minsk II agreement received the endorsement of the UNSC, which unanimously called for its implementation (UN, 2015). It somehow stabilized the situation, but it was never fully implemented since fighting in eastern Ukraine continued (ICG, 2015; Carnegie Europe, 2018). The agreement formally remained in place until 2022, when Russia officially recognized the self-proclaimed Luhansk and Donetsk 'People's Republic' on 21 February 2022, and Putin – on 22 February, two days ahead of the start of his war of aggression – declared that the Minsk agreements no longer existed (CNN, 2022).

Germany's low reluctance in the Ukraine crisis

Over the four phases of the Ukraine crisis of 2014–15 analysed in this section, the German government pursued a policy that displayed only low levels of reluctance and, as time passed, developed to become non-reluctant.

In the months immediately preceding the outbreak of the crisis, that is, at the end of 2013, after the Ukrainian government interrupted preparations for the agreements with the EU and the first protests broke out in Kyiv, Germany did not take the initiative and did not try to defuse the situation before it escalated. According to one of the experts interviewed, the final months of 2013 were a 'transition period' for Germany: 'Westerwelle was not capable of acting and Merkel [was] in hiding'.[13] During those days, the EU's policy on the Ukraine crisis was shaped 'initially by the Commission, later by Poland and the Baltic countries', while Germany played no significant role.[14] However, Germany shed this initial reluctance when the crisis in

---

[13]   Interview G8, German expert, Berlin, 24 April 2015.
[14]   Interview G12, German academic, Hamburg, 27 April 2015.

Ukraine escalated, and its later policies did not display any of the features of reluctance outlined in Chapter 2, as it was neither hesitant (lack of initiative, delaying, flip-flopping) nor recalcitrant (ignoring or rejecting requests, obstructionism). Quite the contrary, several initiatives emerged from Berlin, among others an early proposal on the part of German Foreign Minister Frank-Walter Steinmeier in a meeting on 14 February 2014 with Russian Foreign Minister Sergey Lavrov and President Vladimir Putin to establish an OSCE observer mission for Ukraine (Rinke, 2014b: 37).

More importantly, Germany played a major role in mediating a compromise that put an end to the Maidan violence (Malik and Gani, 2014). Reportedly, the initiative for the mediation by the foreign ministers of the Weimar Triangle (Germany, France, Poland) originated on 19 February 2014 during the Franco–German Ministerial Council, and Steinmeier played 'a very active role ... and pressed for his French colleague, Laurent Fabius, and the Polish foreign minister, Radosław Sikorski, to travel to Kiev with him' (Rinke, 2014b: 38). On 20–21 February, the Weimar Triangle foreign ministers mediated negotiations between Ukrainian President Yanukovych and representatives of the opposition, and also managed to get the agreement approved by a Russian representative. The diplomatic initiative by the Weimar Triangle did not involve a recalcitrant attitude vis-à-vis the requests of other European countries. On the contrary, the initiative was backed by the EU, which on 20 February decided to impose sanctions on the Yanukovych regime (European Council, 2014a).

Russia's annexation of Crimea in March 2014 was an important catalyst in the formation of an increasingly consistent policy on the part of Berlin. During the two weeks that preceded the formal annexation of Crimea, the USA and the EU became more closely involved in the crisis. For Germany, this implied closer coordination efforts with Washington, on the one hand, as exemplified by Steinmeier's visit to Washington for consultations with John Kerry on 27 February (Klingst, 2014) and Chancellor Merkel talking on the phone to President Obama on 2 March (Bundesregierung, 2014a). On the other hand, it involved Germany's acceptance of a three-steps approach to sanctions (Gotev, 2014) in the EU context. While on 3 March Steinmeier had called for sanctions to be just threatened but not actually imposed (Rinke, 2014b: 41), at the extraordinary meeting of EU Heads of State or Government on Ukraine on 6 March, Merkel showed a new openness towards far-reaching economic sanctions in the case of 'any further steps by the Russian Federation to destabilise the situation in Ukraine' (European Council, 2014b; Rinke, 2014b: 41–2; Bundesregierung, 2014b).

Still, during this phase, some indicators of recalcitrance and hesitation can be identified in Germany's approach. For example, in early March 2014, Germany took a while to join the USA, the UK, France and Canada in their refusal to take part in a preparatory meeting for the planned G8 summit at

Sochi (Schmitz and Wittrock, 2014). The German government, moreover, initially expressed its opposition to the US proposal of expelling Russia from the G8 (Baker, 2014b). Berlin was also initially sceptical with regard to the imposition of sanctions due to the huge economic interests and investments of German companies in Russia (Hesse et al, 2014). These moderate signs of recalcitrance (initially not conforming to the requests of international partners) and hesitation (delay) are indicators of low-level reluctance on the part of Germany during this phase of the Ukraine crisis.

At the same time, Germany continued to play an active role in international crisis management efforts, including several journeys by Steinmeier in early March 2014 to promote the idea of a contact group (an initiative that had emerged from a Franco–German meeting; see Rinke, 2014b: 41). More importantly, during this phase of low-level reluctance, we can observe the gradual consolidation of what became the German position on the Ukraine crisis for the months to come. This position entailed: (1) a focus on negotiations, based on the notion that the crisis could not be solved militarily and that ties with Moscow should not be completely broken; (2) support for Ukraine; and (3) increased pressure on Moscow through the threat and the adoption of sanctions. These three main points, which were outlined by Merkel in her speech in front of the Bundestag on 13 March 2014 (see Bundesregierung, 2014b), formed the backbone of Germany's approach to Ukraine in the following phases.

During the third phase, while violence in eastern Ukraine escalated, Germany played a less visible international leadership role, but shed several of the elements of reluctance that had emerged during the phase of the annexation of Crimea. For a short period, in April 2014, the USA was a driving force in the effort to find a negotiated solution to the crisis, but pro-Russian separatists rejected a US-promoted agreement signed in Geneva on 17 April (BBC News, 2014a). After that, 'Washington participated ... in all steps of imposing sanctions and frequently even went a step further than the EU, but essentially left talks with Moscow to the Germans' (Rinke, 2015: 12). According to one of the experts I interviewed, 'the United States were not there. [It was] a real vacuum. ... The US [stood by Germany's side, but] as a sniper, not as a leading power'.[15] Some initiatives were taken by the French side, for example inviting Putin to the commemorations for the 70th anniversary of the Normandy landings (Baker, 2014a) – thereby leading to the first meeting between Putin and Ukraine's new president Petro Poroshenko (and to the establishment of what later came to be called the 'Normandy format', that is, meetings involving representatives from Russia, Ukraine, Germany and France). Germany, for its part, pursued its

---

[15] Interview G13, German expert, telephone interview, 29 April 2015.

mixed approach of negotiations and sanctions – with an increasing focus on sanctions as a response to escalation. On the one hand, therefore, Germany continued its negotiation efforts, among others, through repeated telephone contact with government representatives from Ukraine and Russia (Kundnani and Pond, 2015). Germany also served as a host for a foreign minister-level meeting in the Normandy format in July 2014 to discuss a ceasefire against the backdrop of increased violence (*Spiegel Online*, 2014). On the other hand, after the kidnapping of several members of an OSCE observer mission, four of whom German, in eastern Ukraine and an unsuccessful telephone conversation with Putin, on 25 April 2014 Merkel announced that the EU would prepare the second stage of sanctions (Rinke, 2015: 11) – and indeed, on 29 April the EU expanded its sanctions list (Flikke, 2015).

After the shooting down of the MH17 aeroplane on 17 July 2014, Germany became increasingly supportive of sanctions, and even 'became the clear leader in consolidating a common sanctions policy in the second half of 2014' (Koeth, 2016: 113). The confirmation that Russian soldiers were fighting in eastern Ukraine reportedly induced Chancellor Merkel to 'fight for a determined response' (Rinke, 2015: 16) at the special meeting of the European Council on 30 August 2014, trying to overcome the scepticism of countries like Austria and Italy towards sanctions. On 10 September 2014, Merkel insisted on the need to swiftly implement the sanctions that the EU had approved but then delayed at Finland's request (Reuters, 2014; Rinke, 2014a). Importantly, therefore, Germany was pushing for the implementation of tougher sanctions in 2014. While it was not necessarily responsive to the demands of its fellow European countries that opposed a harder approach towards Russia, Berlin was no longer hesitant. Overall, Berlin pursued an increasingly consistent policy and its 'brokerage' with regard to a tightening of sanctions and increased NATO presence in Poland and the Baltic countries 'was skillful and determined' (Seibel, 2015: 67).

Finally, the fourth phase of the crisis corresponds to further diplomatic engagement on the part of Berlin, with Merkel and Steinmeier engaging in close consultations with their counterparts in the Normandy format. On 5–6 February 2015, German Chancellor Merkel and French President Hollande travelled to Kyiv and to Moscow and obtained the consent of President Putin on the elaboration of a new document on the implementation of the Minsk I agreement (*Spiegel Online*, 2015). Immediately thereafter, Merkel travelled to Washington and got US President Obama's support for the mediation mission – against the backdrop of increasing pressure within the USA for the delivery of weapons to the Ukrainian army (BBC News, 2015). Ultimately, on 12 February 2015, negotiations took place in Minsk, leading to the signing of the Minsk II agreement. While Germany operated in tandem with France in its mediation efforts, several indicators reveal that the German government played a crucial and leading role in negotiations.

For example, the preparatory meetings among high-ranking bureaucrats from the 'Normandy' countries took place in Berlin (and later in Minsk) (Gebauer and Weiland, 2015), and it was actually Merkel who travelled to Washington to get support from the US president.[16] Again, German foreign policy was also not hesitant in this phase. Berlin followed the principles of pursuing a negotiated solution while keeping sanctions in place. To a certain extent Berlin was recalcitrant (rejection of requests), particularly concerning the issue of weapons supplies for the Ukrainian government forces. In her speech at the Munich Security Conference on 7 February 2015, Merkel reiterated 'The crisis cannot be resolved by military means' (Bundesregierung, 2015). This opposition to weapons supplies also stood in stark contrast to calls for such supplies from several US senators, and it was clear that a failure of the Franco–German mediation effort would make it extremely difficult for President Obama to continue resisting to such pressures. Again, however, recalcitrance was paired with determination, so that during this phase Germany's approach cannot be considered reluctant.[17]

Overall, therefore, Germany's approach to the Ukraine crisis of 2014–15 initially displayed some degree of reluctance, but hesitation was gradually left to one side as Berlin took an increasingly active role in negotiations and consistently embraced a policy of sanctions vis-à-vis Russia. With the benefit of hindsight, after the start of Russia's war of aggression against Ukraine in 2022, the wisdom of pursuing such policy of dialogue with Russia looks questionable. Nevertheless, combining sanctions with negotiations is not an uncommon practice and does not in itself have to be an indication of a contradictory policy. Measured by the standards of the definition proposed in this book, the consolidation of a policy consistently focused on a combination of diplomacy and sanctions corresponds to a less and less reluctant approach. Berlin increasingly took the initiative, it acted in a timely manner and it did not oscillate in its fundamental positions. While the German government

---

[16] According to two interviewees, however, it was very important for Germany to have France on board – because the German–French tandem was a 'sacred cow' to Berlin, something not to be called into question (Interview G1, senior German diplomat, Federal Foreign Office, Berlin, 20 April 2015); and also because Germany wanted to avoid the impression of exclusive German–Russian negotiations over Ukraine (Interview G1; and Interview G5, German government official, Federal Chancellery, Berlin, 23 April 2015). Also, according to a German government official (Interview G9, Federal Ministry for Economic Affairs and Energy, Berlin, 24 April 2015), getting France on board was mainly a 'tactical' decision.

[17] Germany's approach to the Ukraine crisis during this phase also stands in stark contrast to its highly reluctant approach in February 2022 and the following months, when Berlin tried to resist pressures on the delivery of weapons, but gradually backtracked, ultimately pursuing a piecemeal policy of hesitant support to the Ukrainian government (see also Chapter 1).

was recalcitrant vis-à-vis the preferences of countries that opposed tougher sanctions, it ultimately managed to push them towards a common European line. All this did not solve the Ukraine crisis, but at that time it certainly marked a shift away from previously high levels of reluctance on the part of Berlin. To some extent, German activism and leadership in Europe went so far as to even surprise German diplomats. As one interviewee told me, 'that's remarkable, that Germany is so active!'[18]

Explaining Germany's decreasing reluctance in the Ukraine crisis of 2014–15

How can we explain Germany's initially low and then gradually decreasing and disappearing reluctance in the Ukraine crisis of 2014–15? First of all, the political weakness explanation discussed in Chapter 3 applied during the very first phase of the Ukraine crisis: when the Euromaidan protests broke out, the Merkel II cabinet (the CDU/CSU/FDP coalition government) was still in power, but only as a caretaker government. The new grand coalition government (Merkel III cabinet) took over on 17 December 2013. It is thus unsurprising that still-Foreign Minister Westerwelle did not start any major new diplomatic initiatives. The political weakness argument therefore explains Germany's hesitation during the very beginning of the Ukraine crisis in late 2013. In the months that followed, Germany could gradually leave aside its reluctance since it was governed by a very stable 'grand coalition', which entailed the two largest parties, the CDU/CSU and the SPD. This coalition government had developed a broad agreement on the need for Germany to pursue a more decisive foreign policy and to take up greater leadership responsibilities in regional and global affairs.

The coordinated speeches at the Munich Security Conference of 31 January–2 February 2014 involved not only the head of state, President Joachim Gauck, but also Foreign Minister Steinmeier of the SPD and Defence Minister Ursula von der Leyen of the CDU, thereby reflecting a broad consensus on the overall direction of German foreign policy within the newly formed governing coalition. As mentioned, the statements about a sea change in German foreign policy certainly put the German government under pressure to act during the Ukraine crisis, and this also contributes to explain why the new German government shed its almost proverbial reluctance in foreign policy.

Capacity problems did not constitute an issue during the Ukraine crisis, or possibly only in a limited way. According to one expert I interviewed, Germany 'initially did not pay [enough] attention, maybe also because

---

[18] Interview G1, senior German diplomat, Federal Foreign Office, Berlin, 20 April 2015.

expertise on Russia had declined'.[19] However, compared to other European countries, Germany, with its long-term close relations with Russia, was likely in a better position to assess the situation. Steinmeier had already served as foreign minister in the first grand coalition (Merkel I) of 2005–09. During those years, he had pursued a particularly Russia-friendly policy, for which he was heavily criticized.[20] Nevertheless, this had certainly earned him a high degree of expertise on Russia, which also contributes to explain why the German government was able to pursue a highly influential policy during the Ukraine crisis of 2014–15. When it comes to the bureaucracy, the Federal Foreign Office and the Chancellery had different approaches: 'In the Federal Foreign Office, [diplomats] learn that we always have a close relationship with Russia. ... At the OSCE, German diplomats were always mocked as the "Russia understanders"',[21] while the Chancellery was less Russia-friendly. But according to my interviewees, these differences did not go so far as to produce bureaucratic quarrels that would hamper the formation of a consistent German preference.[22] Instead, they contributed to the compromise solution of privileging a combination of negotiations and sanctions.

Germany's somewhat reluctant policies in the immediate aftermath of Russia's annexation of Crimea can, to some extent, be explained with the 'cognitive problems' argument. In fact, this was certainly one of the most serious security crises that had affected Europe since the end of the Cold War, and the very fact that it involved territorial annexation – something that had almost been ruled out as a possibility in Europe's neighbourhood – produced a high degree of uncertainty among German (but also other European) decision makers. To some extent, it also led to fears in Germany due to territorial proximity and to Putin's perceived 'unpredictability' (Erler, 2014). The very lack of transparency of developments on the ground in Crimea in the process of annexation likely complicated the assessment of the situation, as Germany was caught by surprise by the annexation.

The most plausible explanation for Germany's (low) reluctance in crisis management in Ukraine in 2014–15 is related to the competing norms driving Germany foreign policy, which ultimately touched on the issue of how to deal with Russia and were reflected in divergences between the two governing parties. In fact, there are indications about differences between Merkel and Steinmeier in their approach to the imposition of sanctions

---

[19]   Interview G12, German academic, Hamburg, 27 April 2015.
[20]   The SPD's closeness to Russia also earned the party severe criticism after Russia's aggression against Ukraine in 2022. See, for example, Kinkartz (2022).
[21]   Interview G11, German academic, Hamburg, 27 April 2015.
[22]   Interview G3, expert, German Council on Foreign Relations, Berlin, 21 April 2015.

shortly after the annexation of Crimea, with Steinmeier pursuing a more Russia-friendly course than Merkel, and initially calling for sanctions to be only threatened, but not imposed. As one interviewee put it, 'Steinmeier ... pursued the broad line "We will always negotiate, always communicate with Russia"'.[23] Forsberg (2016: 31) points out that differences between Merkel and Steinmeier were visible particularly at the beginning of the crisis, but were later reduced, with the two even 'assur[ing] the Bundestag that there was no difference between their views, and that all their actions had been coordinated and mutually agreed'. Nevertheless, Steinmeier continued to be more Russia-friendly than Merkel, warning of the dangers of crippling the Russian economy and arguing in 2015 that Russia's return to the G8 would be 'desirable' (Forsberg, 2016: 31).

This reflected underlying differences in the approach of the two political parties forming Germany's grand coalition government (the SPD had traditionally been more open towards the idea of negotiating with Russia in the tradition of Willy Brandt's 'Ostpolitik' as compared to the CDU) and overall strong differences between so-called 'Russia understanders' and proponents of a harder course of action towards Putin (*The Economist*, 2014). At the same time, Germany's industry was concerned about the potential negative consequences of sanctions given that 300,000 jobs in Germany were dependent on business relations with Russia, and that 36 per cent of German oil and 35 per cent of German gas imports at that time came from Russia (Hesse et al, 2014: 26). Moreover, the debate was accompanied by different normative stands, which cut across party lines and in parallel: on the one hand, members of all the major parties emphasized the need for negotiations and diplomacy in addressing the crisis. In a debate in the Bundestag on 13 March 2014, Merkel stressed 'We are working for a political-diplomatic way out of the crisis' (Bundestag, 2014: 1520), and during the same debate the norm of peaceful resolution to disputes was stressed time and again by representatives of all major parties. This was also related to the notion of 'leaving the door open' for Putin's Russia (Bundestag, 2014: 1530). Such emphasis on negotiated solutions was related to Germany's emphasis on presenting itself internationally an 'honest broker, someone all parties trust'.[24] On the other hand, several political actors emphasized the norm of territorial integrity and that the annexation of Crimea constituted a blatant violation of international law. Merkel pointed out 'This is about the territorial integrity of a neighbouring European country, it is about the respect of the principles of the United Nations, the principles and methods of reconciliation of interests in the 21st century' (Bundestag, 2014: 1519).

---

[23] Interview G11, German academic, Hamburg, 27 April 2015.

[24] Interview G1, senior German diplomat, Federal Foreign Office, Berlin, 20 April 2015.

Such a position was echoed most forcefully by other members of the Union as well as by the more Russia-sceptical Greens, but it was not called into question by SPD representatives. In a nutshell, those who emphasized the sanctity of international law and Germany's commitment to a 'rules-based international order'[25] called for greater pressure to be applied to Russia to punish it for violating the sovereignty and territorial integrity of Ukraine.[26]

All this initially led to an indecisive approach on the part of Berlin. However, the shock of territorial occupation and annexation in the EU's neighbourhood ultimately led to greater convergence between the positions of the political parties in the grand coalition and to a policy reconciling the position of both 'camps'. The fact that Foreign Minister Steinmeier and SPD leader Sigmar Gabriel were disappointed by talks with Russian government representatives in early March 2014, induced the SPD to more decisively endorse the idea of sanctions and of a generally more determined approach towards Putin (Rinke, 2014b: 42). Moreover, the annexation of Crimea galvanized public opinion and German industry. On 14 March 2014, Merkel held a meeting with representatives of German industry, who ended up supporting her course since 'violations of international law cannot be accepted without further comments or reactions' (*Manager Magazin*, 2014: 9). As the situation in eastern Ukraine escalated, none of the major political actors in Berlin seriously called into question the policy of sanctions, given that it was clear to everybody that a military option was not on the table (Rinke, 2015: 9).

The fact that Germany chose to pursue a mixed approach that combined negotiation efforts with sanctions played an important role in reconciling normative struggles: it satisfied both the proponents of negotiated solutions and those who called for a tougher approach vis-à-vis Russia.[27] Moreover, the German government resisted the contrasting pressures of domestic actors who accused it of not talking enough to Moscow (this accusation came from former SPD chancellors Helmut Schmidt and Gerhard Schröder as well as from the CSU) and of pursuing a policy of appeasement (this accusation came from within the CDU itself and from the Greens) (Rinke, 2015).

A gradually less reluctant and ultimately non-reluctant foreign policy on the part of Berlin in the crisis of 2014–15 was also made possible by a broad convergence of international expectations about greater German engagement in crisis management. As Pond (Kundnani and Pond, 2015: 173) puts it,

---

[25] Interview G12, German academic, Hamburg, 27 April 2015.

[26] Interview G14, German academic, telephone interview, 12 May 2015.

[27] What ultimately differentiates German policy in the Ukraine crisis of 2014–15 from the much more reluctant approach in took in 2022 (see Chapter 7 for some reflections) is the consistency with which this two-tiered approach (negotiations plus sanctions) was pursued in 2014–15.

'Obama, fully occupied with other world crises, essentially outsourced [Western diplomacy] to Berlin' as the USA stopped playing a major diplomatic role after their April 2014 initiative in Geneva. EU institutions were paralysed ahead of the May 2014 EU Parliament elections, given that the tenure of the Commission was coming to an end (Rinke, 2015: 9). Moreover, within the EU, Germany did not encounter much opposition to its policies and was able to rally support for sanctions (Szabo, 2014: 117; Münkler, 2015: 152–3), mediating between the countries that wanted tougher sanctions and those that wanted milder sanctions.[28] With the escalation of violence in eastern Ukraine and the kidnapping of the OSCE observers, convergence between the positions of the EU, the G7 and the USA grew further, so Germany was not subjected to diverging international pressures by its partners (Rinke, 2015: 11). And even Russia saw Berlin as the most acceptable Western interlocutor – as one interviewee put it, 'Putin listens to Germany – who else should do it then?'[29] Germany at that time, however, did not react to calls for the provision of weapons to Ukraine, and only a few voices in Berlin (for example, Wolfgang Ischinger, a German diplomat and chair of the Munich Security Conference; see *Zeit Online*, 2015) called for an engagement of this kind on Germany's part.[30]

All this coalesced with domestic expectations for Germany to play an important role in the crisis. With the speeches on a 'faster, more decisive and more substantial' German foreign policy, 'the bar had been set high', as a senior government official in the Federal Foreign Office put it, and Germany 'was in a tight spot' and had to act.[31] According to Steinmeier's own assessment, Germany had been facing a 'tension between a dramatically changing world, high expectations from abroad as to our performance, and high domestic expectations as to our creativity in finding a sound, realistic, and wherever possible straightforward path' (Steinmeier, 2014: 3). Ultimately, the compromise solution of pursuing a mix of diplomatic negotiations and sanctions was a middle way that most relevant actors could accept. All this allowed the German government to consistently pursue this course of action, and thereby to gradually leave its reluctance behind in this crisis.

This is how Germany, albeit for a short period, took over a leadership role in Europe. In the interviews I carried out in Berlin in April 2015, the interlocutors in German ministries emphasized that they considered this to

---

[28] Interview G14, German academic, telephone interview, 12 May 2015.

[29] Interview G5, German Government official, Federal Chancellery, Berlin, 23 April 2015.

[30] According to one prescient interviewee, 'many in the Federal Foreign Office would agree with Ischinger: it was wrong to leave Ukraine like that [without providing it with weapons], and it will haunt us later on. Putin will come again' (Interview G11, German academic, Hamburg, 27 April 2015).

[31] Interview G6, senior German diplomat, Federal Foreign Office, Berlin, 23 April 2015.

be a major change in German foreign policy. According to a senior diplomat, up until that point the German position had always been 'to go with the flow. The typical bureaucratic formulation for this was "We will agree with an emerging consensus position". [But now things have changed.] Our partners want to follow Germany and to know where Germany stands. … For the bureaucracy, this is a real cultural transformation'.[32] At the same time, there was a high degree of awareness about the potential backlash of German leadership in Europe, as it had emerged during the Eurozone crisis.[33] Other observers pointed out that the German government still had difficulties in adjusting to its newfound leadership role,[34] and that the Merkel government was still only 'managing' foreign policy,[35] also because of Merkel's 'strategic indifference'.[36] As an official in the Federal Ministry for Economic Affairs and Energy put it, Germany was highly oriented towards compromise, and 'the cautious end up dominating in a system based on compromise'.[37] Other interviewees pointed out that, despite its prominent role in the Ukraine crisis of 2014–15, Germany was unsure about how to deal with its new-found power and its sudden leadership role in Europe.[38] And, in fact, despite Germany's non-reluctant policies in the Eurozone crisis and its sudden leadership role in the so-called 'refugee crisis' of 2015, events following Russia's attack against Ukraine in 2022 show that the issue of German reluctance has again come centre stage. German leadership therefore was short-lived and possibly related to the specific conditions of those crises, but the debate on German reluctance started over again a few years later.

---

[32] Interview G6, senior German diplomat, Federal Foreign Office, Berlin, 23 April 2015.
[33] Interview G6, senior German diplomat, Federal Foreign Office, Berlin, 23 April 2015.
[34] Interview G8, German expert, Berlin, 24 April 2015.
[35] Interview G8, German expert, Berlin, 24 April 2015.
[36] Interview G13, German expert, telephone interview, 29 April 2015.
[37] Interview G10, German government official, Federal Ministry for Economic Affairs and Energy, Berlin, 24 April 2015.
[38] Interview G3, expert, German Council on Foreign Relations, Berlin, 21 April 2015.

6

Brazil's Non-Reluctant Approach to Regional Crisis Management

The case of Brazil is analysed in this chapter as a case of non-reluctance in regional crisis management. The analysis will focus on Brazil's approach to the two most severe crises in the country's extended regional neighbourhood: on Brazil's leadership of the UN Stabilization Mission in Haiti (MINUSTAH), and on Brazil's approach to the Colombian civil war between the Fuerzas Armadas Revolucionarias de Colombia (FARC, Revolutionary Armed Forces of Colombia – People's Army) and the Colombian government. As for the other cases analysed in this book, I will address crisis management in a period of political stability. In the case of Brazil, the years of the first presidency of Luiz Inácio Lula da Silva (often just called 'Lula') were indeed a period of stability, and one in which Brazil clearly wanted to become engaged in international affairs. President Lula of the leftist Partido dos Trabalhadores (PT, Workers' Party), a former labour leader who had already run for the presidency of Brazil three times without success, was elected president in the general election of 2002 defeating his rival of the centre-right Brazilian Partido da Social Democracia Brasileira (PSDB, Social Democracy Party) in a landslide in the second round. In the 2006 general election, Lula was re-elected, again after failing to prevail in the first round, but winning a landslide in the second round.

The eight years of Lula's first presidency (2003–10) were a period of great stability for Brazil for several reasons. Lula's leftist government promoted a series of social schemes such as the famous Bolsa Família (Family Allowance) and the Fome Zero (Zero Hunger) programme, which contributed to a remarkable drop in poverty levels in the country. Economic growth rose steadily in the early 2000s, reaching 7.5 per cent in 2010 (Kaufman and García-Escribano, 2013). Correspondingly, and most importantly, Lula's government was extremely popular, with approval ratings of 80 per cent of respondents in December 2010, and a remarkable personal approval rate of 87 per cent for the president (Reuters, 2010).[1]

In parallel to social and economic development, the years 2003–10 were also characterized by an entirely new intensity in Brazil's engagement in world politics. Brazil played a leading role in negotiations in the World Trade Organization (WTO) alongside other emerging powers, it acted as a norm entrepreneur on the topic of Responsibility to Protect (R2P) by trying to promote its own notion of 'responsibility while protecting' (Kenkel and Stefan, 2016), it engaged as a mediator in the dispute over Iran's nuclear programme, and forcefully called for a reform of the UNSC (see, for example, the overview of Brazilian foreign policy provided by the then-Foreign Minister, Celso Amorim, 2010a). Status seeking, that is, the aspiration to get international acceptance as a great power, was one of the main drivers of this activist foreign policy, which also included an unprecedented outreach to Africa (Stolte, 2015). Membership in the BRICS (Brazil, Russia, India, China, South Africa), IBSA (India, Brazil, South Africa), the so-called BASIC (Brazil, South Africa, India, China) group on climate change at the Copenhagen summit and the G20 illustrate the extent of Brazil's international engagement in minilateral forums and global governance (see, for example Bernal-Meza, 2010: 198–9). Indeed, in the 2000s, Brazil's activist foreign policy contributed to its broad recognition as an emerging power (see, for example, Hurrell, 2006; Kahler, 2013; Menezes and Vieira, 2022).

At the regional level, Brazil was clearly the predominating 'regional power' (Nolte, 2010), but it did not promote regionalism beyond a certain point. Indeed, while Brazil had been one of the drivers in the formation of MERCOSUR (the Southern Common Market) and of what later became UNASUR (Union of South American Nations), during the second term of Lula's government (and even more so under his successor Dilma Rousseff), we saw increasing disengagement from regional organizations (Burges, 2017: 169–70). As Burges (2015: 195) put it, Brazil displayed a 'simultaneous rhetoric of solidarity and unwillingness to build robust regional multilateral institutions'. Instead, Brasília seemed to increasingly prefer a bilateral approach to South American countries, sometimes leading to suspicions among its smaller neighbours (Spektor, 2010). Overall, however, despite this hesitation to engage multilaterally, Brazil was unequivocally very much engaged in regional crisis management, which is the main focus of the analysis here.

---

[1]   It was only after a series of corruption scandals under Lula's successor Dilma Rousseff that Brazil rapidly lost its domestic stability as well as its international profile.

Under the government preceding Lula's, Brazil had already played a constructive role in addressing regional crises. Brazil's engagement included the prevention of coups in Paraguay (1997) and Venezuela (2002), as well as assuming the role of mediator in a territorial dispute between Ecuador and Peru in 1995–98 (Spektor, 2010: 193). Lula himself repeatedly created 'groups of friends' to find solutions to some of the crises in Brazil's neighbourhood, thereby choosing an intergovernmental approach and bypassing regional organizations (Zilla, 2011: 14).

In the following, I will address Brazil's approach towards crisis management in what were arguably the most severe crises in Brazil's extended neighbourhood during the years of Lula's first presidency. In particular, I will focus on the Brazilian leadership of MINUSTAH as well as on its approach vis-à-vis the longstanding intrastate conflict in Colombia. In both cases, Brazil did not pursue a reluctant policy but, quite to the contrary, a rather consistent and determined as well as responsive approach. For each of the cases, after providing some background information about the crisis, I will sketch out Brazil's approach and discuss why it was not reluctant. I will then proceed to assess whether this non-reluctant approach to crisis management can be explained in the light of my theoretical framework. As we will see, Brazil was able to pursue a non-reluctant policy in both cases because the government did not face problems with preference formation and, at the same time, was confronted with homogeneous or not particularly pressing international expectations concerning its crisis management approach.

Brazil's leadership of MINUSTAH

One of the most severe crises in Brazil's extended neighbourhood during the years of Lula's presidency took place in Haiti. The country had been plagued by decades of political instability and several coups d'état. Its 'Dysfunctional institutions, poor and corrupt governance, lack of transparency, and pervasive crime' (ICG, 2004: 1) contributed to societal tensions and a high degree of political polarization. The country's first democratically elected president, Jean-Bertrand Aristide, who had repeatedly been in office since 1991, had lost popular support over time. After his re-election in 2000, the country was plagued by human rights violations as well as by increasing violence between supporters of the government as well as 'government-supported gangs' (ICG, 2004: 9) and other paramilitary and opposition groups. Amidst ever more frequent episodes of political violence, targeted killings and attacks on anti- and pro-government supporters in 2003, armed resistance started to form. In February 2004, the rebel group Front pour la Libération et la Reconstruction Nationale (FLRN, National Liberation and Reconstruction Front) and other opponents of Aristide, especially former members of the armed forces who had been dismissed by the president, took over control of the city of Gonaïves (UCDP, 2022b). Within a few days, the rebels also conquered Cap Haïtien, the country's second-largest city, hardly encountering any substantial resistance from the Haitian National Police. Faced with the military advancement of his opponents as well as with intense pressure from international actors (most notably the USA and France), Aristide ultimately signed a letter of resignation on 29 February 2004 and left the country on a plane chartered by the USA (ICG, 2004: 11). The role of the USA and France has been the object of much controversy, with Aristide claiming to have been kidnapped by the USA in a coup, Washington denying this allegation, and the Caribbean Community (CARICOM) demanding a UN investigation on the events.

In the weeks and months following the departure of Aristide, Haiti further sank into chaos. A Multinational Interim Force (MIF) immediately deployed with UNSC Resolution 1529 (UNSC, 2004a) failed to stabilize the situation. The Interim Force was led by the USA and comprised soldiers from Canada, Chile and France. A mostly technocratic interim government headed by the long-time UN diplomat Gérard Latortue was not able to gain much legitimacy or to stabilize the country. Given that with Resolution 1529 the UNSC had already declared its 'readiness to establish a follow-on United Nations stabilization force to support continuation of a peaceful and constitutional political process and the maintenance of a secure and stable environment' (UNSC, 2004a: 2), corresponding steps were taken in the following weeks. Ultimately, on 30 April 2004, the UNSC passed Resolution 1542 (UNSC, 2004b: 2), with which it decided to 'establish the United Nations Stabilization Mission in Haiti (MINUSTAH), the stabilization force called for in resolution 1529 (2004), for an initial period of six months, with the intention to renew for further periods'. MINUSTAH was supposed to operate under Chapter VII of the UN Charter, which entails the possibility to use force with the UNSC mandate, and was, as we will see, one of the most controversial issues for Brazil. MINUSTAH's mandate included the following points:

(a) in support of the Transitional Government, to ensure a secure and stable environment within which the constitutional and political process in Haiti can take place; (b) to assist the Transitional Government in monitoring, restructuring and reforming the Haitian National Police …; (c) to assist the Transitional Government, particularly the Haitian National Police, with comprehensive and sustainable Disarmament, Demobilisation and Reintegration (DDR) programs …; (d) to assist with the restoration and maintenance of the rule of law, public safety and public order in Haiti. (UNSC, 2004b: 2–3)

Moreover, the resolution envisaged the protection of civilians, support for the political process and assistance to the Transitional Government, as well as support for the promotion of human rights (UNSC, 2004b: 3). Ultimately, Brazil took over the leadership of the military component of MINUSTAH and provided the successive force commanders for the mission. The troops deployed to the mission were mostly from Latin American countries. MINUSTAH was formally established on 1 June 2004, and it remained in place until October 2017 (UN Peacekeeping, 2022a).[2] In the following sections, I will focus on Brazil's approach to the mission during the Lula years, and particularly on the important decision to take over its leadership.

Brazil and MINUSTAH

For the Brazilian government, the decision to take over the military leadership of MINUSTAH was a major foreign policy initiative in the field of regional crisis management, and it constituted an important opportunity for Brazil to display regional leadership and the readiness to take over international responsibilities.[3] When it came to the management of the crisis, the Brazilian government initially displayed some degree of hesitation and some inconsistencies in its approach.[4] In fact, Brazil voted in favour of Resolution 1529 on the establishment of the MIF, but it refused to participate in that force, mentioning the fact that the resolution referred to Chapter VII of the UN Charter and thereby to the possibility of using force without the consent of the conflict parties involved (Gauthier and John de Sousa, 2006: 1). The Brazilian government argued that the 'imposition' of peace went against its fundamental foreign policy principles, most notably against Article 4 of the Brazilian Constitution (Gauthier and John de Sousa, 2006: 1). The latter, in fact, envisages the principles of self-determination of peoples and of non-intervention, which successive Brazilian governments have interpreted as preventing Brazil from participating in peacekeeping missions under Chapter VII (Andrade et al, 2019: 27). Brazil has a long history of engagement in UN peacekeeping missions, but had always avoided being involved in peace enforcement.

---

[2]   Prolongation was also related to the devastating earthquake of 2010, which led the UN to further reinforce MINUSTAH in order to help with reconstruction and stabilization (UN Peacekeeping, 2022a). After 2017, MINUSTAH was followed by a much smaller mission called the United Nations Mission for Justice Support in Haiti (MINUJUSTH).

[3]   Interview B1, expert on Brazilian foreign and defence policy, online, 5 July 2022.

[4]   A scholar based in Brazil highlighted this initial reluctance on the part of Brazil, pointing out that it was only in the last few years of the mission, from 2013–14 onwards, that Brazil started openly acknowledging that this was, in fact, a Chapter VII mission. Interview B8, online, 27 September 2022.

Despite this initial refusal to participate in a Chapter VII mission, however, in April 2004 the Brazilian government ultimately voted in favour of Resolution 1542 on the establishment of MINUSTAH – even though MINUSTAH was explicitly a Chapter VII mission. Much more than that, Brazil took over the military leadership of the mission and became the largest provider of troops. Between 2004 and 2017, Brazil ultimately deployed to Haiti a total of 6,335 members of the navy, 30,553 members of the army, 438 members of the air force and 52 members of the military police (Ministério da Defesa, 2022).[5] This was a major departure from Brazil's previous approach to peacekeeping. Since the 1990s, Brazil had consistently deployed some troops to UN peacekeeping missions, for example to East Timor and Angola under Lula's predecessor Cardoso (Villa and Viana, 2010: 96), but on average it had only sent a few dozen soldiers (see UN Peacekeeping, 2022b).

Moreover, it had not previously taken over the leadership of peacekeeping missions (Gauthier and John de Sousa, 2006: 6), with all the responsibilities this implied. While this was therefore a new situation, and despite substantive domestic resistance and criticism, the Lula government managed to pursue a non-reluctant approach to crisis management in Haiti. Indeed, throughout the duration of MINUSTAH, Brazil remained the largest provider of troops most of the time, and towards the end of the mission in 2016, it still had the largest contingent (981 soldiers out of 2,361 provided by 19 countries; see MINUSTAH, 2022). Moreover, Brazil kept the leadership of the mission until its conclusion in 2017, even though MINUSTAH faced considerable criticism over the years, for not acting decisively enough (Gauthier and John de Sousa, 2006: 4), for killing civilians during raids such as those in the slum of Cité Soleil in 2005 (Stargardter, 2018), and for the perpetration of sexual violence by peacekeepers (King et al, 2021). Overall, therefore, Brazil adopted a consistent policy in addressing the crisis in Haiti, not displaying the indicators of hesitation that are typical of reluctance. As we will see, Brazil did not disappoint specific expectations voiced by important international partners, which implies that it was not recalcitrant. In the following sections,

---

[5]   According to a high-ranking Brazilian military officer interviewed, Brazil acted swiftly: 'the mobilization in Brazil was very, very fast, forces arrived very early. ... Brazil moved fast, but some of the other countries did not move that fast, so in the first months of the mission we had less than 30 per cent of the personnel we needed for the mission. The US left the Multinational Interim Force immediately after the fall of the president [Aristide]. ... The French and the Canadian, they were there for a little bit more, and the Chileans transitioned [from MIF] to the UN hat. Even for the UN this transition was very slow, the mobilization of troops was very slow. For the first 6–7 months the mission was struggling' (Interview B7, high-ranking officer in the Brazilian Armed Forces, online, 26 September 2022).

I will apply the theorization of reluctance developed in Chapter 3 to make sense of this non-reluctant approach to crisis management.

Explaining Brazil's non-reluctant approach

Among the possible explanatory factors for hesitation, the one related to government weakness does not apply in the case of Brazil under Lula during the period analysed. Quite to the contrary, in 2004 Lula had just been elected and did not face any substantial challenges to his presidency by domestic political opponents: he had 'a strong allied base and a disarticulated opposition that screamed a lot, but had few victories' (Mazenotti and Lourenço, 2010; author's own translation). Moreover, Lula enjoyed the support of the private sector, and, according to one interviewee, the very fact that he remained in power despite the Mensalão scandal, which involved vote-buying by Lula's PT, reveals how stable Lula's position in power was.[6]

This does not mean that the decision to lead MINUSTAH was uncontested. Indeed, before the decision on Brazil's military leadership of the mission was made, this topic was the object of substantial domestic political debates. The main opponents were intellectuals, members of parliament (including some of Lula's own PT) and union leaders of the Central Única dos Trabalhadores (CUT, Workers' Central Organization) and of the Movimento dos Trabalhadores Rurais Sem Terra (Landless Rural Workers' Movement), who, in April 2004 wrote a manifesto against Brazil's leadership of the mission and carried out protest actions to oppose it (Gauthier and John de Sousa, 2006: 3). Their main arguments focused on the norms of non-interventionism and the respect of Haiti's sovereignty.

The sociologists Emir Sader and Demétrio Magnoli, as well as the PT congressman Ivan Valente, furthermore argued that leading the mission would make Brazil an executor of the imperialistic policies preferred by the USA (see, for example, Magnoli, 2004). Similar arguments were voiced by PT Senator Serys Slhessarenko, who claimed that 'this episode is part of the North American policy of military and economic colonization of the continent' and that the Lula administration would send troops to Haiti 'in the name of Franco-Americans' to 'impose the semi-colonial submission of another Latin American nation' (Slhessarenko, 2004). Other critics argued that Brazil's leadership of MINUSTAH would legitimize what they considered to have been a coup d'état against Aristide (Gauthier and John de Sousa, 2006: 3).[7] Further arguments included the high costs of such a

---

[6]   Interview B1, expert on Brazilian foreign and defence policy, online, 5 July 2022.

[7]   As one interviewee put it, 'some sectors within the PT were against the mission. They were very preoccupied with the way Aristide had been removed from power. But these were

mission, with opponents claiming that those resources should have been invested in the pacification of Brazil's own cities instead. This statement by Senator Jefferson Péres illustrates well this criticism:

> Haiti is the poorest Country in Latin America, of all the Americas, in fact. We will be going to that country in an act of solidarity, but it is paradoxical that Brazil is going to be responsible for policing Haiti and does not have enough police to put order in a privileged city such as Rio de Janeiro – not to mention all the 'haitis' that extend throughout this country. (Senado Federal, 2004: 15249)

These criticisms, however, met a comparably unified government, in which different agencies concurred in supporting the mission.[8] Moreover, there was a high degree of convergence between, on the one hand, Brazil's presidency and its foreign policy bureaucracy, and, on the other, Brazil's military (Miyamoto, 2008: 389). The presidency was particularly important in the decision-making process:

> As far as I heard when I was in the ministry ... it was Lula's personal decision. He was a believer in increasing Brazil's role in the international system. He had a personal agenda. ... He thought that Brazil should participate more in regional efforts. And MINUSTAH came to Brazil as an opportunity because [Haiti] was a country that was not far away [and] it was seen as an easier peacekeeping operation as compared to [those in] some places in Africa. But in Haiti you have an easier agenda, and a lot of people in the government associated the problems in Haiti, social problems, with some problems we have at home. So Lula thought that was a good idea.[9]

The military obviously saw advantages in a mission that was poised to provide it with additional resources and the possibility of training its troops (Harig and Kenkel, 2017: 636; see also Aguilar, 2015: 127). The civilian government

---

a minority and they were invited to visit Haiti and they changed their mind' (Interview B6, Brazilian scholar, online, 19 September 2022).

[8] A scholar based in Brazil cautioned against considering Brazil a unitary actor: 'Basically, you have Lula, who has an idea, very anti-Western, anti-American ideas. Then you have the foreign ministry, which is interested in not giving up its old traditions. And the military wants combat experience' (Interview B8, online, 27 September 2022). The key point here is that there was a remarkable convergence of interests among most of these actors, and that the more sceptical ones could ultimately be convinced of the merits of the mission.

[9] Interview B4, Brazilian academic and former government adviser, online, 8 September 2022.

was primarily driven by the desire to gain international recognition for Brazil as a responsible emerging power and, by extension, as an ideal candidate for a permanent seat at the UNSC. For example, Luiz Carlos Da Silva, the government leader in the Chamber of Deputies, claimed that leadership of the mission was 'a unique opportunity for Brazil to continue competing for a permanent seat at the UN, which has invited our country not only to send troops, but to command them in Haiti' (quoted in Gauthier and John de Sousa, 2006: 1). Faced with criticism, Foreign Minister Amorim (2008a) claimed that Brazil's aspiration to gain a permanent seat in the UNSC was not a driver for the government's decision to lead MINUSTAH, which, he argued, was driven by solidarity with a fellow Latin American country. In fact, norms such as international solidarity and responsibility were frequently mentioned in speeches by Brazil's government representatives. As Amorim put it,

> We believe that a foreign policy of solidarity is both humanistic and in the best interests of Brazil, since a country is better perceived when it contributes to global stability and to the reduction of asymmetries between countries. To the principle of non-intervention, we add 'non-indifference' in relation to peoples experiencing situations of difficulty, provided that this solidarity is provided through legitimate channels and with the approval of the recipient country. The reform of global governance is a key aspect of Brazil's current foreign policy. We want to contribute to building an international order that is fairer, more democratic and inclusive of developing countries. (quoted in Portari and Garcia, 2010)[10]

Other factors mentioned by supporters of the initiative included the common African cultural heritage of Brazil and Haiti as well as the desire to avoid spillovers of the conflict to Brazil and other countries of the region. Again, Amorim argued:

> Look, we are there to help a country in the region, in Latin America and the Caribbean, which was threatened with becoming a totally failed state. ... Haiti is much more like Brazil, in many aspects – of course with many more problems, with much more backwardness in many aspects – but with cultural aspects, even of ethnic origin ... cultural aspects very similar to us, even religious in some regards. It was the first country in the Americas to free the slaves, which is also a reason for us to reflect, so I think it is a country that we should help

---

[10] See also, for example, Amorim (2010b).

and we can help because of this factor, that Brazil is a country that brings people together. (Amorim, 2008b)

Moreover, Lula framed the mission as an opportunity to promote regional cooperation in the field of security and defence – framed in highly normative terms: 'We must articulate a vision of defense in the region founded on common values and principles, such as respect for sovereignty, self-determination, the territorial integrity of States and non-intervention in internal affairs' (quoted in Oliveira and Damé, 2008).

Ultimately, the turning point in explaining why the Brazilian government was not hesitant in its decision to take over the leadership of MINUSTAH can be found in its argument concerning the mission. In fact, the government allayed the fears of those who pointed to the potential unconstitutionality of a Chapter VII mission by arguing that there was a fundamental difference between Resolution 1529 and Resolution 1542: in the former, Chapter VII was mentioned in the preamble, while in the latter, it was only mentioned in paragraph 7. According to the government, therefore, the resolution that mandated the formation of MINUSTAH was a resolution on 'peacekeeping', since Chapter VII appeared only in an 'operative clause' (de Lucena, 2014: 138). This was obviously legal quibbling (Harig and Kenkel, 2017: 635), but ultimately the government managed to assert its position and critics were largely sidelined. Also vis-à-vis Brazilian public opinion, the government was careful to present the mission as primarily humanitarian. Chapter VII was downplayed by defining MINUSTAH as an 'operation with Chapter VII elements' or a 'Chapter 6.5 mission' (Kawaguti, 2015: 47).

Formally, the decision to participate in a UN-mandated mission involves a number of institutional actors in Brazil: the request from the UN is directed at the Ministry of Foreign Affairs; the Ministry of Defence, the Ministry of Planning, Development and Management and the Ministry of Finance are involved in the development of a proposal; if such proposal is approved by the UN, the Ministry of Foreign Affairs and the Ministry of Defence will issue an Inter-Ministerial Explanatory Statement, which has to be approved by the president of the Republic. Then, both houses of the National Congress (Chamber of Deputies and Federal Senate) need to vote on such document. If a simple majority is reached in both houses, a legislative degree can be issued, which is then returned to the president of the Republic, who will finally issue a presidential decree (see Andrade et al, 2019: 16). In other words, different sections of the executive as well as the legislative were involved in the decision on MINUSTAH, as required by Brazil's legal provisions. However, according to observers, the Brazilian decision to take over the military leadership of the mission and to dispatch a substantial number of soldiers was clearly driven by the president (Diniz, 2009, as cited in Lucena, 2014: 139–40): 'Congressional approval ... was not very difficult for Lula to get'.[11] Civil society was not significantly involved in the debate,[12] as defence policy issues have traditionally not been the object of much public scrutiny in Brazil:

> 'I don't think that our society ... was ready to make this debate. Foreign and defence policy are not issues that are discussed, they are not issues that bring votes. They are not issues that are on the agenda, in a country that is so poor. That is why we did not have many discussions going on. In academia there is a lot of artificial support for the ministry of foreign affairs when we are in normal [conditions – now different under Bolsonaro]. We don't see much criticism on these issues, [academics] see Brazil is finally becoming a global player. There wasn't a lot of debate about it.'[13]

Overall, therefore, the absence of all the conditions that would usually explain hesitation helps us make sense of how the Brazilian government could adopt a non-reluctant approach to the crisis in Haiti. The government was stable and criticism could be overcome thanks to these arguments. Second, concerning the 'limited capacity' explanation, none of the elements envisaged by this approach applied to the Brazilian case. Brazil's Ministry of Foreign Affairs, Itamaraty, is usually considered to be composed of well-trained diplomats and to have adequate resources to manage Brazilian foreign policy. As Cason and Power (2009: 119) put it, 'the ministry is admired both inside and outside Brazil for the high level of professionalization of its diplomats'. Indeed, during the Lula years, we saw a veritable explosion of Brazil's foreign policy activities, with the number of diplomatic representations abroad growing from 150 to 225 (Martins y Miguel, 2010).

Bureaucratic infighting or competition among different ministries similarly were not factors that hampered the decision-making process on MINUSTAH leadership and deployment, especially given the great convergence of interests between Itamaraty and the Ministry of Defence. As one of the experts I interviewed put it,

> 'MINUSTAH was a moment of unity because both Itamaraty and the Ministry of Defence had a common interest. Both were interested and they wanted this at any cost. ... The foreign ministry hoped to

---

[11] Interview B6, Brazilian scholar, online, 19 September 2022.
[12] Interview B8, scholar based in Brazil, online, 27 September 2022.
[13] Interview B4, Brazilian academic and former government adviser, online, 8 September 2022. Also, according to another interviewee, political parties did not use the issue for mobilization because 'Messing with the military makes you lose votes' (Interview B8, scholar based in Brazil, online, 27 September 2022).

136

[increase Brazil's international] prestige, and for the military it was an opportunity to get better funding [and active experience].'[14]

The third possible explanation for hesitation, cognitive problems, similarly was not in place in the case of Brazil's decision on MINUSTAH. While for Brazil the leadership of a UN mission was a novelty, the relative distance from Haiti and the limited spillover effects of domestic instability in that country to Brazil did not put decision makers under high pressure, and did not lead to the perception of a severe crisis that might have led to disorientation and stress and therefore induced decision makers to adopt cognitive shortcuts and the other strategies discussed in Chapter 3.[15]

Finally, normative struggles are another possible explanation for hesitation – and indeed in the debates over Brazilian leadership of MINUSTAH, we find a clash between different normative arguments being made. While proponents of Brazilian engagement mostly highlighted international responsibility and solidarity, opponents mentioned non-interventionism, respect of Haiti's sovereignty and territorial integrity (Oliveira and Damé, 2008), as well as anti-imperialism as key norms that should drive Brazilian foreign policy. Moreover, the need to conduct an independent foreign policy and not to bend to international pressures was also mentioned by critics of Brazil's engagement in MINUSTAH. However, these evident normative disagreements and struggles did not go so far as to lead to hesitation, as ultimately the government was able to successfully promote its view by portraying MINUSTAH as a peacekeeping mission, thereby downplaying its peace enforcement elements related to Chapter VII.

When it comes to international expectations, these played an important role in driving Brazil's engagement in Haiti, and the Brazilian government was actually very responsive to those expectations. The strongest expectations about Brazilian leadership came from the USA and France. The USA had a long history of involvement in Haiti: it had militarily intervened in 1915 and occupied the country for 19 years, and in 1994 it had mediated a compromise leading to the reinstatement of President Aristide after a military coup d'état; moreover, the USA had led a UN-mandated mission to promote democratic consolidation, which ultimately had not managed to stabilize the country (ICG, 2004: 3). Overall, US meddling

---

[14] Interview with expert B1, online, 5 July 2022.
[15] See also Interview B1, expert, online, 5 July 2022. According to another interviewee, 'Haiti also provided an excuse to decline participation in other UN missions that were more politically sensitive. So it also became a very convenient excuse as Brazil continued its contribution, there was this positive image' (Interview B6, Brazilian scholar, online, 19 September 2022).

in Haiti in the 1990s was rather detrimental to the stability of the country, and controversies within the USA also hampered the efforts of the Clinton administration (ICG, 2004: 5).

This history of past engagement (and meddling) in Haiti contributes to explain both why the USA in 2004 still had a great interest in the situation in Haiti, and also why Washington was aware that direct engagement would not be welcomed in the country. Moreover, the US administration was mainly focusing on the Middle East at that time, and limited capacities induced it not to focus on Haiti, a much less salient issue.[16] According to a high-ranking Brazilian military officer, 'the US was very, very committed to the situation in Iraq, Afghanistan, so they wanted to get rid of Haiti as soon as possible. Their troops were sent to Haiti [in the context of the MIF, in February–July 2014] as emergency, [they were actually on their way to the Middle East] and needed to go to the Middle East as soon as possible'.[17] Therefore, according to the same officer:

'... as soon as there was a good possibility for Brazil to take part in MINUSTAH a lot of people from the US and France were providing liaison and information about what was going on in the country. There was a real effort of the countries in MIF to make sure that Brazil accept the mission and that the transition would be as fast and smooth as possible. There was a sincere commitment.'[18]

France, the formal colonial power, was concerned that an intervention would lead to resistance in Haiti (Carroll, 2004). Against this backdrop, it is no surprise that in March 2004 French President Jacques Chirac made a phone call to Lula, asking for Brazil to take over the leadership of the mission (Fernández Moreno et al, 2012: 382). This request reportedly had the backing and support of UN Secretary-General Kofi Annan (Andrade, 2004). Overall, therefore, expectations by the USA, France and the UN on Brazil's leadership of MINUSTAH were converging. When it comes to Latin American countries, some of them, most notably Chile and Argentina, were initially critical of Brazilian leadership of MINUSTAH (Hirst, 2007). However, ultimately both countries, together with several other Latin American countries, participated in the mission. As one interviewee argued, joining the mission became a matter of pride for Chile and Argentina: 'There is this rivalry, it's historical, there is always this

[16] Interview B3, Brazilian scholar, online, 23 August 2022.
[17] Interview B7, high-ranking officer in the Brazilian armed forces, online, 26 September 2022.
[18] Interview B7, high-ranking officer in the Brazilian armed forces, online, 26 September 2022.

looking at what your neighbour is doing. So there was this feeling that if Brazil goes [to Haiti] in the name of the region, then we also have to go. And we have to join properly [with adequate resources]'.[19] Moreover, for countries like Chile, participating in the mission also implied signalling to the USA that regional problems were being solved by regional countries, and that regional solidarity was in place.[20]

All in all, therefore, there was a broad convergence of international expectations concerning Brazil's role in Haiti, which also continued after the establishment of the mission. This was demonstrated when in 2005 UN Secretary-General Annan and other international actors agreed to a continuation of Brazil's leadership of the mission (Oswald, 2005). In 2006, after General Urano Teixeira da Matta Bacellar, the Brazilian commander of the mission, died, Jordan signalled its interest in taking over leadership of the mission, but ultimately leadership remained with Brazil, confirming its continued international backing (Miyamoto, 2008). Indeed, the Organization of American States (OAS) issued a statement a few days after the General's death, to declare that it 'continue[d] to support the Brazilian military command of MINUSTAH' (OAS, 2006).[21] In the course of the mission, however, Brazil started being faced with divergent expectations: the USA, Canada and France 'actively and intensely pressured for more aggressive and robust military actions. This pressure was ostensive and exerted in many ways: diplomatic demarches, constant visits and conversations, among others' (Fernández Moreno et al, 2012: 385; see also Kawaguti, 2015: 48). This approach stood in opposition to Brazil's emphasis on the humanitarian dimensions of the mission and also to the preferences of the other Latin American countries involved. Ultimately, Brazil ended up pursuing a more robust approach, 'but not at the levels of frequency and intensity intended by the Northern countries' (Fernández Moreno et al, 2012: 385). A high-ranking Brazilian military officer interviewed described the dilemma as follows:

'[On the one side,] you had US and France and even Canada who were strong advocates of a higher level of the use of force. And I had the opportunity to participate in many meetings with military and diplomatic authorities from the US, France, and the message was always the same [that MINUSTAH needed to become more robust]. And parts of the elite in Haiti were also advocating for more use of force because they wanted more security. On the other side, the governments

---

[19] Interview B2, scholar based in Chile, online, 14 July 2022.
[20] Interview B2, scholar based in Chile, online, 14 July 2022.
[21] The fact that the leadership of the mission did not rotate was actually quite unusual. Interview B8, scholar based in Brazil, online, 27 September 2022.

of the countries that had troops there were very careful about the use of force, about casualties, but also for people in Haiti. You had human rights organizations, international and national (from Haiti), who were pushing for not using force [even] against any cockroach. They even threatened to send the force commander to the international criminal court. So ... to modulate the use of force, was very complicated. I always advocate that if the troops are challenged and you cannot use force, you lose your credibility. It's not easy.'[22]

Despite these challenges, however, Brazil's engagement in Haiti can clearly be considered as a case of non-reluctance. This determined and responsive approach was made possible by a combination of a clear domestic preference on the matter and largely converging international expectations. The preferences of important international actors (France, USA) dovetailed with the Brazilian government's ambition to be recognized as a responsible actor, willing to take the leadership in managing a crisis in its extended regional neighbourhood in the context of a UN-mandated mission.

Brazil's approach to the conflict in Colombia

The civil war in Colombia has been the most virulent traditional intra-state armed conflict in South America during the past decades. While Colombia has had a history of political violence since its independence in the 19th century, a number of leftist rebel groups started forming in the 1960s in particular. Some of these guerrilla organizations disarmed in the early 1990s, but others continued their armed fight. The most important rebel organization was FARC (Fuerzas Armadas Revolucionarias de Colombia, Revolutionary Armed Forces of Colombia), a leftist armed group that over the years combined typical guerrilla tactics with terrorist attacks, started resorting to kidnapping to generate funding, but was also involved in drug production and trafficking. Another relevant group was the ELN (Ejército de Liberación Nacional, National Liberation Army).

During the period of the first presidency of Lula da Silva in Brazil, that is, 2003–10, the Colombian civil war experienced an intense phase. Those years corresponded to the administration of hardline right-wing President Álvaro Uribe in Colombia (Kajsiu, 2019). Uribe began a massive military offensive against FARC and ELN after the failure of peace talks, and in 2004 the government stepped up its operations under the Plan Patriota (Patriot Plan). This contributed to comparably high-conflict intensity in

---

[22] Interview B7, High-ranking officer in the Brazilian armed forces, online, 26 September 2022.

2002–05 (UCDP, 2022c). An attempt to restart peace negotiations in 2005 failed after an attack on a military facility in Bogotá in October of that year. Further negotiation attempts took place in 2007, with a mediation effort by Venezuela's President Hugo Chávez. In particular, Chávez conveyed to the Colombian government that it would be necessary to recognize FARC as a legitimate organization, instead of labelling it a terrorist group (La Nación, 2008) – one of the main bones of contention in the on-and-off peace negotiations with FARC in the course of the 2000s. Ultimately – looking beyond the time frame analysed in this chapter – peace negotiations between the Colombian government and FARC resumed in 2012, and a historic peace agreement was signed with FARC (but not with ELN) in 2016.

The civil war in Colombia obviously had implications for the country's direct neighbours, including Brazil. Even though the conflict did not represent a direct threat to Brazil, it was a source of preoccupation to Brazilian policy makers due to the long common border and to the conflict's potential to destabilize the region (Tarapués Sandino, 2012: 433). Around 2010, and also earlier, the Colombian military had pushed FARC fighters back so far that they had crossed into Brazilian territory. Moreover, FARC was reportedly involved in drug trafficking in Brazil via connections to Brazilian drug gangs such as Comando Vermelho (Rabello, 2010). Perhaps even more importantly, apart from these immediate (if minor) spillover effects of the Colombian civil war to Brazil, the Brazilian government was interested in the conflict as it wanted to avoid its internationalization – and most obviously excessive meddling by the USA (Flemes, 2015), which, through Plan Colombia, were already extremely influential in Colombia. Brazil was worried about a potential 'internationalization of the Amazonas', especially after a US military base was shifted from Ecuador to Colombia in 2009 (Martins Filho, 2006: 14). For different reasons, therefore, the civil war in Colombia constituted a crisis in Brazil's neighbourhood that could not be ignored by policy makers in Brasília.

Overall, the Brazilian government displayed a high degree of consistency in approaching the issue of the civil war in Colombia. Under Lula's two terms in office during his first presidency, Brazil took a consistent and non-reluctant approach to crisis management in Colombia, albeit a very different one as compared to the crisis in Haiti. In fact, throughout the years of Lula's first presidency and also beyond, Brazil limited its conflict management approach to a low-key role, offering to mediate between the conflict parties and to support the peace process.[23] As one interviewee put it, Brazil's approach

---

[23] One interviewee emphasized that Brazil and Colombia have had a very good working relationship in matters of security at the tactical and operative levels, cooperating on issues like border security or de-mining. But he also confirmed that Brazil's political

was very 'discreet'.[24] In particular, the Brazilian government insisted on defining the conflict as a domestic issue of Colombia, thereby rejecting external interventions and signalling that it was not interested in meddling with what it considered to be Colombia's domestic affairs (see, for example, Ministério das Relações Exteriores, 2008b). Moreover, much in line with the norms enshrined in the Brazilian constitution, the Lula administration kept expressing support for a negotiated solution to the conflict (Soares de Lima and Hirst, 2006: 35). Despite pursuing this low-key approach, Brazil was not hesitant. In fact, we cannot observe the elements of delaying, flip-flopping or a complete lack of initiative, which are typical of hesitation. This consistent, but low-key, approach to the conflict might have been related to the relatively low degree of interaction between the Brazilian and the Colombian governments.

Leftist President Lula and right-wing President Uribe had little in common, and Brazil was highly critical of Colombia's reliance on US involvement in its war on drugs. The disconnect between Colombia and Brazil ultimately contributed to make the two countries 'distant neighbours' (Carpes, 2015: 176). The relationship, however, improved over time, especially after the departure of Uribe in August 2010. His successor Juan Manuel Santos took a less militaristic approach to the conflict, favouring a negotiated solution, which also corresponded to Brazil's long-held preference (Carpes, 2015: 177).

The idea that the armed conflict in Colombia should be addressed via negotiations was already well established in Brazil before Lula came to power. President Fernando Cardoso, Lula's predecessor (1995–2003), had already offered to serve as a mediator in the civil war (Carpes, 2015: 166). In 2003, under Lula, Brazil offered to host talks between the conflict parties on Brazilian territory, but such talks never materialized (LatinNews, 2003). Later, Brazil repeated its mediation offers (CIDOB, 2015), but the Colombian government did not accept them, to some extent reflecting the estrangement between Uribe and Lula (Carpes, 2015: 166–7), but also, and perhaps more prominently, Colombia's efforts to keep control of events and to limit external involvement in its domestic conflicts.[25] The Brazilian government was also consistent when it came to the issue of not defining

---

role on broader matters of conflict resolution has been extremely limited. Interview B5, Colombian scholar, online, 16 September 2022.

[24] Interview B6, Brazilian scholar, online, 19 September 2022.

[25] See Interview B2, with a scholar based in Chile, online, 14 July 2022, who emphasized that Colombia put great emphasis on keeping control of the peace process: 'The Colombian elite said, we are not some African failed state, we don't need a peacekeeping mission, we only need help in this peace process. This is why the Colombians did not want some neighbouring countries getting engaged directly'.

FARC as a terrorist organization. Colombia's President Uribe reportedly exercised intense pressure on Brazil to induce it to classify FARC as a terrorist group, but the Lula administration consistently refused to do so. The Brazilian government argued that this would have reduced its own credibility as a potential neutral mediator (Tarapués Sandino, 2012: 432). Moreover, it pointed out that Brazil did not have a terrorism classification on its own and followed that of the UN – and that since the UN did not list FARC as a terrorist group, it could not deviate from this approach (Amorim, 2008b).

Over time, there were some important shifts in Brazil's approach to the civil war in Colombia, mainly implying increased support for the Colombian government on the part of Brazil, but always within the framework of privileging negotiated solutions and taking a low-key approach. These shifts ultimately highlight that longer-term change does not amount to hesitation if it is a linear process and if we don't see flip-flopping and indecision. Brazil's changing attitude towards the conflict was mainly driven by developments on the ground. On the one hand, the intensification of the conflict led to increased preoccupations on the part of Brazil about a potential spread of the conflict across the border. On the other hand, Uribe's military strategy was rather successful in pushing FARC back and liberating hostages, with the most visible success being the rescue of Colombian politician Ingrid Betancourt in July 2008 (RTVE, 2008). Moreover, Brazil was dissatisfied with the USA's involvement in Colombia, so that Lula reportedly 'invited Uribe to rely more on Brazil and less on the United States for help' (Hakim, 2004: 120).

All this ultimately induced the Brazilian government to provide some concrete support to Colombian operations, mainly through the provision of logistical assistance for hostage rescue operations such as the transportation of freed hostages by helicopter (Candeas, 2012: 299; Tarapués Sandino, 2012: 433). Moreover, in 2008, Lula signed several agreements with the Colombian government, including on matters of defence and more specifically on patrolling the borders in the Amazonas (LatinNews, 2008b: 4). In addition, starting from 2008, the Brazilian government made it explicit that it considered the liberation of all hostages by FARC to be a precondition for negotiations (*O Estado de S. Paulo*, 2008). Lula, in that context, called for FARC to renounce violence and to pursue their agenda as a political actor: 'FARC should think about this, that you don't win elections by kidnapping people, that's a fact. You win elections by playing the game of politics, by convincing people, by making proposals, by presenting programmes – this is how you win the game' (Ministério das Relações Exteriores, 2008a). Still, the Brazilian government remained consistent in its approach of refusing to label FARC a terrorist organization. The main argument put forward by the Brazilian government was that banning FARC as a terrorist group would inevitably hamper negotiations and possibly prevent the conflict parties from reaching an agreement (Rossi, 2003). Overall, therefore, while taking a slightly tougher stance vis-à-vis FARC, the Brazilian government had a highly consistent approach to the civil war in Colombia characterized by low-key offers of support and a continuous emphasis on negotiated solutions (paired with scepticism about the involvement of external actors, most notably the USA).

Explaining Brazil's non-reluctant approach

Overall, the Brazilian government was able to pursue a non-reluctant, determined course of action in its approach to the civil war in Colombia because it had a clear preference and did not face competing external expectations that pushed it in different directions. In fact, none of the drivers of hesitation and recalcitrance were in place in this case.

As discussed, the government was not weak, but enjoyed substantial popular support and did not face a strong opposition that would have called into question its approach to the conflict. There are only few indications about disagreements among different government bodies on how to approach the conflict in Colombia. According to some reports, there were frictions between the foreign ministry, Itamaraty, and Lula's special adviser for international affairs, the Marxist Marco Aurélio Garcia, who had been criticized for being too sympathetic to leftist governments and too soft on the FARC issue (LatinNews, 2008a).[26] However, these were not confirmed by any of the interviewees. Concerning capacities, the kind of low-key support offered by Brazil certainly did not overstretch its possibilities, while its diplomatic corps and foreign policy bureaucracy were well equipped to address crises in the neighbourhood. However, a more extensive engagement was beyond its reach: 'Brazil also did not have the amount of money to support Colombia to the extent the US was doing. I think it's something that Brazil just accepted'.[27] At the same time, the sheer political distance between Lula and Uribe discouraged the Brazilian government from attempting to engage more explicitly. According to one of the interviewees, the decision to engage in Colombia only to a very limited extent was driven by a very pragmatic calculation on the part of the Brazilian government: 'they [only] went to places where they saw the opportunity to produce a lot of gains'.[28] In other words, the Lula administration preferred to focus on international

---

[26] Such allegations were refuted by Garcia; see Congresso em Foco (2008).

[27] Interview B4, Brazilian academic and former government advisor, online, 8 September 2022.

[28] Interview B4, Brazilian academic and former government advisor, online, 8 September 2022.

engagements that would increase Brazil's status in world politics, and in the case of the civil war in Colombia, it did not see any potential for status gains.

Also, the explanation related to cognitive problems does not apply in this case: the Colombian civil war was not a sudden crisis that caught Brazilian decision makers by surprise, forcing them to act at short notice and to make difficult foreign policy decisions. Quite to the contrary, the war had been going on for decades, with ups and downs in levels of violence, and the peak of fatalities in Colombia had been reached immediately before Lula came to power (UCDP, 2022a). Overall, therefore, despite the certainly more assertive policies adopted by the Uribe administration, the situation was not particularly novel to Brazilian policy makers. Nor was time pressure a major issue that could have induced Brazilian policy makers to become hesitant in their approach to Colombia.

Finally, normative struggles were not in place since the low-key approach adopted by the Lula administration was not really controversial. The declared prioritization of negotiated solutions was much in line with Brazil's constitution, which, in Article 4, items IV and VII stipulates that the country's international relations approach should be governed by the principles of non-intervention and peaceful settlement of conflicts.

Despite the overall agreement on the policies of the Lula administration, this does not mean that the issue of Brazil's approach to the Colombian civil war was not discussed in Brazil. Critics of the Lula administration pointed out that Lula had been close to FARC, which in the past had belonged to a group of leftist Latin American organizations founded by Lula and Fidel Castro in 1990, called the São Paulo Forum (de Almeida, 2010: 162–3). Commentaries in the magazine *Veja* and the newspaper *O Estado de S. Paulo* argued that Lula's shift towards a more critical approach vis-à-vis FARC and its more explicit support for the Colombian government came far too late, basically free-riding on the military successes of the Uribe administration (LatinNews, 2008b: 4). There also were reports in Brazilian media critical of the government about a presumed connection between FARC and Lula's PT, which had allegedly been supported financially by the Colombian rebels (LatinNews, 2005: 7; Feuerwerker, 2010), but those comments were mostly made to discredit the government as there was no evidence of such a connection. Still, despite such criticism, there were no actors in Brazil vocally arguing in favour of greater, possibly military, involvement of Brazil in supporting Colombia's fight against FARC.

This all dovetailed with widespread criticism in Brazil of the USA's influence in Latin America, which made the option of siding with the US-backed Uribe government unpalatable to most relevant political actors in Brazil (*Veja*, 2011). Overall, therefore, the Brazilian approach to the conflict corresponded to the widely held normative preference for peaceful negotiated solutions to conflicts, for non-interference and for sovereignty.

In the Federal Senate, references to the Colombian civil war mostly entailed criticism of the role of the USA in that country and in the region, while there was no substantial disagreement on Brazil's policies. An analysis of the news section of the internet site of the Federal Senate reveals that most reports refer to the discontent expressed by Brazilian senators and politicians over the USA's influence in Colombia (see, for example, Senado Noticias, 2009)

Such broad consensus at the domestic level was paired with a lack of strongly competing international expectations. The Colombian government obviously expected greater support from Brazil, for example requesting it to label FARC a terrorist organization (Tarapués Sandino, 2012: 433). Here, the Brazilian approach displayed some degree of recalcitrance (see, for example, Sander, 2008). However, apart from the issue of the classification of FARC as a terrorist group, the Colombian government did not put much pressure on Brazil, and did not call for greater engagement – mostly because of the political distance between the Lula and Uribe administrations. Bilateral relations between Brazil and Colombia improved gradually, in parallel with Lula's slightly more explicit support for Uribe's fight against FARC, but also, and more explicitly, after the new Obama administration in the USA gave less support to Uribe's hardline approach. This ultimately forced Uribe to rely more on regional partners, for example by joining the UNASUR Defence Council.

This body had been created in 2009 at the initiative of Brazil after Colombia had carried out attacks against FARC camps in Ecuador, thereby violating that country's sovereignty. The Defence Council had set itself the objective of becoming 'a primary forum to prevent and mediate conflicts within South America' (LatinNews, 2009b: 1) and the 30-point Declaration of Santiago de Chile, signed in 2009, emphasized the principle of 'unconditional respect for the sovereignty, integrity and territorial inviolability of states, non-intervention in their internal affairs, and the self-determination of peoples' (UNASUR, 2009) – a signal against the meddling of external powers (first and foremost the USA) in regional affairs. Uribe had initially set as a precondition for Colombia's participation in the UNASUR Defence Council that all member states should label FARC a terrorist organization – but he ultimately backtracked from that demand (LatinNews, 2009a). He had also wanted UNASUR to explicitly include a focus on drug trafficking issues, which Brazil did not want to subsume under defence policy. In the end, Colombia joined UNASUR after a compromise was reached via the creation of a committee that focused exclusively on narcotrafficking but kept the issue separate from matters of defence.[29] Colombia's accession to the Defence Council therefore also reveals the ongoing rapprochement

---

[29] Interview B3, Brazilian scholar, online, 23 August 2022.

between Brazil and Colombia. Indeed, Uribe had even praised Brazil's 'discreet' handling of a hostage rescue mission in 2009 (Terra, 2009). Still, the improved relationship between Colombia and Brazil did not go so far as to involve calls for much greater Brazilian engagement on the part of the Colombian government.

Other international actors were obviously also interested and involved in the conflict in Colombia to different extents. The USA need to be mentioned in the first place since their Plan Colombia directed against drugs production and trafficking ultimately benefited President Uribe's fight against FARC (Molina, 2021). US relations with Uribe were particularly close, as the USA even provided support for his personal protection, along with that of the vice-president and the minister of defence, by delivering equipment (bulletproof vehicles, alarms, and so on) and training – something no other world leader except Hamid Karzai was granted (van Dongen, 2003). However, according to one interviewee, the USA was not really interested in the management of the civil war in Colombia:

> 'Sometimes you would think that, given [close] relations between Colombia and the US, the United States are omnipresent [in Colombia], but this is … not the case. It is often surprising to see to what extent they are only interested in the drugs issue, and [even] that only from a narrow perspective.'[30]

So it is not surprising that Washington was not particularly interested in seeing a greater involvement in Colombia's civil war on the part of Brazil. There is no evidence of the USA explicitly putting pressure on the Brazilian government to take a specific approach towards the conflict. But, as an interviewee put it, 'The US was very happy that Brazil was having an important role in South America. The US had other problems so if Brazil wanted to get involved more in South American politics, for the US it was OK – one problem less to deal with'.[31] When it comes to the expectations of other international actors, issues such as the kidnapping of Ingrid Betancourt, a Colombian politician and French citizenship holder, led to the involvement of several countries. Among those getting engaged to free her were France, Spain, Switzerland (which had also been collaborating in trying to free other hostages; see Burnard, 2008) as well as Venezuela and Ecuador. But these international actors did not explicitly pressurize Brazil towards getting involved more extensively or in different ways in conflict management in Colombia.

---

[30] Interview B2, scholar based in Chile, online, 14 July 2022; author's own translation.
[31] Interview B3, Brazilian scholar, online, 23 August 2022.

To conclude, Brazil's approach to the Colombian civil war was non-reluctant since the Brazilian government pursued a consistent approach. This was made possible by the broad domestic consensus on offering mediation and support but not engaging too heavily; moreover, it was enabled by the lack of competing pressures and expectations on the part of international actors. In the years following the Lula administration, which are not the object of analysis in this chapter, things changed and Brazil became much more reluctant in regional crisis management. For example, weakened by corruption scandals and internal strife, the Brazilian government was entirely passive and refused to take any initiative in the context of a crisis in Venezuela in 2014, when the government of Chávez' successor, Nicolás Maduro, resorted to the violent suppression of dissent (see Stuenkel, 2014).

Overall, the case of Brazil, in contrast to the cases of India and Germany, shows that powerful regional countries that have stable governments and the necessary capacities, and that do not face huge competing pressures from international actors, are able to adopt consistent and responsive – non-reluctant – policies in the field of regional crisis management.

7

Explaining Reluctance
in Other Contexts

The aim of this book is to make sense of reluctance in world politics and to explain its causes. In order to assess the explanatory power of my theorization of reluctance, I chose to focus on particularly 'hard' cases, in which we would generally not expect to see a reluctant behaviour in foreign policy: on states that are particularly powerful in their regions, and, more specifically, on how they address and manage regional crises. The underlying idea is that we would expect such countries to have an inherent interest in the stabilization of their respective regions, and therefore to engage in regional crisis management in a coherent and decisive manner. However, we actually observe variation: while Brazil was not reluctant in regional crisis management during the years of the first presidency of Lula da Silva, both India and Germany were reluctant regional crisis managers, even in periods of domestic political stability. The analyses in Chapters 4, 5 and 6 reveal that the explanations for the emergence of reluctance developed in Chapter 3 go a long way towards explaining the regional crisis management policies adopted by powerful states: in the cases analysed, reluctance emerged because of a combination of difficulties in preference formation (mostly driven by internal struggles and lack of coordination among different agencies and/or normative disagreements) and competing expectations by external actors.

But can the theory of reluctance developed in this book also be applied to other cases, actors or issue areas? In other words, does it have an explanatory power beyond the cases analysed in this book? This chapter addresses these questions by focusing on (1) different types of crisis; (2) different countries such as small states and great powers, with reluctance being particularly puzzling for the latter; and (3) different types of actors beyond the nation-state. Given space constraints, the following sections will necessarily be less detailed and rely more on secondary sources as compared to the in-depth case studies of the previous chapters. Overall, as we will see, the explanations for reluctance developed in this book are also helpful to make sense of reluctant policies in a broad range of different contexts.

Reluctance in different types of crisis

So far, I have mainly discussed crises that had a security component as they related to (violent) conflicts taking place in the extended neighbourhood of India, Germany and Brazil, and in some cases involved the risk of spillover of the conflict across borders. The theory of reluctance developed in this book, however, is also suitable to explain variations in reluctance in the management of different types of crisis by the same actors.

One remarkable example is Germany's approach to the Eurozone crisis, the debt crisis that shook the EU between 2009 and the mid-2010s. This crisis was the first one that seriously displayed 'the potential to make or break Europe' (Dempsey, 2015) as it touched on the very foundations of the EU by involving issues of solidarity, legitimacy and further integration. Since the outbreak of the crisis in the autumn of 2009, Germany's approach shifted over different phases. If we apply the concept of reluctance to Germany's crisis management approach, we find that during the first months of the crisis, the German government was clearly reluctant, as its policies involved both elements of hesitation and recalcitrance. An indicator of hesitation is the delay with which Germany developed responses to the crisis. Initially, in fact, Chancellor Angela Merkel argued that the crisis was a Greek domestic problem – even though the EU and Germany had already sent consultants to Greece and were dealing with the issue. Furthermore, Merkel explicitly 'delayed common European action' (Schild, 2013: 28).

Moreover, Berlin's approach to the crisis during its early phase was reactive, leading to several contradictions between German government statements and policies. In their statements, government officials time and again tried to reassure the German public that Berlin would not make too substantial concessions, but in many cases the German government then had to eat its words. To cite just one example, on 21 March 2010, Merkel stated 'Help is not on the agenda' (Janssen, 2012) – only to agree, in May 2010, to the first bailout package for Greece and to the establishment of the European Financial Stability Facility with a German guarantee of 27.13 per cent (Paterson, 2011: 69). In between, in April 2010, Merkel replied evasively to Greece's request for a safety net, giving an impression of 'indecisiveness' (Traynor, 2010).

Besides these contradictions between statements and actual policies, several inconsistencies and contradictions emerged among statements by different members of the government, most notably Finance Minister Wolfgang Schäuble and Chancellor Merkel, further contributing to flip-flopping. For example, in March 2010, Schäuble developed a proposal about a European

Monetary Fund modelled along the lines of the International Monetary Fund (IMF) (Schäuble, 2010) – an idea the Chancellery reportedly learned about from the media, and which clearly contradicted Merkel's rejection of financial transfers to debtor countries (Feldenkrichen et al, 2010: 22). Moreover, Schäuble had dismissed the idea of an IMF participation in European crisis management, but was brusquely contradicted by Merkel during a speech in the Bundestag in March 2010 (Feldenkrichen et al, 2010: 21).

When it comes to the third indicator of hesitation, a lack of initiative, this was certainly in place in the early phase of the Eurozone crisis: 'for one, one-and-a-half years not much happened'.[1] However, this hesitation disappeared entirely when the German position on austerity and conditionalities consolidated and was articulated in a more consistent manner. Besides these elements of hesitation, a medium level of recalcitrance was also clearly in place: by initially labelling the crisis as a Greek problem and refusing to help, the German government rejected requests for crisis management and did not respond to those demands that did not fit with its preferences. Just to mention one example, on the issue of Eurobonds Germany's rejection was consistent over time, even though it was articulated in increasingly drastic terms, up to Merkel's infamous June 2012 statement 'no Eurobonds as long as I live' (*Spiegel Online*, 2012b).

While Germany's approach to the Eurozone crisis was initially reluctant, over time its reluctance decreased. On the one hand, Germany's recalcitrance remained constant as Berlin continued to reject requests for greater concessions. On the other hand, however, most elements of hesitation were left aside as the German position towards the crisis increasingly consolidated: delaying became a less explicitly used tactic compared to the 2009–10 period, Germany took the initiative more openly, and flip-flopping became less common.

A first instance of increasing determination was the bilateral German–French informal summit meeting in Deauville in October 2010, the outcome of which was criticized as a 'Franco–German diktat' (Schild, 2013: 37). The meeting paved the way for a period of intense consultations between Merkel and French President Nicolas Sarkozy, in which both sides made concessions and compromises (Schild, 2013: 37), but Germany ultimately pushed through many of its preferences. According to some observers, with the European Council meeting of 8–9 December 2011 and the adoption of the Fiscal Compact, Merkel 'won the battle by "institutionalizing" austerity' (Hübner, 2012: 174) and was certainly no longer reluctant. As Bulmer (2014: 1249) puts it, the management of the Eurozone crisis marked 'a new stage in German European policy' in which 'national interests and assertiveness' as

---

[1]   Interview G12, German academic, Hamburg, 27 April 2015.

well as 'Greater unilateralism' emerged. This holds true for the following years and further developments in the Eurozone crisis as the German government continued to insist on reform programmes and austerity measures, among others, in the case of Greece – in terms that were increasingly perceived as highly intrusive. Indeed, after the negotiations on a third bailout package for Greece in July 2015, there was a huge backlash in terms of perceptions of Germany. As German philosopher Jürgen Habermas put it, 'the German government ... gambled away in one night all the political capital that a better Germany had accumulated in half a century' (cited in Oltermann, 2015).

In sum, Germany shifted from strong reluctance to no reluctance during the Eurozone crisis, as recalcitrance remained constant while hesitation disappeared. How can we explain the country's initial reluctance and the later shift towards a determined approach?

Germany's initial reluctance can best be explained by focusing on the 'cognitive problems' explanation. In particular, the initial delays with which the government reacted to the crisis can certainly be traced back to the uncertainties of the situation. As one interviewee put it, 'There were no established instruments or mechanisms to deal with the crisis. It was uncharted territory. ... We could not have acted faster'.[2] Also, according to Schoeller (2017: 8), 'there was a lot of uncertainty regarding the magnitude as well as the legal and technical features of the bailout', which certainly put pressure on German decision makers.[3] Such pressures were further intensified by competing expectations: in the Eurozone crisis, the German government had to struggle with the contradictions between the expectations of regional actors – most notably of the countries affected by the crisis, which wanted concessions (see Schimmelfennig, 2015: 183–91) – and the expectations of German voters and taxpayers, who were increasingly opposed to further financial support for crisis-ridden economies (Schoeller, 2017: 8). For example, the Greek government called for the adoption of alternative measures, from Eurobonds to a Tobin Tax, a Carbon Tax and the introduction of a Marshall Plan for Green and Sustainable Development for Europe (see Maris and Manoli, 2022: 289).

At the domestic level, expectations by German banks, including the Bundesbank, which would have been endangered by a Greek default, added further pressure on the government (*Spiegel Online International*, 2011). While the difficulties of managing these competing expectations

---

[2]   Interview G9, German government official, Federal Ministry for Economic Affairs and Energy, Berlin, 24 April 2015.

[3]   Schoeller (2017) does not focus on reluctance as I understand it here, but is instead interested in the broader question of German leadership (or the lack thereof), which he explains in terms of rational cost-benefit calculations, while acknowledging some of the aspects I am focusing on in this section such as the uncertainties faced by decision makers.

led to Germany's initial hesitation, over time Germany became less and less reluctant. This might have been related to the German government devising a clear preference, and initially possibly still acting in a reluctant manner in a 'strategic' effort towards appeasing some of the competing expectations (see the discussion on the strategic use of reluctance in Chapter 3). Later, reluctance was entirely left behind. As Schimmelfennig (2015: 177) puts it, 'Whereas negotiations produced a co-operative solution averting the breakdown of the euro area and strengthening the credibility of member state commitments, asymmetrical interdependence resulted in a burden-sharing and institutional design that reflected German preferences predominantly' – in other words, Germany was increasingly assertive and managed to impose its preferences.

On the issue of the Fiscal Compact, ultimately some convergence of expectations among European actors emerged. According to Schoeller (2017: 13),

> ... apart from the United Kingdom (UK), none of the actors was really against the Fiscal Compact. To be sure, in particular France and Italy were skeptical at the beginning. However, against the background of strong market pressures, 'there was a collective recognition' that such a signal was needed to calm the markets and stabilize the Eurozone. ... Although the Commission and the EP [European Parliament] would have preferred a solution within EU law, they had no major objections against the contents of the Fiscal Compact as such. The ECB [European Central Bank] was once again Germany's strongest supporter.

In other words, after the initial shock and confusion provoked by the crisis, the German government devised clear preferences and found ways to implement them. Thereby, it left behind reluctance entirely.

The explanations for reluctance that were empirically tested with reference to crisis management in violent conflicts or crises having security implications therefore also apply for the study of a debt crisis. Explanations referring to cognitive problems would certainly also apply if we wanted to study the initial reactions of several governments to the COVID-19 pandemic, which posed severe challenges to decision makers all over the world in terms of lack of information, time pressure and novelty of the crisis.

The case of Italy, the first European country and the first democracy to be hit by the virus, is a good example. As Bull (2021: 149) put it, 'The government's response, especially in the first wave, was confused, dilatory and inadequate'. In fact, the Italian government, despite being aware of the crisis and having commissioned reports that early on provided models of the possible diffusion of infections, initially delayed the adoption of more stringent measures such as a national lockdown. Instead, a series of regional lockdowns were implemented, with repeated changes and shifts. These led to disastrous consequences such as an exodus of thousands of people from northern to southern Italy as news about an upcoming lockdown in the north were leaked in early March 2020 (*The Guardian*, 2020). The highly hesitant policies adopted by the Italian government reveal a difficulty in devising a clear course of action, which can certainly be attributed to the novelty of the situation, the severity of the crisis and extreme time pressure. It has to be kept in mind that Italy was the first democracy to experience the pandemic, and that the imposition of a strict and wide-ranging lockdown was, at that time, an almost unthinkable measure.

Besides these factors, however, hesitation also emerged because of major disputes on how to deal with the crisis between the central government and those of the regions. In matters of health policy, the central government is responsible for developing legislation and allocating funds, while the regions manage health services and enjoy a considerable degree of autonomy in this field. As Bull (2021: 157) points out, 'Generally speaking, the regions were inclined towards, or proposed, more stringent restrictions being imposed sooner and were frustrated by the slowness of government decision-making, some regional Governors even going ahead and implementing them'. At the same time, several regional governments disagreed among themselves, further complicating the development of clear preferences on the management of the pandemic. Besides cognitive problems and internal struggles, other capacity problems also played a role in complicating decision making: the government initially simply did not have the capabilities to efficiently implement a set of measures that would have been suitable to contain the transmission of the virus (Bull, 2021: 156). Overall, therefore, the Italian government was highly reluctant in its management of the pandemic during the first months, and such reluctance was driven by a mix of the explanations as developed in Chapter 3. This theoretical framework is therefore also applicable to the analysis of governments' crisis management in other types of crisis, including a major health crisis.

Reluctance by small states and great powers

The empirical analysis in Chapters 4–6 focused on India, Germany and Brazil as powerful countries in their respective regional contexts. The conceptualization and theorization of reluctance can, however, also be applied to other types of countries, from small states to great powers.

Small states have by definition much more limited capabilities as compared to larger ones, and this will automatically reduce their room to manoeuvre in international politics. However, it would be wrong to expect all small states to pursue reluctant policies all the time. Importantly, as discussed in Chapters 2 and 3, reluctance does not amount to the unwillingness or impossibility of exercising leadership. It is about pursuing policies that are hesitant and recalcitrant. Correspondingly, small states that adopt a very consistent policy of low-key engagement in international affairs, focusing mainly on issues such as domestic economic development and displaying a high degree of continuity in their foreign policy, will not count as reluctant. There are many examples of such non-reluctant small states that simply keep a low profile in international affairs, but do so in a consistent manner. Think of the foreign policies of Austria during the Cold War: the notion of permanent neutrality was inscribed into its constitution in 1955 and was kept up consistently throughout the Cold War, with Austria trying to position itself as a bridge between the East and the West, even though quite apparently and consistently tilting towards the West (see Rainio-Niemi, 2014; Pelinka et al, 2017).

This is not to say that small states, as realism in International Relations (IR) has long assumed, have no choice but to bandwagon with larger powers (for a critical stance on this position, see, for example, Braveboy-Wagner, 2010; Long, 2022). In fact, there are also many examples of small states that stand out for pursuing a particularly activist foreign policy in specific issue areas, and that adopt such an agenda without hesitation. Among them is Norway, which, since the 1990s, has pursued a 'foreign policy of peace' (Leira, 2013), serving as a mediator or facilitator in conflicts worldwide – a strategy that has proved useful 'to support Norway's standing, relevance and influence in international relations' (Stokke, 2012: 227). The same applies for Switzerland, which has enshrined the promotion of peace in its constitution, making it one of its five central foreign policy objectives (Graf and Lanz, 2013). This policy has been pursued very consistently and intensely: between 2000 and 2012, Switzerland engaged in as many as 20 peace processes in 15 different countries worldwide (Lanz and Mason, 2012).

At the same time, there are also instances of dramatic but longer-term foreign policy change in small states, as in the case of Bolivia's rejection of its traditional partnership with the USA after the formation of the left-wing populist government of Evo Morales. Here, since the new foreign policy was consistently implemented over many years and was pursued without any flip-flopping, we cannot talk about a reluctant approach (John, 2020). And, of course, there are cases like that of Cuba, in which a small state has pursued such a determined and consistent foreign policy over decades, challenging a superpower despite huge costs.[4]

---

[4] Notably, non-reluctant policies are not necessarily successful. They can also lead to failure and, especially in small states, increased dependence. For example, when the SYRIZA government in Greece was forced to accept a €86 billion rescue package and harsh austerity measures in 2015, this was not a consequence of reluctance on its part. Quite to the contrary, the government had clear preferences and did not display much hesitation. Yet it

But there are obviously also instances in which small states adopt hesitant and recalcitrant policies due to capacity problems, as they simply do not have the resources to navigate the complexities of international politics or to cope with changing circumstances or mounting and competing international pressures. Among a number of small states unsuccessfully trying to assert themselves vis-à-vis predominant powers is Gabon (Long, 2022), whose government tried to move away from dependence on the former colonial power France in the 2000s, but was unable to build a lasting alternative partnership with China. The outcome was a reluctant policy, in which the government of Gabon oscillated between France and China and was highly recalcitrant vis-á-vis French expectations, but ultimately reverted back to French protection (see RFI, 2010, 2012). The main drivers of reluctance in this case were the weakness of a corrupt government and serious capacity problems (Long, 2022: 85–6).

In a more extreme case, in the 1990s and 2000s the government of Zambia pursued policies that can be classified as extremely reluctant, ultimately because it was so weak that it was entirely driven by donors and their sometimes diverging priorities: 'donor preferences grew less cohesive as divisions emerged between multilateral lenders and bilateral donors over what to emphasize in assessing Zambia – democratic governance or economic liberalization' (Long, 2022: 119). The Movement for Multi-party Democracy (MMD) government ultimately became more and more fragmented and its leadership 'accepted donor priorities and compromised their stated position even when political stakes were high' (Long, 2022: 121).

More interesting than reluctant small states, however, are reluctant great powers. These countries are in most cases the object of various and often competing international expectations. Reluctance can occur if these competing expectations meet political weakness, limited capacities (which will most likely emerge as a consequence of bureaucratic infighting and coordination problems among various agencies), cognitive problems by decision makers in particularly severe and new crisis situations, or if there are normative struggles going on, possibly about a new course to be imparted to foreign policy. Indeed, different variants of these drivers of reluctance can be observed in various instances in the foreign policies of great powers.

First of all, the governments of great powers are not immune from political weakness, which can be in place if a government is dependent on coalition partners or, for example in the case of the USA, if the president faces a Congress dominated by the opposing party. This will make it much more

---

was forced to bow to the demands of the Troika composed of the European Commission, the European Central Bank (ECB) and the IMF (see, for example, Aslanidis and Rovira Kaltwasser, 2016).

difficult to pursue a consistent and determined course of action. In the USA, generally speaking, the president has traditionally been the predominant force in foreign policy making (see Lindsay, 1992: 609). However, the balance between the presidency and Congress over foreign policy issues has repeatedly shifted over time (Lindsay, 2018: 149), and there are, indeed, instances in which the Congress has exerted considerable influence on foreign policy making. Struggles between the executive and the legislative have at times led to highly reluctant policies.

A good example is the USA's approach to the Cyprus crisis between 1974 and 1977. The crisis was unleashed by a coup sponsored by the Greek military junta, which was followed by a Turkish military response that led to the occupation of the northern part of Cyprus by Turkish troops in two waves starting on the 20 July and 14 August 1974, respectively. This major breach of international law meant the USA faced a dilemma: 'The US government had to figure out how to restrain its two allies from going to war against each other without straining relations with either one of them' (Katsoulas, 2022: 318). The US response to the crisis was highly reluctant, with its reluctance mainly emerging from political weakness. First, as events unfolded in the summer of 1974, Washington's response to the dilemma of whether to align with Greece or Turkey was to simply take an indifferent approach towards the crisis (Kassimeris, 2008: 94). This obviously amounts to a lack of initiative and thereby to hesitation. At the same time, recalcitrance towards pressures to take action in either direction was in place. This initial reluctance can mainly be explained with the precarious situation of the Nixon administration, with the president resigning on 9 August 1974 in the midst of the Watergate scandal, and Vice-President Gerald Ford succeeding him in the presidency. These events practically coincided with the Turkish invasion of Cyprus on 20 July and 14 August.

According to Katsoulas (2022: 326), 'President Nixon's involvement in the management of the Cyprus crisis was minimal. Confronted with either impeachment or resignation, Nixon was utterly consumed by the Watergate scandal'. Yet, the Ford administration did not manage to pursue a less reluctant policy in the unfolding Cyprus crisis either. After the occupation of the northern part of the island by Turkish troops, the main dilemma for the USA was the issue of weapons deliveries to Turkey, which led to a rift between the Republican Ford presidency and a Congress dominated by Democrats. In particular, Congress called for the imposition of an arms embargo on Turkey, while the executive was against such a measure. The result was a hesitant policy, marked by the adoption of an arms embargo on 5 February 1975, which was, however, watered down on 2 October 1975, as Turkey was allowed to receive weapons that had been ordered before the imposition of the embargo; still, in an obviously contradictory policy, Turkey could continue to import arms, including US military equipment, from Italy and Germany in the context of NATO. On 30 June 1976, with the introduction of the Foreign Aid Act, the embargo was partially lifted, but it was conclusively removed only in September 1978, when President Jimmy Carter took over and the gridlock ended (for an overview of these twists and turns, see Kassimeris, 2008). The USA's highly reluctant and inconsistent policy can be primarily explained with the political weakness argument: the president's hands were tied by Congress or, as Rodman (1985: 28) puts it, President Ford was 'wrestling with the Congress'. An end to reluctance became possible only after a Democrat became president and managed to convince the Congress that the USA needed to cultivate a good relationship with Turkey in the face of the Soviet threat, and therefore to lift the embargo (see Kassimeris, 2008: 106).

Besides political weakness, great powers are also not immune from the capacity problems issue, understood not necessarily in terms of a lack of resources to successfully implement foreign policy, but mainly in terms of coordination problems among various actors and agencies, which can hamper the adoption of a consistent foreign policy line. China, which, in many respects, can be considered a great power (Mearsheimer, 2001; Bijian, 2005), has been defined as a 'conflicted' state (Shambaugh, 2011). Jones and Hameiri (2021) argue that China's foreign policy has often displayed elements of contradiction and inconsistency. For example, they show that China's approach to the South China Sea, which has sometimes been described as becoming increasingly assertive and robust over the past decades (see, for example, Yahuda, 2013; Chubb, 2021), was actually characterized by a remarkable number of shifts in conflict intensity between the 1990s and 2010s, essentially amounting to a back-and-forth in China's approach (flip-flopping) (Jones and Hameiri, 2021: 74–5). Indeed, the authors themselves point to 'the erratic nature of Chinese conduct, with conflict escalating and deescalating, often within the space of a single year' (Jones and Hameiri, 2021: 76). Such inconsistencies, according to the authors, can be traced back to 'evolving struggles for power and resources within the Chinese-style regulatory state', with the latter being defined as a system in which 'top leaders rarely control state outputs directly, but rather seek to "steer" and coordinate a diverse array of actors towards often vaguely defined ends' (Jones and Hameiri, 2021: 20). In such a system, 'different elements of the party-state often operate at crosspurposes, even under the notional guidance of central policy frameworks' (Jones and Hameiri, 2021: 45). In the case of China's approach to the South China Sea, a remarkable number of agencies was involved in policy making (see also ICG, 2012b) and operated in a context lacking clear decision-making structures or a system of institutionalized consultation. This led to open contradictions, for example between the China National Petroleum Corporation (CNPC), which, in 2014, placed a mobile oil rig in waters disputed by Vietnam, at the same time as the Chinese government was carrying out a policy of rapprochement towards Vietnam and other ASEAN (Association of Southeast Asian Nations) countries (Jones and Hameiri, 2021: 100–1).

Cognitive problems can explain reluctance on the part of great powers, especially in very grave crisis situations. According to some interpretations, this applied in the case of US President Barack Obama's approach to the early phase of the Libya crisis, ahead of the vote on UNSC Resolution 1973 (see also Chapter 5). In fact, the Obama administration initially pursued an indecisive approach and was put under huge pressure by France and the UK. Later on, calls for a no-fly zone also came from Libya's National Transitional Council (NTC) and the Gulf Cooperation Council (GCC) as well as from the Arab League (Payandeh, 2011: 376; Vaughn and Dunne, 2014; Chivvis, 2015: 15). Ultimately, it was only on 15 March 2011 that the US administration decided to support a no-fly zone and the use of 'all necessary means' in Libya. This reluctance can be explained with difficulties in getting clarity about the situation on the ground and problems in making a decision under time constraints, given the imminent threat of Gaddafi perpetrating a massacre on Libyan civilians (see Chapter 5). But also the decisiveness of many other countries took the US administration by surprise:

As one senior official recounted, 'The whole thing ramped up so quickly I don't think anybody saw the speed [with which] the two UNSCRs [United Nations Security Council Resolutions] passed. Everybody was expecting a couple of nations in the Security Council to block it. ... That took everybody by surprise.' Only a week before, the expectation in the US Department of Defense (DoD) had been that any operations would be largely humanitarian in nature. (Chivvis, 2015: 21)

Finally, the fourth driver of hesitation, the existence of struggles over the norms that should guide foreign policy, can also help in explaining reluctance in the foreign policies of great powers. For example, US President Joe Biden's approach to China during his first two years in office was described as 'muddling through' (Rovner, 2022) given the lack of a clear orientation and of explicitly articulated goals (Fontaine, 2022). More specifically, the Biden administration's approach to China was characterized by contradictory statements, primarily concerning Taiwan.

The USA had pursued a policy of 'strategic ambiguity' on the Taiwan issue since 1979. This entailed a combination of an acknowledgement of the One China policy, on the one hand (Pinsker, 2003: 355–6), and a number of security provisions entailed in the Taiwan Relations Act (TRA), on the other. This policy of strategic ambiguity had allowed the USA to leave all options open, but also 'leaders in Beijing and Taipei were generally if not always enthusiastically complicitous with the ambiguity, for both believed it was preferable to a starker demarcation of policy' (Pollack, 1996: 115). Ultimately, notwithstanding its deliberate ambiguity, such a policy had been pursued quite consistently over several decades.

Biden, after taking office, gave a number of speeches and interviews on China in which he explicitly broke with the tenets of strategic ambiguity, declaring that the USA would support Taiwan militarily in the case of a Chinese attack. In all cases, members of Biden's staff afterwards publicly backtracked, pointing out that the USA was still acknowledging the One China policy (Kine, 2022). In May 2022, Biden himself retracted from a previous statement he had made, declaring that 'the policy has not changed at all' (Thiessen, 2022). A few days later Secretary of State Antony Blinken 'repeated that the US position on Taiwan has not changed, despite Biden saying days earlier that the United States is bound to come to Taiwan's defense' (Johnson, 2022). All these contradictions and sudden turnabouts conveyed the impression that the US administration was no longer pursuing strategic ambiguity but was instead engulfed in 'strategic confusion' (Smith, 2022).

Competing norms driving US foreign policy are sometimes mentioned as an explanation for reluctance in this case:

> The Biden administration is trying to uphold conflicting values in its approach to great-power competition. It wants to deter military aggression by issuing credible threats, and it wants to rally the world's democracies against America's authoritarian rivals. Yet it also wants to encourage cooperation with those same rivals, given the urgent need to make progress on climate change and other transnational threats. So far it has not hinted that it is ready to seek any of these values and the expense of another [sic]. (Rovner, 2022)

Other competing norms driving US foreign policy under the Biden administration that are mentioned to explain the reluctant approach towards China are 'internationalism' versus 'restraint' (Rovner, 2020), reflecting a more general tension that surfaced time and again in US foreign policy.

Overall, these examples of reluctant foreign policy reveal that reluctance is a phenomenon that goes beyond the cases analysed in Chapters 4–6, which concerned powerful regional countries and crisis management. We can indeed also find reluctance in the foreign policies of very different types of states, from small to great powers. And also in these cases, reluctance can emerge as a result of the combination of competing expectations and difficulties in preference formation.

Reluctance beyond the nation-state

Finally, the mix of hesitation and recalcitrance that is typical of reluctance is not necessarily limited to the policies of nation-states. Reluctance can, in fact, also be found in the behaviour of a range of other actors, both above and below the level of the nation-state. Again, these will be addressed here only by way of example in order to provide an illustration of the workings of the theory of reluctance in other cases.

The EU is the prime example of an actor that has been frequently criticized for not being able to follow a consistent course of action, ultimately being unresponsive to the multiple expectations and requests addressed to it (see, for example, Koenig, 2011; Galariotis and Gianniou, 2022). In the context of multilevel governance of the EU, which adds further layers of complexity to decision making, reluctance is even more likely than in nation-states. As Maull (2017: 66) puts it with reference to the EU's approach to China, 'European policies towards China suffer from fragmentation, incoherence and inconsistencies that are caused by divergence of commercial preferences and the pluralistic character of policy-making within the EU'.

Among the many other examples that could be cited, the European Neighbourhood Policy (ENP) is a good case in point. Schumacher (2020) points out that in the recent past there was a clear discrepancy between, on the one hand, the ambitious goals set by the revised ENP of 2015, the Global Strategy of 2016 and the new strategic agenda for 2019–24, which emphasized the EU's ambition to pursue a norm-driven agenda in the neighbourhood, promoting democracy and human rights, and to keep up the perspective of accession to the EU for countries in the neighbourhood; and, on the other hand, the EU's actual policies on the ground, which, in many cases, disregarded violations of human rights and fundamental liberties in strategically important neighbouring countries, and failed to follow up on promises of accession. For example, in October 2019, the European Council decided not to give the Republic of North Macedonia and Albania an unequivocal date on which to start formal accession negotiations, despite previous commitments and positive evaluations (Schumacher, 2020: 189). Europe's approach to Libya in 2019 was characterized by a high degree of hesitation – mainly flip-flopping, resulting from French and Italian competing and one-sided policies vis-à-vis various Libyan factions. In fact, while the EU official policy was to support only the Government of National Accord (GNA) in Libya, single member states such as Italy and France also cultivated relations with General Khalifa Haftar and his Libyan National Army (LNA). Furthermore, France has even protected Egypt, Haftar and the UAE from official condemnation or sanctions from the EU and the UN (el-Gomati, 2022). Italy, in turn, pursued its own policies aimed at reducing migration inflows from Libya, and to that end provided support to empower

Libyan authorities to intercept migrants, regardless of massive human rights violations (Human Rights Watch, 2019).

Schumacher (2020: 198) argues that the entire ENP was a 'mere muddling through exercise', primarily driven by a lack of coordination among member states, but also by a lack of coordination among EU institutions. A series of institutional shifts in the late 2010s contributed to such lack of coherence:

> EU institutions were marked by new mandates commencing over the course of 2019: the arrival of a new and more fragmented European Parliament in the first half of 2019, the belated coming into power of a self-proclaimed geopolitical Commission in December 2019, and the appointments of a new High Representative for Foreign and Security Policy and a new President of the European Council. (Schumacher, 2020: 188)

Therefore, among the four possible explanations for reluctance developed in this book, the EU's reluctant neighbourhood policy can best be explained by focusing on what I have labelled the 'capacity problems' explanation. In particular, this refers to the difficulties in acting consistently that emerge as a consequence of poor coordination among the actors involved. While in nation-states these are usually different branches of the bureaucracy, in the context of EU multilevel governance, they are EU member states and various EU institutions.

But a range of other actors can also display reluctance. This goes from local administrations to non-profit associations, in which exactly the same difficulties in devising clear preferences might emerge, and which might be faced with a number of competing expectations. A discussion of all possible types of actors displaying this kind of behaviour would go well beyond the scope of this chapter and this book. Just to give an example, the state-level government of Berlin took an extremely reluctant approach in the management of the COVID-19 pandemic in 2020. The delays and flip-flopping that could be observed at the national level in many countries (including in the case of Italy described earlier) also applied to other levels of decision making. In Germany, the implementation of most measures during the pandemic was a competence of the federal states (Länder), and Berlin was one of them. While Berlin had a mid-range position in most COVID-19-related statistics among German federal states in the early phase of the pandemic (Gegg et al, 2020), its chaotic crisis management became almost proverbial, both in the first and the second COVID-19 wave. Between 2016 and 2021, Berlin was governed by a 'red-red-green' coalition composed of the SPD, Die Linke (The Left) and Bündnis 90/Die Grünen (The Green Party). During the first wave, there was a high degree of flip-flopping and many inconsistencies between the positions of health senator Dilek Kalayci of the SPD and the rest of the governing coalition, with Kalayci making a number of proposals that diverged, among others, from the positions of the mayor Michael Müller (Rosenfelder and Teevs, 2020). During the second wave of the pandemic, reluctance also manifested itself via flip-flopping on issues such as the introduction of social distancing measures in early December: two days after having declared that he did not see any need for further measures, the mayor had to backtrack and declared that he would not exclude new social distancing rules. Two days later, he announced a partial lockdown, with the closing of shops and schools. In early January, further flip-flopping concerned the potential reopening of schools in Berlin (see Betschka et al, 2021).

Exactly as it happened at the national level, the local government of Berlin also faced huge problems in devising a clear course of action during the pandemic. Besides the difficulties related to decision making in an entirely new situation and under extreme time pressure, other explanatory factors also played a role in this case. Among them are capacity problems, with the Berlin administration being notoriously underfunded and poorly organized (Keilani and Eckstein, 2021), as well as competing expectations related to deep normative disagreements. In the eastern part of Germany in particular, there was huge resistance towards social distancing measures and the vaccination campaign. All this culminated in an episode in August 2020, when far-right protesters almost managed to storm the parliament building (Bennhold, 2020).

Reluctance can therefore also be found in the policies of actors below the level of the nation-state, and in a range of issue areas. For example, there is a study that applies the concept developed in my previous research (Destradi, 2017) to the analysis of the city of Athens' recalcitrance and hesitation in implementing a refugee housing policy (Kiddey, 2019). Deeper analysis of a broader range of actors and policy fields, however, goes well beyond the scope of a book that is primarily interested in how this phenomenon manifests itself in world politics.

To conclude, the conceptualization of reluctance, which I developed with a focus on the field of International Relations and Foreign Policy Analysis, and with an interest in the empirical analysis of powerful countries' approach to regional crisis management, can be applied to very different crises, settings and actors. The explanations for reluctance that were developed in Chapter 3 can also 'travel' well to other cases and levels, if a few necessary modifications are made. In other words, the concept and the theory of reluctance can help illuminate some of the hesitant and recalcitrant behaviour that we often observe in the most different contexts.

8

Conclusion

This book started from the observation of contradictory, flip-flopping, muddling-though behaviour in international politics, and from the assessment that the existing theoretical repertoire in International Relations (IR) and Foreign Policy Analysis (FPA) does not really help us to make sense of these phenomena, which we nevertheless frequently observe. To address this gap, I proposed a conceptualization of reluctance that tries to move away from the often polemic and politically charged use of this notion. Building on different stages of concept reconstruction and concept building, in Chapter 2 I proposed an understanding of reluctance that focuses on two constitutive dimensions: hesitation and recalcitrance. Since both dimensions can be operationalized and observed empirically, my conceptualization of reluctance can be used for the classification of foreign policy, and can be usefully applied in empirical analyses.

Chapter 3 was devoted to developing a theory of reluctance in order to explain why this phenomenon originates and why it can be observed in different intensities across various cases. Building on a range of theoretical approaches from IR and FPA more broadly, I argued that a reluctant foreign policy will emerge if governments are faced with difficulties in devising clear preferences and, at the same time, a number of different and competing expectations by external actors. Such difficulties in preference formation can, in turn, emerge for a number of reasons.

For one, governments might be politically weak, which makes it difficult for them to devise a clear foreign policy course and to implement it. Second, states might have capacity problems of various kinds. They might have a weak bureaucratic apparatus and insufficient resources to implement a coherent foreign policy; or the state apparatus might be well equipped, but fundamentally divided. Forms of bureaucratic infighting such as struggles among different ministries can lead to problems in devising a clear foreign policy course and ultimately to flip-flopping or contradictory policies and statements on the part of various actors. A third possible driver of reluctance has to do with the individuals involved in decision making, and especially with their cognitive abilities. These can be seriously hampered in grave crisis situations that require swift decision making, and this can lead to a range of psychological mechanisms that ultimately result in ambiguous and hesitant policies. Finally, hesitation can be the result of normative struggles among various actors within a society over the best course of action to follow in a specific crisis. If the fundamental norms driving a country's approach to the world are being contested and renegotiated, this will inevitably lead to frictions and to policies that, at least for a certain time, are not determined and straightforward. These are, of course, alternative explanations for the emergence of hesitation, and therefore alternative pathways towards reluctance, which can be distinguished analytically but often also reinforce each other.

The main part of the book, Chapters 4–6, was devoted to the application of this theory to the analysis of the foreign policies of India, Germany and Brazil. I chose to focus on countries that are relatively powerful in their respective regions, and I decided to analyse their policies in crises that took place in their regional neighbourhoods, because these would be particularly hard test cases for my theory: we can easily expect reluctance to occur in the foreign policies of small states, or on secondary foreign policy issues, but when it comes to countries that are predominant in their regions and to crises that have the potential to spill over across borders and to create instability, hesitant and recalcitrant policies are rather surprising.

In the case of India, the grave deterioration of the security situation in Afghanistan was met in 2014–21 with a surprisingly high degree of reluctance. Under the Bharatiya Janata Party (BJP)-led government of Prime Minister Narendra Modi, India pursued policies that were essentially similar to those of the preceding government. Such reluctance was mainly driven by a combination of competing expectations (especially those of Pakistan as opposed to those of successive Afghan governments and Western powers, even with some variations) and normative struggles between sections of the Indian political establishment on how to deal with the various challenges faced by Afghanistan, from its deteriorating security situation to the issue of negotiating with the Taliban. The dramatic events of August 2021, when the Taliban took over Kabul, initially led to a highly reluctant approach on the part of New Delhi, which adopted a series of contradictory policies on how to issue visas to Afghan refugees. Later, India took the bold move of reopening its de facto embassy in the country, thereby signalling its intention to remain engaged in Afghanistan despite the changed political situation.

The case of Nepal is instructive of a highly asymmetrical relationship, in which India, as the clearly preponderant power, was still not able to devise a determined and responsive foreign policy. Quite to the contrary, during the crisis related to the adoption of new constitution in Nepal in 2015–17, India pursued a zig-zagging approach that alienated most Nepalese political actors and seriously limited India's influence in the country. In that case, competing expectations came not so much from the international community, which was barely interested in the issue, but from various Nepalese constituencies and political actors. At the same time, India's hesitation mainly derived from a lack of coordination and from competing approaches taken by various actors within India, who pursued distinct agendas, while the prime minister long neglected the issue. Paradoxically, the deep connections between India and Nepal contributed to capacity problems, hampering India's ability to speak with one voice and devise a clear course on Nepal.

Germany was analysed in this book as a reluctant power when it came to crisis management in its extended neighbourhood, focusing on the crises in Libya (2011) and Ukraine (2014–15). In the first case, Germany's abstention on UNSC Resolution 1973 can partly be explained by focusing on cognitive problems of decision making under high time pressure and information constraints, with competing expectations further complicating things for the government in Berlin. Beyond that, however, broader normative debates on Germany's role in the world, and the tension between norms such as loyalty to allies or responsibility and non-interventionism played an important role in shaping Germany's continued reluctance with regard to the crisis in Libya.

The Ukraine crisis, by contrast, shows a shift in Germany's foreign policy towards a gradually less reluctant approach. This transition was made possible by the government's efforts to convince both domestic opponents and international partners of the usefulness of combining diplomacy and sanctions. This reduced competing expectations and allowed for a reconciliation of opposed positions in normative debates about the role of Germany in that crisis.

Chapter 6 focused on Brazil and on its approach to the management of the crises in Haiti and Colombia during the years of the first Lula presidency. Brazil differed from India and Germany as it pursued policies that were not reluctant but overall determined and responsive. In those cases, my theoretical framework is also helpful as it reveals that the preconditions for reluctance were not in place, thereby making it possible for the Brazilian government to adopt a clear and consistent course of action. In particular, the Brazilian government did not face obstacles in taking over the leadership of the UN Stabilization Mission in Haiti (MINUSTAH) because most international actors (both extra-regional and regional) were happy with (or agreed to) Brazilian leadership and, at the same time, there was no substantial domestic opposition to it, or divisions within the government. At a time when Brazil was striving to be recognized as a great power in international politics and as a responsible regional actor, leading a UN mission in the region was a perfect signal to the world. The few domestic opponents who claimed that such a mission went against the core normative tenets of Brazilian foreign policy could ultimately be convinced of the merits of the mission.

When it comes to the civil war in Colombia, things were different. Brazil pursued a low-key approach, basically not engaging beyond offers of mediation and some support to the Colombian government with rescue logistics. Despite being so low-key and certainly not ambitious, this foreign policy was not reluctant: in fact, it was pursued very consistently over time, without flip-flopping, delays or a total lack of initiative (which would be indicators of hesitation); moreover, it was not a policy that disappointed other actors (which means it was not recalcitrant), since there were no major expectations directed at Brazil by other countries or by major political players from Colombia. This low-key but non-reluctant policy did not therefore require any particular capabilities, but it also did not lead to difficult or contentious decision processes.

In Chapter 7, I discussed to what extent my theory of reluctance 'travels' beyond powerful states' regional crisis management initiatives. In other words, I was interested in finding out if it has some explanatory power beyond the cases analysed in depth in this book. I therefore applied the theory to a number of illustrative cases that refer to the management of different types of crisis; to reluctance on the part of small states and great powers; and to reluctance on the part of actors beyond the nation-state. While not being able to study those cases in the same depth as my main case studies, those examples nevertheless help illustrating that the basic logic I developed in my theory can certainly be employed to explain reluctance in very different settings.

Lessons learned: reluctance, rising powers and issue salience

The analysis in this book has demonstrated that reluctance is a phenomenon in world politics that deserves greater attention. Reluctance is quite common, and it is important to understand its causes. The empirical analysis of three powerful regional countries and of varying degrees of reluctance in their regional crisis management leads to a number of more general observations. First of all, the study of India and Brazil provides some fresh insights into rising powers' foreign policy, as it highlights some of the constraints these countries are subjected to. They are often asked to assume international responsibility, but are frequently unwilling or unable to wholeheartedly conform to such expectations (see Kenkel and Destradi, 2019). In particular, rising powers face tensions between, on the one hand, their established foreign policy norms and traditions, and on the other, expectations of appropriate behaviour for aspiring 'great' powers. This has become evident in the discussion of norms of sovereignty and non-intervention as opposed to notions of responsibility and solidarity, especially in the case of Brazil's engagement in Haiti, but also in debates about India's approach to Afghanistan.

Conforming to the standards of appropriate behaviour of a reference group is a typical social mobility strategy that helps gain higher status (see Larson and Shevchenko, 2010). In some cases, as with Brazil's leadership of MINUSTAH, emerging powers manage to reconcile external expectations with their own domestic goals and ambitions, and this can lead them to pursue determined and responsive policies. In other cases, however, that process is more complicated and troubled. Admittedly, the case of India's engagement in Afghanistan is clearly an exceptionally hard case, given that the conflict in Afghanistan is so deeply intertwined with the long-standing bilateral conflict between India and Pakistan, and that for a long time the USA actively sought to limit India's influence against the backdrop of their own reliance on Pakistan. Still, the notion of reluctance helps us grasp some of the difficulties faced by rising powers in their very process of 'rise', as they navigate the complexities of high external expectations and important domestic normative shifts and adjustments.

Germany is obviously not a rising power, but the Eurozone crisis arguably catapulted Germany back centre stage in Europe and forced the country's leadership to rethink Germany's role in European and international politics. In many ways, the two crises analysed in Chapter 5, Libya (2011) and Ukraine (2014–15), were key points in Germany's process of reconsidering its position in international affairs and rethinking some of its basic tenets in foreign policy. The harsh international criticism that came as a reaction to Germany's abstention on UNSC Resolution 1973 contributed to unleashing such debate, which ultimately culminated in the coordinated speeches at the Munich Security Conference of 2014. That debate revolved around the need for Germany to take over greater international responsibilities given its features as an economic powerhouse in Europe, and it started calling into question the notion of 'civilian power' with its rejection of the use of military power and its ambition to be a moral force in international politics. Those discussions, which have their roots in the imperative to avoid any resurgence of German nationalism and militarism after the horrors of Germany's past, are far from concluded. In many ways, the renewed reluctance of Germany in the Ukraine war in 2022 and all the heated debates about a *Zeitenwende* (turning point) in German security policy are still part of that process. Despite a very different context, therefore, also Germany has been faced with quite fundamental domestic debates about how to position itself in international politics, and those debates have arguably had repercussions on the country's willingness and ability to pursue a less hesitant and recalcitrant foreign policy.

At the same time, the analysis has revealed that reluctance is not some kind of inherent or durable attribute of certain states. As opposed to some parts of the literature on 'reluctant hegemons', which seems to imply that reluctance – mostly equated with an unwillingness to lead – is a general feature of these countries, I have shown that reluctance is clearly context- and issue-specific. The same government can display different degrees of reluctance in the management of different crises given variations in their severity and in time pressure, in the very specific normative debates associated with them, in the bureaucratic agencies involved, as well as in the intensity of competing external expectations. Moreover, the analysis has revealed that reluctance is not a permanent feature of foreign policy and therefore does not last indefinitely. It can be overcome if expectations change and compromises can be achieved among the relevant actors involved.

The analysis of reluctance also points to another issue that has often been addressed only implicitly in the literature in IR and FPA: the salience of specific foreign policy issues or relationships. Quite obviously, not all crises and topics enjoy the same importance in the eyes of decision makers, and their prioritization differs widely. India's highly reluctant approach to Nepal reveals that, without international pressures on an issue, this might lose salience. Especially in the context of personalized leadership, as in the case of Modi's India (Plagemann and Destradi, 2019), if the leader is not personally interested in a crisis, its management might be left to a number of competing lower-ranking actors. Under 'normal' conditions, in the everyday business of international politics, this can work well for a long time: keeping foreign relations going and guaranteeing continuity is ultimately what foreign policy bureaucracies are tasked with. However, in crisis situations, if tough decisions need to be made, leaving foreign policy making to a number of (uncoordinated) actors will inevitably lead to hesitant and recalcitrant policies, with potentially detrimental effects.

Policy implications

From these thoughts and the book's overall findings, we can derive a number of conclusions that are relevant for policy making. The muddling through that we observe in world politics is, in fact, much more than an interesting phenomenon for academic research in IR and FPA. It has very tangible political consequences. The desperate appeals by the Ukrainian government in the weeks preceding Russia's attack in 2022 as well as the repeated calls that came in the following months, asking partners in the West for more help and support, and requesting countries such as Germany to take a clear stand and to overcome their hesitation, are obvious examples. Dealing with a reluctant international partner is frustrating, and the flip-flipping and contradictions that are typical of hesitation by definition make foreign policy unpredictable. What are the lessons that the theory of reluctance developed in this book yields for decision makers who have to deal with reluctant international partners?

First of all, the normative dimension of foreign policy was an important element in most cases analysed: if the expectations and requests articulated by international actors clash with long-held normative commitments, reluctant policies will be very likely. In fact, normative struggles can also reinforce competition among different actors within a government or within the bureaucracy, and thereby they ultimately have the potential to limit a government's ability to follow a consistent course of action. What is required, then, is first of all a deep understanding of the norms underpinning a country's foreign policy, including its very specific ideological foundations. Cases like the shifts from Nehruvianism to a Hindu nationalist ideology in India's foreign policy, and first signs that this shift is also taking place within the foreign policy bureaucracy (Huju, 2022), reveal the importance of a deep knowledge of the specificities and subtleties of such ideational foundations of foreign policy (see also Leader Maynard and Haas, 2023). This is fundamental for foreign policy making, and should be accompanied by a broader cultivation of area studies and regional expertise in academia and think tanks.

Second, the analysis has shown that reluctance can be overcome if there is a broad convergence between international expectations and preferences as well as the normative commitments of the most influential domestic actors. This also implies that governments can be nudged towards engaging, for example in crisis management, by articulating expectations that do not clash with their core domestic foreign policy norms. Far too often, established powers have called for countries from the Global South or for emerging powers to finally take over responsibility commensurate with their grown power capabilities. Unsurprisingly, this kind of exhortation has led to a high degree of disaffection and resistance as it was often perceived as patronizing and not sensitive to local constraints and specificities. If the normative foundations of emerging powers' foreign policies had been taken more seriously, and if the dangers of forcefully articulating expectations vis-à-vis those governments had been recognized, some tensions might have been avoided.

Third, established powers or, more generally, international partners should recognize that reluctance might be an inherent feature of processes of 'rise' in international politics, or of phases of normative transition and readjustment in foreign policy. These are often things that simply take time, and reluctance is frequently the expression of an ongoing genuinely democratic process. Therefore, it would be wrong to dismiss reluctance as a foreign policy failure. In some cases, especially if there is no dramatic and imminent crisis to be resolved, it might be more helpful to let such processes unfold, even though it is sometimes precisely through crises and increased pressure for action that they get a new dynamic and that readjustments take place.

Avenues for further research: what are the consequences of reluctance?

This book was mainly interested in conceptualizing the phenomenon of reluctance and in explaining its causes, but obviously the hesitant and recalcitrant foreign policy that was analysed here can also have important consequences. Assessing and also theorizing those consequences would have gone beyond the scope of this book, but at least some aspects related to the effects of reluctance were indirectly addressed in some of the case studies. Here, I would like to briefly discuss some of the potential implications of reluctance since their analysis opens up a number of important avenues for further research.

First of all, reluctance can have unintended consequences. In particular, it can be interpreted as a sign of weakness and lead to disconcert and criticism among international partners. This is how, for example, US President Joe Biden's hesitant approach to the Taiwan issue has been interpreted in much commentary: 'That flip-flopping makes it unclear whether Beijing will take anything away from this point other than that the United States is playing games, or that Biden is muddleheaded' (Johnson, 2022). In other words, reluctance can be misinterpreted as always entailing a lack of resolve, even if it emerges in cases where political weakness or capacity problems are not its major drivers. In fact, as has become clear from the cases analysed in this book, reluctance not only emerges from weakness or helplessness in crisis management; in the case of normative struggles, it can also be part of a process of discussion and deliberation on the fundamental norms that should guide an actor's policies – or, in the cases primarily discussed in this book, a state's foreign policy. Still, reluctance can have unintended consequences by signalling a lack of resolve to international partners and competitors. Exploring the unintended consequences of reluctance via a rationalist or even a game-theoretical framework might be an interesting avenue for further research.

Another area for further research concerns the relationship of reluctance and leadership in world politics. While reluctance is a phenomenon that can be found in the foreign policies of all sorts of states, and, in fact, even in the policies of other actors beyond the nation-state (see Chapter 7), the main cases analysed in this book referred to states that are particularly strong or predominant in a certain regional context. They were chosen because reluctance is particularly surprising on the part of actors that seem to possess sufficient power capabilities to pursue consistent and determined policies. In cases like these, reluctance is often equated with a lack of leadership: if the most powerful actors muddle through, who will take the lead? While I have discussed at several points in this book that reluctance goes well beyond an unwillingness or inability to lead, it is certainly true that a lack of leadership can be one of its implications, especially in asymmetric collective settings. This is how reluctance has frequently been discussed with reference to a lack of leadership on the part of Germany in the early phases of the Eurozone crisis, or a lack of leadership on the part of India in South Asian politics. And obviously, there is something to the observation that an indecisive and recalcitrant regional power that does not engage with its region in a consistent manner will not exactly help promoting regional cooperation and integration. This is especially true if we think of multilateral settings. India is a case in point: beyond its reluctance in crisis management in cases such as Afghanistan and Nepal, India has been extremely hesitant in matters of regional multilateralism. Successive Indian governments have contributed to hampering the activities of SAARC (South Asian Association for Regional Cooperation), be it by initially requesting that all contentious and political issues be removed from its remit, or later by neglecting the organization and even by looking for alternative forums for regional cooperation that exclude Pakistan (Michael, 2013; see Khan, 2021: 159).

This leads to the broader question of the long-term effects of reluctance on the part of powerful actors. What are the consequences of reluctance for regional cooperation and integration, and also for the provision of global public goods? Inspired by hegemonic stability theory (Kindleberger 1973), one could argue that reluctance on the part of powerful countries, which do not provide public goods in a consistent manner, leads to a loss of their credibility as leaders. This might, in turn, reduce traditional followers' readiness to follow (see, for example, Ikenberry and Kupchan, 1990), and ultimately weaken international cooperation in a sort of downward spiral of distrust. Theories of collective action would interpret reluctance to cooperate as creating an incentive structure that leads to an undersupply of collective goods (Rhinard, 2009), or at least to time lags in cooperation outcomes. All this can have detrimental consequences for global governance. From an alternative vantage point, emerging powers' reluctance might also lead to an ambiguous situation in which existing norms developed by established powers are increasingly contested, but emerging powers are still caught in the process of devising and shaping new norms. This all reflects preoccupations in policy circles about the 'reluctance' of the world order's traditional 'guardians' and the absence of new actors willing to engage in global public goods provision (Bunde and Oroz, 2015). How exactly reluctance plays out in multilateral settings or in complex global governance fields like climate change mitigation, however, awaits further exploration. In many ways, the notion of reluctance is a useful starting point to develop a better understanding of some of the dynamics that characterize current world politics.

Appendix: List of Interviewees

India

I1: Indian expert, New Delhi, 18 October 2013.

I2: Retired Nepalese diplomat, New Delhi, 29 October 2013.

I3: Afghan academic, New Delhi, 31 October 2013.

I4: Indian scholar, New Delhi, 12 November 2013.

I5: Retired Indian diplomat, New Delhi, 14 November 2013.

I6: Former high-ranking government official, New Delhi, 14 November 2013.

I7: Former high-ranking government official, New Delhi, 22 November 2013.

I8: Indian scholar, New Delhi, 26 November 2013.

I9: Indian scholar, online, 8 November 2022.

I10: Indian scholar, online, 15 November 2022.

I11: Afghan scholar, online, 16 November 2022.

I12: Indian scholar, online, 18 November 2022.

I13: Nepalese scholar, online, 20 November 2022.

Germany

G1: Senior German diplomat, Federal Foreign Office, Berlin, 20 April 2015.

G2: Expert, German Council on Foreign Relations, Berlin, 21 April 2015.

G3: Expert, German Council on Foreign Relations, Berlin, 21 April 2015.

G4: Expert, Federal Academy for Security Policy, Berlin 22 April 2015.

G5: German government official, Federal Chancellery, Berlin, 23 April 2015.

G6: Senior German diplomat, Federal Foreign Office, Berlin, 23 April 2015.

G7: German diplomat, Federal Foreign Office, Berlin 23 April 2015.

G8: German expert, Berlin, 24 April 2015.

G9: German government official, Federal Ministry for Economic Affairs and Energy, Berlin, 24 April 2015.

G10: German government official, Federal Ministry for Economic Affairs and Energy, Berlin, 24 April 2015.

G11: German academic, Hamburg, 27 April 2015.

G12: German academic, Hamburg, 27 April 2015.

G13: German expert, telephone interview, 29 April 2015.
G14: German academic, telephone interview, 12 May 2015.

Brazil

B1: Expert on Brazilian foreign and defence policy, online, 5 July 2022.
B2: Scholar based in Chile, online, 14 July 2022.
B3: Brazilian scholar, online, 23 August 2022.
B4: Brazilian academic and former government adviser, online, 8 September 2022.
B5: Colombian scholar, online, 16 September 2022.
B6: Brazilian scholar, online, 19 September 2022.
B7: High-ranking officer in the Brazilian Armed Forces, online, 26 September 2022.
B8: Scholar based in Brazil, online, 27 September 2022.

References

Adcock, R. and Collier, D. (2001) 'Measurement validity: A shared standard for qualitative and quantitative research', *American Political Science Review*, 95(3): 529–46.

Afghanistan Times (2019) 'India committed to economic reconstruction of Afghanistan, says Swaraj', 14 January, Available from: www.afghanistantimes.af/india-committed-to-economic-reconstruction-of-afghanistan-says-swaraj [Accessed 24 November 2022].

Aguilar, S.L.C. (2015) 'A participação do Brasil nas operações de paz: Passado, presente e futuro', *Brasiliana: Journal for Brazilian Studies*, 3(2): 113–41.

Alizada, N., Boese, V.A., Lundstedt, M., Morrison, K., Natsika, N., Sato, Y., Tai, H. and Lindberg, S.I. (2022) *Autocratization Changing Nature?*, Democracy Report 2022, V-Dem Institute, Available from: https://v-dem.net/media/publications/dr_2022.pdf [Accessed 26 November 2022].

Allison, G.T. (1971) *Essence of Decision: Explaining the Cuban Missile Crisis*, Boston, MA: Little, Brown & Co.

Allison, G.T. and Halperin, M.H. (1972) 'Bureaucratic politics: A paradigm and some policy implications', *World Politics*, 24: 40–79.

Amann, M., Becker, M., Gebauer, M., Hickmann, C., Höhne, V., Knobbe, M., Medick, V., Reiermann, C., Schult, C., Traufetter, G. and Weiland, S. (2022) 'Deutschlands sicherheitspolitische Wende: Um kurz nach drei liegt der Bündnisfall auf dem Tisch', *Spiegel Politik*, 1 March, Available from: www.spiegel.de/politik/deutschland-und-der-ukraine-krieg-wie-es-zur-sicherheitspolitischen-wende-kam-a-3f5a5000-452d-49db-a5c1-15701dc66808 [Accessed 13 November 2022].

Amorim, C. (2008a) 'Entrevista do Ministro Celso Amorim ao programa Roda Viva', Ministério das Relações Exteriores [Accessed 26 November 2022].

Amorim, C. (2008b) 'Íntegra da entrevista de Celso Amorim (Entrevista do Ministro Celso Amorim ao repórter Luiz Carlos Azenha, 5/5/2008)', Ministério das Relações Exteriores, Available from: www.gov.br/mre/pt-br/centrais-de-conteudo/publicacoes/discursos-artigos-e-entrevistas/minis tro-das-relacoes-exteriores/entrevistas-mre/entrevista-concedida-pelo-ministro-das-relacoes-exteriores-embaixador-celso-amorim-ao-reporter-luiz-carlos-azenha-brasilia-df-05-05-2008 [Accessed 26 November 2022].

Amorim, C. (2010a) 'Brazilian foreign policy under President Lula (2003–2010): An overview', *Revista Brasileira de Política Internacional*, 53(spe): 214–40.

Amorim, C. (2010b) 'O Haiti e o futuro', *Folha de S. Paulo*, Available from: www1.folha.uol.com.br/fsp/opiniao/fz3103201008.htm [Accessed 26 November 2022].

Amorim Neto, O. and Malamud, A. (2019) 'The policy-making capacity of foreign ministries in presidential regimes: A study of Argentina, Brazil, and Mexico, 1946–2015', *Latin American Research Review*, 54(4): 812–34.

Andrade, I. de O., Hamman, E.P. and Soares, M.A. (2019) *A participação do Brasil nas operações de paz das Nações Unidas: Evolução, desafios e oportunidades*, Brasília: IPEA (Instituto de Pesquisa Econômica Aplicada).

Andrade, R. (2004) 'Brasil tem tropa de 1.100 militares para ir ao Haiti', *Gazeta Digital*, Available from: www.gazetadigital.com.br/conteudo/show/secao/10/materia/30135 [Accessed 5 March 2017].

Andreatta, F., Brighi, E. and Forcella, I. (2002) 'The Berlusconi government's foreign policy: The first 18 months', *Italian Politics*, 18: 221–36.

Arora, V. (2015) 'RIP, India's Influence in Nepal', *The Diplomat*, 25 November, Available from: https://thediplomat.com/2015/11/r-i-p-indias-influence-in-nepal [Accessed 25 November 2022].

Ash, T.G. (2011) 'France plays hawk, Germany demurs. Libya has exposed Europe's fault lines', *The Guardian*, 24 March, Available from: www.theguardian.com/commentisfree/2011/mar/24/france-hawk-germany-demurs-libya-europe [Accessed 9 August 2022].

Asia Foundation, The (2017) 'The state of conflict and violence in Asia', Available from: https://asiafoundation.org/wp-content/uploads/2017/10/The_State_of_Conflict_and_Violence_in_Asia-12.29.17.pdf[Accessed 3 February 2023].

Asian Development Bank (2021) *Asian Economic Integration Report 2021*, Available from: https://aric.adb.org/pdf/aeir/AEIR2021_complete.pdf [Accessed 30 August 2021].

Aslanidis, P. and Rovira Kaltwasser, C. (2016) 'Dealing with populists in government: The SYRIZA–ANEL coalition in Greece', *Democratization*, 23(6): 1077–91.

Auswärtiges Amt (2011) 'Bundesminister Westerwelle begrüßt Verschärfung der EU-Sanktionen gegen Libyen', Press release, 7 June, Available from: www.auswaertiges-amt.de/de/newsroom/110607-eu-sanktionen-gegen-libyen/243806 [Accessed 28 November 2022].

Bach, T. and Wegrich, K. (2019) 'Blind Spots, Biased Attention, and the Politics of Non-Coordination', in T. Bach and K. Wegrich (eds) *The Blind Spots of Public Bureaucracy and the Politics of Non-Coordination*, Cham: Palgrave Macmillan, pp 3–28.

Baker, P. (2014a) 'Obama and Putin meet briefly at D-Day event', *The New York Times*, 6 June, Available from: www.nytimes.com/2014/06/07/world/europe/obama-honors-moment-of-liberation-in-normandy.html [Accessed 28 November 2022].

Baker, P. (2014b) 'Pressure rising as Obama works to rein in Russia', *The New York Times*, 2 March, Available from: www.nytimes.com/2014/03/03/world/europe/pressure-rising-as-obama-works-to-rein-in-russia.html?_r=0 [Accessed 2 February 2023].

Barker, A. (2011) 'Raging Gaddafi orders forces to "capture the rats"', ABC News, 22 February, Available from: www.abc.net.au/news/2011-02-23/raging-gaddafi-orders-forces-to-capture-the-rats/1953788 [Accessed 5 November 2022].

Basit, A. (2021) 'Why did India open a backchannel to the Taliban?', Al Jazeera, 7 July, Available from: www.aljazeera.com/opinions/2021/7/7/why-did-india-open-a-backchannel-to-the-taliban [Accessed 24 November 2022].

Basrur, R. (2023) *Subcontinental Drift: Domestic Politics and India's Foreign Policy*, Washington, DC: Georgetown University Press.

Basrur, R. and Sullivan de Estrada, K. (2017) *Rising India: Status and Power*, London: Routledge.

BBC News (2011) 'Libya protests: Defiant Gaddafi refuses to quit', Available from: www.bbc.com/news/world-middle-east-12544624 [Accessed 5 November 2022].

BBC News (2014a) 'Eastern Ukraine militants snub Geneva deal on crisis', Available from: www.bbc.com/news/world-europe-27076226 [Accessed 28 November 2022].

BBC News (2014b) 'Little green men or Russian invaders', Available from: www.bbc.com/news/world-europe-26532154 [Accessed 28 November 2022].

BBC News (2015) 'Ukraine conflict: US "may supply arms to Ukraine"', Available from: www.bbc.com/news/world-europe-31279621 [Accessed 28 November 2022].

BBC News (2018) 'MH17 missile owned by Russian brigade, investigators say', Available from: www.bbc.com/news/world-europe-44235402 [Accessed 28 November 2022].

BBC News (2019) 'Trump mocks India PM over Afghanistan library', Available from: www.youtube.com/watch?v=jGdyxwtX7gI [Accessed 24 November 2022].

Beasley, R.K., Kaarbo, J., Hermann, C.F. and Hermann, M.G. (2001) 'People and processes in foreign policymaking: Insights from comparative case studies', *International Studies Review*, 3(2): 217–50.

Beck, U. (2012) 'Merkiavellis Macht: Das Zögern der Kanzlerin bei der Euro-Rettung', *Der Spiegel*, 41: 50–1.

Bejar, S., Mukherjee, B. and Moore, W.H. (2011) 'Time horizons matter: The hazard rate of coalition governments and the size of government', *Economics of Governance*, 12(3): 201–35.

Bellamy, A.J. (2010) *Responsibility to Protect: The Global Effort to End Mass Atrocities*, Cambridge: Polity Press.

Bennhold, K. (2020) 'Far-Right Germans try to storm Reichstag as virus protests grow', *The New York Times*, 31 August, Available from: www.nyti mes.com/2020/08/31/world/europe/reichstag-germany-neonazi-coro navirus.html [Accessed 29 November 2022].

Benwell, R. (2011) 'The canaries in the coalmine: Small states as climate change champions', *The Round Table*, 100(413): 199–211.

Berger, T.U. (1996) 'Norms, Identity, and National Security in Germany and Japan', in P.J. Katzenstein (ed) *The Culture of National Security: Norms and Identity in World Politics*, New York: Columbia University Press, pp 317–56.

Bernal-Meza, R. (2010) 'International thought in the Lula era', *Revista Brasileira de Política Internacional*, 53(spe): 193–213.

Betschka, J., Brandhofer, B., Kleist-Heinrich, K., Meidinger, D. and Perdoni, S. (2021) 'Ein Jahr Corona: Chronik einer Stadt im Jojo-Lockdown', Tagesspiegel, Available from: https://interaktiv.tagesspiegel.de/lab/ein-jahr-corona-in-berlin [Accessed 29 November 2022].

Bhatia, R., van Deutekom, J., Lee, L. and Kulkarni, K. (2016) 'Chinese investments in Nepal', Gateway House, 16 September, Available from: www.gatewayhouse.in/chinese-investments-nepal-2 [Accessed 25 November 2022].

Bielby, W.T. and Bielby, D.D. (1992) 'I will follow him: Family ties, gender-role beliefs, and reluctance to relocate for a better job', *American Journal of Sociology*, 97(5): 1241–67.

Bijian, Z. (2005) 'China's "peaceful rise" to great-power status', *Foreign Affairs*, 84(5): 18.

Bilefsky, D. and Landler, M. (2011) 'As UN backs military action in Libya, US role is unclear', *The New York Times*, 18 March, Available from: www.nytimes.com/2011/03/18/world/africa/18nations.html [Accessed 4 November 2022].

Biswas, B. (2006) 'The challenges of conflict management: A case study of Sri Lanka', *Civil Wars*, 8(1): 46–65.

Blomdahl, M. (2016) 'Bureaucratic roles and positions: Explaining the United States Libya decision', *Diplomacy & Statecraft*, 27(1): 142–61.

BMWK (Bundesministerium für Wirtschaft und Klimaschutz) (no date) 'Politische Grundsätze der Bundesregierung für den Export von Kriegswaffen und sonstigen Rüstungsgütern', Available from: www.bmwk.de/Redaktion/DE/Downloads/P-R/politische-grundsaetze-fuer-den-exp ort-von-kriegswaffen-und-sonstigen-ruestungsguetern.pdf?__blob=publ icationFile [Accessed 25 November 2022].

Boin, A., 't Hart, P., Stern, E. and Sundelius, B. (2005) *The Politics of Crisis Management: Public Leadership Under Pressure*, Cambridge: Cambridge University Press.

Bösch, F., Deitelhoff, N. and Kroll, S. (2020) *Handbuch Krisenforschung*, Wiesbaden: Springer VS.

Bose, P.R. (2015) 'Will Bihar result end Nepal border crisis?', *The Hindu Business Line*, 9 November, Available from: www.thehindubusinessline. com/news/will-bihar-result-end-nepal-border-crisis/article64348365.ece [Accessed 25 November 2022].

BPB (Bundeszentrale für Politische Bildung)(2014) 'Dokumentation: Das Minsker Memorandum vom 19 September', 2 October, Available from: www. bpb.de/themen/europa/ukraine/192488/dokumentation-das-minsker-memorandum-vom-19-september [Accessed 28 November 2022].

Braumann, N. (2011) 'Libya: The view from Germany', *Atlantic Council*, 24 March, Available from: www.atlanticcouncil.org/blogs/new-atlanticist/libya-the-view-from-germany [Accessed 28 November 2022].

Braveboy-Wagner, J. (2010) 'Opportunities and limitations of the exercise of foreign policy power by a very small state: The case of Trinidad and Tobago', *Cambridge Review of International Affairs*, 23(3): 407–27.

Breuer, F. (2006) 'Between ambitions and financial constraints: The reform of the German armed forces', *German Politics*, 15(2): 206–20.

Brockmeier, S. (2013) 'Germany and the intervention in Libya', *Survival*, 55(6): 63–90.

Brummer, K. and Thies, C.G. (2015) 'The contested selection of national role conceptions', *Foreign Policy Analysis*, 11(3): 273–93.

Bucher, J., Engel, L., Harfensteller, S. and Dijkstra, H. (2013) 'Domestic politics, news media and humanitarian intervention: Why France and Germany diverged over Libya', *European Security*, 22(4): 524–39.

Bull, M. (2021) 'The Italian government response to Covid-19 and the making of a prime minister', *Contemporary Italian Politics*, 13(2): 149–65.

Bulmer, S. (2014) 'Germany and the Eurozone crisis: Between hegemony and domestic politics', *West European Politics*, 37(6): 1244–63.

Bulmer, S. and Paterson, W.E. (2013) 'Germany as the EU's reluctant hegemon? Of economic strength and political constraints', *Journal of European Public Policy*, 20(10): 1387–405.

Bunde, T. and Oroz, A. (2015) *Munich Security Report 2015*, Munich Security Conference, Available from: https://securityconference.org/assets/02_Do kumente/01_Publikationen/MunichSecurityReport_2015.pdf [Accessed 25 November 2022].

Bundesregierung (2014a) 'Concern for Ukraine', Available from: www.bund esregierung.de/breg-en/news/concern-for-ukraine-440204 [Accessed 28 November 2022].

Bundesregierung (2014b) 'Regierungserklärung von Bundeskanzlerin Merkel', Available from: www.bundeskanzler.de/bk-de/aktuelles/regie rungserklaerung-von-bundeskanzlerin-merkel-443682 [Accessed 28 November 2022].

Bundesregierung (2015) 'Speech by Federal Chancellor Angela Merkel on the occasion of the 51st Munich Security Conference', Available from: www.bundesregierung.de/breg-en/chancellor/speech-by-federal-chancellor-angela-merkel-on-the-occasion-of-the-51st-munich-secur ity-conference-400334 [Accessed 28 November 2022].

Bundesregierung (2022) 'Bundesregierung liefert Waffen aus Bundeswehr-Beständen an die Ukraine', 26 February, Available from: www.bundesregier ung.de/breg-de/themen/krieg-in-der-ukraine/bundesregierung-liefert-waffen-aus-bundeswehr-bestaenden-an-die-ukraine-2008214 [Accessed 31 October 2022].

Bundestag (2011a) 'Aussetzung der allgemeinen Wehrpflicht beschlossen', Available from: www.bundestag.de/webarchiv/textarchiv/2011/33831649 _kw12_de_wehrdienst-204958 [Accessed 28 November 2022].

Bundestag (2011b) 'Plenarprotokoll 17/104', Available from: https://dserver. bundestag.de/btp/17/17104.pdf#P.11937 [Accessed 28 November 2022].

Bundestag (2011c) 'Plenarprotokoll 17/95', Available from: https://dserver. bundestag.de/btp/17/17095.pdf#P.10831 [Accessed 28 November 2022].

Bundestag (2011d) 'Plenarprotokoll 17/97', Available from: https://dserver. bundestag.de/btp/17/17097.pdf.

Bundestag (2011e) 'Plenarprotokoll 17/98', Available from: https://dserver. bundestag.de/btp/17/17098.pdf#P.11194 [Accessed 28 November 2022].

Bundestag (2011f) 'Plenarprotokoll 99. Sitzung', Available from: https://dserver. bundestag.de/btp/17/17099.pdf#P.11442 [Accessed 28 November 2022].

Bundestag (2014) 'Plenarprotokoll 18/20', Available from: https://dserver. bundestag.de/btp/18/18020.pdf [Accessed 28 November 2022].

Bundestag (2022) 'Bundeskanzler Olaf Scholz: Wir erleben eine Zeitenwende', Available from: www.bundestag.de/dokumente/textarc hiv/2022/kw08-sondersitzung-882198 [Accessed 28 November 2022].

Bundeswahlleiter (2009) 'Bundestagwahl 2009', Available from: www.bunde swahlleiter.de/bundestagswahlen/2009.html [Accessed 28 November 2022].

Bundeswahlleiter (2013) 'Bundestagwahl 2013', Available from: www. bundeswahlleiter.de/bundestagswahlen/2013/ergebnisse.html [Accessed 28 November 2022].

Burges, S.W. (2015) 'Revisiting consensual hegemony: Brazilian regional leadership in question', *International Politics*, 52(2): 193–207.

Burges, S.W. (2017) *Brazil in the World: The International Relations of a South American Giant*, Manchester: Manchester University Press.

Burnard, F. (2008) 'Swiss offer best hope for Colombian hostages', Swissinfo, 21 May, Available from: www.swissinfo.ch/eng/swiss-offer-best-hope-for-colombian-hostages/6668940 [Accessed 26 November 2022].

Business Standard (2016) 'Bihar leaders' remarks on Madhesis provocative: Nepal', 2 February, Available from: www.business-standard.com/article/pti-stories/bihar-leaders-remarks-on-madhesis-provocative-nepal-116020201529_1.html [Accessed 25 November 2022].

Byman, D. and Waxman, M. (2002) *The Dynamics of Coercion: American Foreign Policy and the Limits of Military Might*, Cambridge: Cambridge University Press.

Candeas, A. (2012) 'Brasil y Colombia: Vecinos otrora distantes descubren el potencial de su relación', in E.P. Buelvas, S. Jost and D. Flemes (eds) *Colombia y Brasil: ¿Socios estratégicos en la construcción de Suramérica?*, Bogotá: Editorial Pontificia Universidad Javeriana, pp 283–308.

Cantir, C. and Kaarbo, J. (2016) 'Unpacking Ego in Role Theory', in C. Cantir and J. Kaarbo (eds) *Domestic Role Contestation, Foreign Policy, and International Relations*, New York, London: Routledge, pp 1–22.

Carnegie Europe (2018) *Eastern Ukraine: Different Dynamics*, Available from: https://carnegieeurope.eu/2018/12/03/eastern-ukraine-different-dynamics-pub-77845 [Accessed 28 November 2022].

Carnegie Europe (2019) *From the Square to Politics After Ukraine's Euromaidan Protests: Pathways Beyond Mass Mobilization*, Available from: https://carnegieeurope.eu/2019/10/24/from-square-to-politics-after-ukraine-s-euromaidan-protests-pub-80144 [Accessed 28 November 2022].

Carpes, M. (2015) 'O papel do Brasil no período pós-conflito na Colômbia', *Iberoamericana*, XV(60): 175–9.

Carroll, R. (2004) 'Exiled Aristide urges Haitian resistance', *The Guardian*, 9 March, Available from: www.theguardian.com/world/2004/mar/09/rorycarroll [Accessed 22 August 2022].

Cason, J.W. and Power, T.J. (2009) 'Presidentialization, pluralization, and the rollback of Itamaraty: Explaining change in Brazilian foreign policy making in the Cardoso-Lula era', *International Political Science Review*, 30(2): 117–40.

Center for Insights in Survey Research (2015) *Public Opinion Survey: Residents of Ukraine*, International Republican Institute, Available from: www.iri.org/wp-content/uploads/legacy/iri.org/wysiwyg/2015_11_national_oversample_en_combined_natl_and_donbas_v3.pdf [Accessed 28 November 2022].

Chatterji, A.P., Hansen, T.B. and Jaffrelot, C. (eds) (2020) *Majoritarian State: How Hindu Nationalism Is Changing India*, London: Hurst & Co.

Chaturvedi, S. (2012) 'India's development partnership: Key policy shifts and institutional evolution', *Cambridge Review of International Affairs*, 25(4): 557–77.

Chaudhuri, R. and Shende, S. (2020) 'Dealing with the Taliban: India's strategy in Afghanistan after US withdrawal', Carnegie India, 2 June, Available from: https://carnegieindia.org/2020/06/02/dealing-with-tali ban-india-s-strategy-in-afghanistan-after-u.s.-withdrawal-pub-81951 [Accessed 23 November 2022].

Chaudhury, D.R. (2017) 'Yogi Adityanath's royal connection: Former royal family of Nepal trace their origin to Guru Gorakshanath', *The Economic Times*, 20 March, Available from: https://economictimes.indiatimes.com/ news/politics-and-nation/yogi-adityanaths-royal-connection-former-royal-family-of-nepal-trace-their-origin-to-guru-gorakshanath/articles how/57722870.cms [Accessed 25 November 2022].

Checkel, J.T. (1997) 'International norms and domestic politics', *European Journal of International Relations*, 3(4): 473–95.

Chivvis, C.S. (2015) 'Strategic and Political Overview of the Intervention', in K.P. Mueller (ed) *Precision and Purpose: Airpower in the Libyan Civil War*, Santa Monica, CA: RAND Corporation, pp 11–42.

Christensen, T.J. and Snyder, J. (1990) 'Chain gangs and passed bucks: Predicting alliance patterns in multipolarity', *International Organization*, 44(2): 137–68.

Chubb, A. (2021) 'PRC assertiveness in the South China Sea: Measuring continuity and change, 1970–2015', *International Security*, 45(3): 79–121.

CIDOB (Barcelona Centre for International Affairs) (2015) 'Processos de paz anteriores (FARC-EP Y ELN)', Available from: www.cidob.org/public aciones/documentacion/dossiers/dossier_proceso_de_paz_en_colombia/ dossier_proceso_de_paz_en_colombia/procesos_de_paz_anteriores_farc_ ep_y_eln [Accessed 26 November 2022].

CNN (2011) 'Germany lends Libyan rebels $144 million as fighting rages', 24 July, Available from: http://edition.cnn.com/2011/WORLD/africa/ 07/24/libya.germany/index.html [Accessed 28 November 2022].

CNN (2022) 'Ukraine–Russia crisis news', 22 February, Available from: https://edition.cnn.com/europe/live-news/ukraine-russia-news-02-22-22#h_39f36c7e88452f3eb41f9d41b8491ab6 [Accessed 28 November 2022].

Cohen, S.P. (2002) *India: Emerging Power*, Washington, DC: Brookings Institution.

Collier, D. (2011) 'Understanding process tracing', *PS: Political Science & Politics*, 44(4): 823–30.

Collier, D., LaPorte, J. and Seawright, J. (2012) 'Putting typologies to work: Concept formation, measurement, and analytical rigor', *Political Research Quarterly*, 65(1): 217–32.

Congresso em Foco (2008) 'Assessor de Lula nega ligação do governo com as Farc', 31 July, Available from: https://congressoemfoco.uol.com.br/proj eto-bula/reportagem/assessor-de-lula-nega-ligacao-do-governo-com-as-farc [Accessed 6 August 2022].

Corbett, J., Xu, Y. and Weller, P. (2019) 'Norm entrepreneurship and diffusion "from below" in international organisations: How the competent performance of vulnerability generates benefits for small states', *Review of International Studies*, 45(4): 647–68.

Council on Foreign Relations (2017) 'A conversation with Shahid Khaqan Abbasi', 20 September, Available from: www.cfr.org/event/conversation-shahid-khaqan-abbasi [Accessed 24 November 2022].

CrisisWatch Database (2022) 'Tracking conflict worldwide', International Crisis Group, Available from: www.crisisgroup.org/crisiswatch/datab ase?location%5B%5D=39&date_range=custom&from_month=01&from_year=2016&to_month=12&to_year=2017 [Accessed 25 November 2022].

Croissant, A. and Merkel, W. (2019) 'Defective Democracy', in W. Merkel, R. Kollmorgen and J. Wagener (eds) *The Handbook of Political, Social, and Economic Transformation*, Oxford: Oxford University Press, pp 437–46.

CRS (Congresional Research Services) (2019) *Afghanistan: Background and US Policy in Brief*, Available from: www.ecoi.net/en/document/2008094. html [Accessed 24 November 2022].

Culp, J. (2016) 'How irresponsible are rising powers?', *Third World Quarterly*, 37(9): 1525–36.

Das, K.N. (2019) 'India rejects Trump's "sermons" on Afghanistan, says it is building lives', Reuters, 4 January, Available from: www.reuters.com/article/us-trump-india-afghanistan-idUSKCN1OY0FZ [Accessed 24 November 2022].

de Almeida, P.R. (2010) 'Never before seen in Brazil: Luis Inácio Lula da Silva's grand diplomacy', *Revista Brasileira de Política Internacional*, 53(2): 160–77.

de Lucena, L.L.M. (2014) 'O Brasil e a MINUSTAH – Ou a busca de novos parâmetros para uma política externa brasileira "altiva" em operações de paz das Nações Unidas', *Século XXI*, 5(1): 129–49.

Dempsey, J. (2015) 'Angela Merkel's Greek tragedy', Carnegie Europe, 29 June, Available from: http://carnegieeurope.eu/strategiceurope/?fa=60523 [Accessed 28 April 2016].

Dempsey, J. (2022a) 'German ambiguity is deciding Ukraine's future', Carnegie Europe, Judy Dempsey's, Strategic Europe, 31 May, Available from: https://carnegieeurope.eu/strategiceurope/87215 [Accessed 22 November 2022].

Dempsey, J. (2022b) 'Judy asks: Is Germany damaging Europe's position on Ukraine?', Carnegie Europe, Judy Dempsey's Strategic Europe, 27 January, Available from: https://carnegieeurope.eu/strategiceurope/86288 [Accessed 13 November 2022].

Der Derian, J. (1987) *On Diplomacy: A Genealogy of Western Estrangement*, Hoboken, NJ: Wiley Blackwell.

Destradi, S. (2010) 'Regional powers and their strategies: Empire, hegemony, and leadership', *Review of International Studies*, 36(4): 903–30.

Destradi, S. (2012a) 'India as a democracy promoter? New Delhi's involvement in Nepal's return to democracy', *Democratization*, 19(2): 286–311.

Destradi, S. (2012b) *Indian Foreign and Security Policy in South Asia*, London, New York: Routledge.

Destradi, S. (2014) 'India: A reluctant partner for Afghanistan', *The Washington Quarterly*, 37(2): 103–17.

Destradi, S. (2015) *Reluctant Powers: A Concept-Building Approach and an Application to the Case of Germany*, EUI Working Paper RSCAS 2015/46.

Destradi, S. (2017) 'Reluctance in international politics: A conceptualization', *European Journal of International Relations*, 23(2): 315–40.

Destradi, S. (2018) 'Reluctant powers? Rising powers' contributions to regional crisis management', *Third World Quarterly*, 39(12): 2222–39.

Destradi, S. and Plagemann, J. (2019) 'Populism and International Relations: (Un)predictability, personalisation, and the reinforcement of existing trends in world politics', *Review of International Studies*, 45(5): 711–30.

Destradi, S. and Plagemann, J. (2023) 'Ideology and Indian Foreign Policy', in J. Leader Maynard and M.L. Haas (eds) *The Routledge Handbook of Ideology and International Relations*, Abingdon, New York: Routledge, pp 299–312.

Deutsche Welle (2011) 'Berlin's stance on Libya has isolated Germany in NATO', 13 April, Available from: www.dw.com/en/berlins-sta nce-on-libya-has-isolated-germany-in-nato/a-14985036-0 [Accessed 9 August 2022].

Deutschlandfunk (2011) 'Ich möchte nicht, dass Deutschland Teil eines Krieges in Libyen wird',17 March, Available from: www.deutschlandfunk. de/ich-moechte-nicht-dass-deutschland-teil-eines-krieges-in-100.html [Accessed 28 November 2022].

Deutschlandfunk (2022) 'Botschafter Melnyk: Deutschland muss die "russische Brille" ablegen', Kriegsangst der Ukraine, 13 February, Available from: www.deutschlandfunk.de/interview-der-woche-andrij-melnyk-bots chafter-ukraine-krise-krieg-angriff-russland-waffenlieferungen-100.html [Accessed 31 October 2022].

Diez, T. (1999) 'Speaking "Europe": The politics of integration discourse', *Journal of European Public Policy*, 6(4): 598–613.

Diniz, E. (2009) 'O Brasil e a MINUSTAH', *Pontifícia Universidade Católica de Minas Gerais*, Available from: http://www.cprepmauss.com.br/documen tos/obrasileaminustha98283.pdf [Accessed 4 September 2013].

Dixit, K. (2015) 'India and Nepal have no choice but to end their border dispute and move on', *Time*, 17 November, Available from: https:// time.com/4115801/nepal-india-border-blockade-madhesh [Accessed 24 November 2022].

Drezner, D.W. (2019) 'Present at the destruction: The Trump administration and the foreign policy bureaucracy', *The Journal of Politics*, 81(2): 723–30.

D'Souza, S.M. (no date) 'India's role in the economic stabilisation of Afghanistan', Friedrich-Ebert-Stiftung, Available from: https://library.fes.de/pdf-files/bueros/kabul/12959.pdf [Accessed 24 November 2022].

Dueck, C. (2006) *Reluctant Crusaders: Power, Culture, and Change in American Grand Strategy*, Princeton, NJ, Oxford: Princeton University Press.

Dutch Safety Board (2015) 'Buk surface-to-air missile system caused MH17 crash', Press release, 13 October, Available from: www.onderzoeksraad.nl/nl/media/inline/2018/10/11/press_release_buk_surface_to_air_missile_system_caused_mh17_crash.pdf [Accessed 28 November 2022].

Dyson, T. (2011) 'Managing convergence: German military doctrine and capabilities in the 21st century', *Defence Studies*, 11(2): 244–70.

Economic Times, The (2019) 'India hasn't shown inclination to pursue deeper defence ties with Afghanistan: US report', 4 May, Available from: https://economictimes.indiatimes.com/news/defence/india-hasnt-shown-inclination-to-pursue-deeper-defence-ties-with-afghanistan-us-report/articleshow/69171572.cms?utm_source=contentofinterest&utm_medium=text&utm_campaign=cppst [Accessed 24 November 2022].

Economist, The (2013) 'The reluctant hegemon', 13 June, Available from: www.economist.com/special-report/2013/06/13/europes-reluctant-hegemon [Accessed 13 February 2015].

Economist, The (2014) 'How very understanding', 8 May, Available from: www.economist.com/europe/2014/05/08/how-very-understanding [Accessed 26 November 2022].

Economist, The (2022) 'Olaf Scholz's dithering is damaging Germany's international image', 31 May, Available from: www.economist.com/europe/2022/05/31/olaf-scholzs-dithering-is-damaging-germanys-international-image [Accessed 26 November 2022].

el-Gomati, A. (2022) 'Libya – Mapping European leverage in the MENA region', European Council on Foreign Relations, Available from: https://ecfr.eu/special/mapping_eu_leverage_mena/libya [Accessed 28 November 2022].

Embassy of India (2020) 'India–Afghanistan Relations', Indo–Afghan Relations, Kabul, Available from: https://eoi.gov.in/kabul/?0354?000 [Accessed 24 November 2022].

Engberg, K. (2014) *The EU and Military Operations: A Comparative Analysis*, London, New York: Routledge.

Erler, G. (2014) 'Gernot Erler: "Wladimir Putin hat Russland unberechenbar gemacht"', IPG, 14 October, Available from: www.ipg-journal.de/kommentar/artikel/gernot-erler-wladimir-putin-hat-russland-unberechenbar-gemacht-623 [Accessed 28 November 2022].

Esterhuyse, A. (2010) 'South Africa: The reluctant leader', Limes: Rivista italiana di geopolitica, Available from: https://www.limesonline.com/en/south-africa-the-reluctant-leader [Accessed 24 March 2023].

European Commission (2011) 'Extraordinary European Council 11 March 2011 Declaration', Available from: https://ec.europa.eu/commission/presscorner/detail/en/DOC_11_2 [Accessed 9 August 2022].

European Council (2011) 'Joint statement by President of the European Council Herman Van Rompuy, and EU High Representative Catherine Ashton on UN Security Council resolution on Libya', 17 March, Available from: www.consilium.europa.eu/uedocs/cms_data/docs/pressdata/en/ec/120012.pdf [Accessed 16 November 2022].

European Council (2014a) 'Statement by the President of the European Council Herman Van Rompuy and the President of the European Commission in the name of the European Union on the agreed additional restrictive measures against Russia', 29 July, Available from: www.consilium.europa.eu/uedocs/cms_data/docs/pressdata/en/ec/144158.pdf [Accessed 28 November 2022].

European Council (2014b) 'Statement of the Heads of State or Government on Ukraine Brussels, 6 March 2014', 6 March, Available from: www.consilium.europa.eu/media/29285/141372.pdf [Accessed 28 November 2022].

Fair, C.C. (2018) 'Afghanistan in 2017', *Asian Survey*, 58(1): 110–19.

FAZ (*Frankfurter Allgemeine Zeitung*) (2011) 'Unruhen in Libyen: Gaddafi lässt Greuel-Beweise vernichten', 26 February, Available from: www.faz.net/aktuell/politik/ausland/naher-osten/unruhen-in-libyen-gaddafi-laesst-greuel-beweise-vernichten-1597687.html [Accessed 28 November 2022].

FAZ (2022) '"Deutliches Signal": Lambrecht verspricht der Ukraine 5000 Helme', 26 January, Available from: www.faz.net/aktuell/politik/ausland/lambrecht-verspricht-ukraine-5000-helme-im-konflikt-mit-russland-17752622.html [Accessed 13 November 2022].

Federal Foreign Office (Germany) (2015) *Review 2014: Crisis, Order, Europe*, Available from: www.auswaertiges-amt.de/blob/692042/cef1f6308ebdb0d2d7c62725089c4198/review2014-data.pdf [Accessed 28 November 2022].

Fehl, C. (2012) *Living with a Reluctant Hegemon: Explaining European Responses to US Unilateralism*, Oxford: Oxford University Press.

Feldenkrichen, M., Reiermann, C., Sauga, M. and Schlamp, H.-J. (2010) 'Machtkampf in der Kulisse', *Der Spiegel*, 22: 20–3.

Fernández Moreno, M., Braga, C.C.V. and Gomes, M.S. (2012) 'Trapped between many worlds: A post-colonial perspective on the UN mission in Haiti (MINUSTAH)', *International Peacekeeping*, 19(3): 377–92.

Feuerwerker, A. (2010) 'O Brasil e as FARC', Correio Braziliense, 21 July, Available from: www2.senado.leg.br/bdsf/bitstream/handle/id/46319/noticia.htm?sequence=1&isAllowed=y [Accessed 26 November 2022].

Finnemore, M. and Sikkink, K. (1998) 'International norm dynamics and political change', *International Organization*, 52(4): 887–917.

Fischer, S. (2019) *The Donbas conflict*, SWP Research Paper, 2019(RP 05), Berlin: Stiftung Wissenshaft und Politik [German Institute for International and Security Affairs].

Fix, L. (2018) 'The different "shades" of German power: Germany and EU foreign policy during the Ukraine conflict', *German Politics*, 27(4): 498–515.

Flemes, D. (2015) 'Brasil-Colombia: ¿de vecinos distantes a socios estratégicos?', *Iberoamericana*, XV(60): 171–4.

Flikke, G. (2015) *A Timeline for the Conflict and War in Ukraine*, Oslo: The Norwegian Atlantic Committee.

Fontaine, R. (2022) 'Washington's missing China strategy: To counter Beijing, the Biden administration needs to decide what it wants', *Foreign Affairs*, 14 January, Available from: www.foreignaffairs.com/articles/china/2022-01-14/washingtons-missing-china-strategy [Accessed 28 November 2022].

Forsberg, T. (2016) 'From Ostpolitik to "frostpolitik"? Merkel, Putin and German foreign policy towards Russia', *International Affairs*, 92(1): 21–42.

Franchini, M.A. and Viola, E. (2019) 'Myths and images in global climate governance, conceptualization and the case of Brazil (1989–2019)', *Revista Brasileira de Política Internacional*, 62(2): e005.

Freedom House (2022) 'India', in *Freedom in the World 2021*, Available from: https://freedomhouse.org/country/india/freedom-world/2021 [Accessed 23 November 2022].

Fuchs, A. and Vadlamannati, K.C. (2013) 'The needy donor: An empirical analysis of India's aid motives', *World Development*, 44: 110–28.

Gady, F.-S. (2016) 'US General asks India for more military assistance in Afghanistan', *The Diplomat*, 14 August, Available from: https://thediplomat.com/2016/08/us-general-asks-india-for-more-military-assistance-in-afghanistan [Accessed 24 November 2022].

Gady, F.-S. (2019) 'India delivers two Mi-24V attack helicopters to Afghanistan', *The Diplomat*, 21 May, Available from: https://thediplomat.com/2019/05/india-delivers-two-mi-24v-attack-helicopters-to-afghanistan [Accessed 23 November 2022].

Galariotis, I. and Gianniou, M. (2022) 'EU Foreign Policy Incoherence in the United Nations: The Case of the Middle East', in D. Bouris, D. Huber and M. Pace (eds) *Routledge Handbook of EU–Middle East Relations*, Abingdon, New York: Routledge, pp 169–80.

Ganguly, S. (2002) *Conflict Unending: Indo–Pakistani Tensions Since 1947*, New York, Chichester: Columbia University Press.

Gaouette, N., Hansler, J., Starr, B. and Liebermann, O. (2021) 'The last US military planes have left Afghanistan, marking the end of the United States' longest war', CNN Politics, 31 August, Available from: https://edition.cnn.com/2021/08/30/politics/us-military-withdraws-afghanistan/index.html [Accessed 23 November 2022].

Gaskarth, J. (2017) 'Rising powers, responsibility, and international society', *Ethics & International Affairs*, 31(3): 287–311.

Gauck, J. (2014) 'Deutschlands Rolle in der Welt – Anmerkungen zu Verantwortung, Normen und Bündnissen', Der Bundespräsident, 31 January, Available from: www.bundespraesident.de/SharedDocs/Reden/DE/Joachim-Gauck/Reden/2014/01/140131-Muenchner-Sicherheitsko nferenz.html [Accessed 28 November 2022].

Gauthier, A. and John de Sousa, S. (2006) 'Brazil in Haiti: Debate over the peacekeeping mission', *FRIDE Comment*.

Gebauer, M. and Weiland, S. (2015) 'Angela Merkel und Wladimir Putin: Ukraine-Gipfel droht zu platzen', Spiegel Online, 9 February, Available from: www.spiegel.de/politik/deutschland/angela-merkel-und-wladimir-putin-ukraine-gipfel-droht-zu-platzen-a-1017510.html [Accessed 28 November 2022].

Gegg, M., Wittlich, H., Salmen, I., Meidinger, D. and Lehmann, H. (2020) 'Grafiken zum Coronavirus in Berlin: Der Anstieg bei den Infizierten lässt nach – aber nicht der bei den Todesfällen', Tagesspiegel, 17 April, Available from: www.tagesspiegel.de/berlin/der-anstieg-bei-den-infizierten-lasst-nach--aber-nicht-der-bei-den-todesfallen-8107201.html [Accessed 29 November 2022].

Gellner, D.N. (2007) 'Nepal and Bhutan in 2006: A year of revolution', *Asian Survey*, 47(1): 80–6.

Ghimire, Y. (2009) 'India, US interfering in Nepal's internal matter', The Indian Express, 23 April, Available from: http://archive.indianexpress.com/news/-india-us-interfering-in-nepal-s-internal-matter-/450173 [Accessed 25 November 2022].

Gladstein, D.L. and Reilly, N.P. (1985) 'Group decision making under threat: The tycoon game', *Academy of Management Journal*, 28(3): 613–27.

Goertz, G. (2006) *Social Science Concepts: A User's Guide*, Princeton, NJ, Oxford: Princeton University Press.

Goertz, G. and Mazur, A. (2008) 'Mapping Gender and Politics Concepts: Ten Guidelines', in G. Goertz and A. Mazur (eds) *Politics, Gender, and Concepts: Theory and Methodology*, Cambridge: Cambridge University Press, pp 14–44.

Gokhale, V. (2021) 'India's fog of misunderstanding surrounding Nepal–China relations', Carnegie India, 4 October, Available from: https://carneg ieindia.org/2021/10/04/india-s-fog-of-misunderstanding-surrounding-nepal-china-relations-pub-85416 [Accessed 25 November 2022].

Goren, N. (2020) 'It's time to empower Israel's Foreign Ministry – Opinion', *The Jerusalem Post*, 9 December, Available from: www.jpost.com/opinion/its-time-to-empower-the-foreign-ministry-651640 [Accessed 6 June 2022].

Gotev, G. (2014) 'EU leaders losing "propaganda war", says diplomat', Euractiv, 20 March, Available from: www.euractiv.com/section/global-eur ope/news/eu-leaders-losing-propaganda-war-says-diplomat [Accessed 28 November 2022].

Graf, A. and Lanz, D. (2013) 'Conclusions: Switzerland as a paradigmatic case of small-state peace policy?', *Swiss Political Science Review*, 19(3): 410–23.

Gstöhl, S. (2002) *Reluctant Europeans: Norway, Sweden, and Switzerland in the Process of Integration*, Boulder, CO, London: Lynne Rienner Publishers.

Guardian, The (2014) 'Russian armoured vehicles on the move in Crimea', 28 February, Available from: www.theguardian.com/world/2014/feb/28/gunmen-crimean-airports-ukraine [Accessed 26 November 2022].

Guardian, The (2020) 'Leaked coronavirus plan to quarantine 16m sparks chaos in Italy', 8 March, Available from: www.theguardian.com/world/2020/mar/08/leaked-coronavirus-plan-to-quarantine-16m-sparks-chaos-in-italy [Accessed 13 November 2022].

Haass, R.N. (1997) *The Reluctant Sheriff: The United States after the Cold War*, New York: Council on Foreign Relations Press.

Hachhethu, K. and Gellner, D.N. (2010) 'Nepal: Trajectories of Democracy and Restructuring of the State', in P.R. Brass (ed) *Routledge Handbook of South Asian Politics: India, Pakistan, Bangladesh, Sri Lanka, and Nepal*, London: Routledge, pp 131–46.

Hagan, J.D., Everts, P.P., Fukui, H. and Stempel, J.D. (2001) 'Foreign policy by coalition: Deadlock, compromise, and anarchy', *International Studies Review*, 3(2): 169–216.

Haidar, S. (2020) 'Experts raise concerns for India over US–Taliban agreement', The Hindu, 1 March, Available from: www.thehindu.com/news/international/experts-raise-concerns-for-india-over-us-taliban-agreement/article61968226.ece [Accessed 24 November 2022].

Haidar, S. (2021) 'India supports Afghan–Taliban dialogue, says Jaishankar', The Hindu, 2 April, Available from: www.thehindu.com/news/national/india-supports-afghan-taliban-dialogue-says-jaishankar/article61919348.ece [Accessed 24 November 2022].

Haidar, S. (2022a) 'For India, the buzzword now is "all-alignment"', The Hindu, 14 September, Available from: www.thehindu.com/opinion/lead/for-india-the-buzzword-now-is-all-alignment/article65887072.ece [Accessed 22 November 2022].

Haidar, S. (2022b) 'India reopens Embassy in Kabul', The Hindu, 24 June, Available from: www.thehindu.com/news/national/india-reopens-emba ssy-in-kabul/article65558557.ece [Accessed 24 November 2022].

Haidar, S. and Peri, D. (2016) 'Afghan army chief coming to India with revised wish list', The Hindu, 1 October, Available from: www.thehindu. com/news/national/Afghan-Army-chief-coming-to-India-with-revised-wish-list/article14507929.ece [Accessed 24 November 2022].

Hakim, P. (2004) 'The reluctant partner', Foreign Affairs, 83(1): 114–23.

Hall, I. (2016a) 'Multialignment and Indian foreign policy under Narendra Modi', The Round Table, 105(3): 271–86.

Hall, I. (2016b) 'The Persistence of Nehruvianism in India's Strategic Culture', in A.J. Tellis, A. Szalwinski and M. Wills (eds) Understanding Strategic Cultures in the Asia-Pacific, Seattle and Washington, DC: National Bureau of Asian Research, pp 141–67.

Halperin, M.H. and Boyer, S.P. (2007) 'Introduction: A World of Rules', in M.H. Halperin (ed) Power and Superpower: Global Leadership and Exceptionalism in the 21st Century, New York: Century Foundation Press, pp 1–13.

Hansel, M. and Oppermann, K. (2016) 'Counterfactual reasoning in foreign policy analysis: The case of German nonparticipation in the Libya intervention of 2011', Foreign Policy Analysis, 12(2): 109–27.

Harig, C. and Kenkel, K.M. (2017) 'Are rising powers consistent or ambiguous foreign policy actors? Brazil, humanitarian intervention and the "graduation dilemma"', International Affairs, 93(3): 625–41.

Harnisch, S. (2012) 'Conceptualizing in the minefield: Role theory and foreign policy learning', Foreign Policy Analysis, 8(1): 47–69.

Harnisch, S. (2015) 'Deutschlands Rolle in der Libyen-Intervention: Führung, Gefolgschaft und das angebliche Versagen der Regierung Merkel', in M. Kneuer (ed) Standortbestimmung Deutschlands: Innere Verfasstheit und internationale Verantwortung, Baden Baden: Nomos, pp 85–122.

Hellmann, G. (2016) 'Germany's world: Power and followership in a crisis-ridden Europe', Global Affairs, 2(1): 3–20.

Hellmann, G., Jacobi, D. and Stark Urrestarazu, U. (eds) (2015) "Früher, entschiedener und substantieller"? Die neue Debatte über Deutschlands Aussenpolitik, Wiesbaden: VS.

Helms, L., van Esch, F. and Crawford, B. (2019) 'Merkel III: From committed pragmatist to "conviction leader"?', German Politics, 28(3): 350–70.

Hermann, C.F. (2012) 'What We Do When Things Go Wrong', in C.F. Hermann (ed) When Things Go Wrong: Foreign Policy Decision Making under Adverse Feedback, New York: Routledge, pp 1–10.

Herszenhorn, D.M. (2013) 'Amid unrest, Ukrainian president defends choice on accords', The New York Times, 2 December, Available from: www.nyti mes.com/2013/12/03/world/europe/ukraine-unrest.html?_r=0 [Accessed 28 November 2022].

Hesse, M., Neubacher, A., Neukirch, R., Pauly, C., Reiermann, C. and Schepp, M. (2014) 'Teure Führung', Spiegel Online, 16 March, Available from: www.spiegel.de/politik/teure-fuehrung-a-9d0e5b16-0002-0001-0000-000126014785?context=issue [Accessed 4 November 2022].

Hindu, The (2016) 'Avoid interference: Nepal to India', 3 November, Available from: www.thehindu.com/news/national/Avoid-interference-Nepal-to-India/article60619377.ece [Accessed 25 November 2022].

Hindustan Times (2017) 'India never interferes in Nepal's internal matters: Envoy', 26 January, Available from: www.hindustantimes.com/world-news/india-never-interferes-in-nepal-s-internal-matters-envoy/story-PIjpGs5AAGo7dt6M2mL3WL.html [Accessed 25 November 2022].

Hirst, M. (2007) 'La intervención Sudamericana en Haiti', FRIDE Comentario, April.

Holsti, K.J. (1970) 'National role conceptions in the study of foreign policy', *International Studies Quarterly*, 14(3): 233–309.

Holsti, K.J. (2010) 'Exceptionalism in American foreign policy: Is it exceptional?', *European Journal of International Relations*, 17(3): 381–404.

House of Commons (2016) *HC 119 Libya: Examination of Intervention and Collapse and the UK's Future Policy Options*, London.

Hübner, K. (2012) 'German crisis management and leadership: From ignorance to procrastination to action', *Asia Europe Journal*, 9(2–4): 159–77.

Hudson, V.M. (2005) 'Foreign policy analysis: Actor-specific theory and the ground of International Relations', *Foreign Policy Analysis*, 1(1): 1–30.

Huju, K. (2022) 'Saffronizing diplomacy: The Indian Foreign Service under Hindu nationalist rule', *International Affairs*, 98(2): 423–41.

Human Rights Watch (2015) *"Like We Are Not Nepali": Protest and Police Crackdown in the Terai Region of Nepal*, New York, Available from: www.hrw.org/sites/default/files/report_pdf/nepal1015_forupload.pdf [Accessed 24 November 2022].

Human Rights Watch (2019) *No Escape from Hell: EU Policies Contribute to Abuse of Migrants in Libya*, 21 January, Available from: www.hrw.org/report/2019/01/21/no-escape-hell/eu-policies-contribute-abuse-migrants-libya [Accessed 28 November 2022].

Hurrell, A. (1992) 'Brazil As a Regional Great Power: A Study in Ambivalence', in I.B. Neumann (ed) *Regional Great Powers in International Politics*, London: Macmillan, pp 16–48.

Hurrell, A. (2006) 'Hegemony, liberalism and global order: What space for would-be great powers?', *International Affairs*, 82(1): 1–19.

Hurrell, A. and Sengupta, S. (2012) 'Emerging powers, North–South relations and global climate politics', *International Affairs*, 88(3): 463–84.

ICG (International Crisis Group) (2004) *A New Chance for Haiti?*, ICG Latin America/Caribbean Report 10, 18 November. Available from: https://www.ecoi.net/en/file/local/1285957/2107_1306313630_neu.pdf [Accessed 3 February 2023].

ICG (2012a) *Nepal's Constitution (I): Evolution Not Revolution*, Available from: www.crisisgroup.org/asia/south-asia/nepal/nepal-s-constitution-i-evolution-not-revolution [Accessed 24 November 2022].

ICG (2012b) *Stirring up the South China Sea (I)*, Available from: www.crisisgroup.org/asia/south-east-asia/south-china-sea/stirring-south-china-sea-i [Accessed 28 November 2022].

ICG (2015) *The Ukraine Crisis: Risks of Renewed Military Conflict after Minsk II*, Available from: www.crisisgroup.org/europe-central-asia/eastern-europe/ukraine/ukraine-crisis-risks-renewed-military-conflict-after-minsk-ii [Accessed 28 November 2022].

ICG (2016) *Nepal's Divisive New Constitution: An Existential Crisis*, Available from: www.crisisgroup.org/asia/south-asia/nepal/nepal%E2%80%99s-divisive-new-constitution-existential-crisis [Accessed 24 November 2022].

ICG (2022) 'CrisisWatch Nepal', Available from: www.crisisgroup.org/crisiswatch/database?location[]=39 [Accessed 26 November 2022].

Ikenberry, G.J. (1999) 'Institutions, strategic restraint, and the persistence of American postwar order', *International Security*, 23(3): 43–78.

Ikenberry, G.J. and Kupchan, C.A. (1990) 'The Legitimation of Hegemonic Power', in D.P. Rapkin (ed) *World Leadership and Hegemony*, Boulder, CO: Lynne Rienner, pp 49–69.

Ischinger, W. (2022) 'Germany's Ukraine problem: Europe's largest country needs time to adjust to a dangerous new world', Foreign Affairs, 10 August, Available from: www.foreignaffairs.com/germany/germanys-ukraine-problem [Accessed 30 October 2022].

Jacob, H. (2022) 'Narendra Modi government's neighbourhood policy', *International Politics*, 59(1): 24–43.

Jaffrelot, C. (2010) 'Hindu Nationalism and Power', in N.G. Jayal and P.B. Mehta (eds) *The Oxford Companion to Politics in India*, New Delhi: Oxford University Press, pp 205–18.

Jaffrelot, C. (2021) *Modi's India: Hindu Nationalism and the Rise of Ethnic Democracy*, Princeton, NJ: Princeton University Press.

Jaleel, M. (2015) 'Why Bihar is tracking a group of protesters on a border bridge', The Indian Express, 4 October, Available from: https://indianexpress.com/article/political-pulse/why-bihar-is-tracking-a-group-of-protesters-on-a-border-bridge [Accessed 26 November 2022].

Janis, I.L. and Mann, L. (1979) *Decision Making: A Psychological Analysis of Conflict, Choice, and Commitment*, New York: Free Press, Collier Macmillan.

Janssen, H. (2012) 'Die Schönredner', Spiegel Politik, 19 November, Available from: www.spiegel.de/politik/deutschland/muenchhausen-check-merkel-und-schaeuble-ueber-die-euro-krise-a-867147.html [Accessed 28 April 2016].

Jervis, R. (ed) (1976) *Perception and Misperception in International Politics*, Princeton, NJ: Princeton University Press.

Jha, P. (2015) 'Nepali secularism has pronounced Hindu tilt', Hindustan Times, 16 September, Available from: www.hindustantimes.com/analysis/nepali-secularism-has-pronounced-hindu-tilt/story-W4C6pf4mDCK7eJsYvnGfOL.html [Accessed 25 November 2022].

Jha, P. (2016a) 'End of the Madhesi blockade: What it means for Nepal', Hindustan Times, 6 February, Available from: www.hindustantimes.com/opinion/end-of-the-madhesi-blockade-what-it-means-for-nepal/story-JixO1gsdWLprj8Lc6G0hQL.html [Accessed 24 November 2022].

Jha, P. (2016b) 'Opinion: A Maoist's burden in Nepal', The New York Times, 7 August, Available from: www.nytimes.com/2016/08/08/opinion/a-maoists-burden-in-nepal.html [Accessed 25 November 2022].

Jha, P. (2017a) 'How India steadily lost all its leverage in Nepal', Hindustan Times, 23 December, Available from: www.hindustantimes.com/opinion/how-india-steadily-lost-all-its-leverage-in-nepal/story-eyZcX3OOVJRVqJvP7EXH0O.html [Accessed 25 November 2022].

Jha, P. (2017b) 'India "shifts" stance, asks Madhesis to drop demand for changes in constitution', Hindustan Times, 16 May, Available from: www.hindustantimes.com/india-news/india-shifts-stance-asks-madhesis-to-drop-demand-for-changes-in-constitution/story-29xYUN0YoCCnRFTSiyOWOP.html [Accessed 25 November 2022].

Jha, P. (2017c) 'India must firmly push for Madhesi inclusion with the Nepali president', Hindustan Times, 18 April, Available from: www.hindustantimes.com/authors/india-must-firmly-push-for-madhesi-inclusion-with-the-nepali-president/story-WHz8glB8xIJSepSqf3CcnI.html [Accessed 25 November 2022].

Jha, P. (2017d) 'Nepal PM Deuba's visit reflects a changed political context between India and its neighbour', Hindustan Times, 24 August, Available from: www.hindustantimes.com/india-news/nepal-pm-deuba-s-visit-reflects-a-changed-political-context-between-india-and-its-neighbour/story-mlqdYFC6U8Kgkl102RZjCK.html [Accessed 25 November 2022].

Jobe, J.B. (2003) 'Cognitive psychology and self-reports: Models and methods', *Quality of Life Research: An International Journal of Quality of Life Aspects of Treatment, Care and Rehabilitation*, 12(3): 219–27.

Joffe, J. (2011) 'Eine Regierung ohne Kiel und Kompass', Zeit Online, 25 March, Available from: www.zeit.de/politik/ausland/2011-03/deutschland-libyen-aussenpolitik [Accessed 28 November 2022].

John, R.B.S. (2020) *Bolivia: Geopolitics of a Landlocked State*, Abingdon: Routledge.

Johnson, I. (2022) 'Biden's grand China strategy: Eloquent but inadequate', Council on Foreign Relations, 27 May, Available from: www.cfr.org/in-brief/biden-china-blinken-speech-policy-grand-strategy [Accessed 28 November 2022].

Jones, E. (2010) 'Merkel's folly', *Survival: Global Politics and Strategy*, 53(3): 21–38.

Jones, L. and Hameiri, S. (2021) *Fractured China: How State Transformation is Shaping China's Rise*, Cambridge: Cambridge University Press.

Joshi, S. (2016) 'The pivot through Kabul', The Hindu, 1 November, Available from: www.thehindu.com/opinion/lead/The-pivot-through-Kabul/article15881161.ece [Accessed 24 November 2022].

Kaarbo, J. (2012) *Coalition Politics and Cabinet Decision Making: A Comparative Analysis of Foreign Policy Choices*, Ann Arbor, MI: University of Michigan Press.

Kaarbo, J. and Beasley, R.K. (2008) 'Taking it to the extreme: The effect of coalition cabinets on foreign policy', *Foreign Policy Analysis*, 4(1): 67–81.

Kaarbo, J. and Cantir, C. (2013) 'Role conflict in recent wars: Danish and Dutch debates over Iraq and Afghanistan', *Cooperation and Conflict*, 48(4): 465–83.

Kahler, M. (2013) 'Rising powers and global governance: Negotiating change in a resilient status quo', *International Affairs*, 89(3): 711–29.

Kajsiu, B. (2019) 'The Colombian Right: The political ideology and mobilization of Uribismo', *Canadian Journal of Latin American and Caribbean Studies*, 44(2): 204–24.

Kamradt-Scott, A. (2018) 'What Went Wrong? The World Health Organization from Swine Flu to Ebola', in A. Kruck, K. Oppermann and A. Spencer (eds) *Political Mistakes and Policy Failures in International Relations*, Cham: Palgrave Macmillan, pp 193–215.

Kapur, S.P. and Ganguly, S. (2010) *India, Pakistan, and the Bomb: Debating Nuclear Stability in South Asia*, New York: Columbia University Press.

Kassimeris, C. (2008) 'The inconsistency of United States foreign policy in the aftermath of the Cyprus invasion: The Turkish arms embargo and its termination', *Journal of Modern Greek Studies*, 26(1): 91–114.

Katju, V. (2015) 'Ghani and India: Circles of separation', Gateway House, 29 April, Available from: www.gatewayhouse.in/ghani-and-india-circles-of-separation [Accessed 24 November 2022].

Katsoulas, S. (2022) 'The "Nixon letter" to Ecevit: An untold story of the eve of the Turkish invasion of Cyprus in 1974', *The International History Review*, 44(2): 318–34.

Katzenstein, P.J. (ed) (1996) *The Culture of National Security: Norms and Identity in World Politics*, New York: Columbia University Press.

Kaufman, M. and García-Escribano, M. (2013) 'Unleashing Brazil's growth', IMF Blog, 27 November, Available from: www.imf.org/en/Blogs/Artic les/2013/11/27/unleasing-brazils-growth [Accessed 26 November 2022].

Kaul, I., Grunberg, I. and Stern, M.A. (1999) *Global Public Goods: International Cooperation in the 21st Century*, New York: Oxford University Press.

Kaura, V. (2017) 'India–Afghanistan relations in the Modi-Ghani era', *Indian Journal of Asian Affairs*, 30(1/2): 29–46.

Kaura, V. and Rani, M. (2020) 'India's neighbourhood policy during 2014–2019: Political context and policy outcomes', *Indian Journal of Public Administration*, 66(1): 10–27.

Kawaguti, L.M.V. (2015) 'A tensa relação entre militares e jornalistas no início da missão no Haiti', in E.P. Hamman (ed) *Brasil e Haiti: Reflexões sobre os 10 anos da missão de paz e o futuro da cooperação após 2016*, Rio de Janeiro: Instituto Igarapé, pp 44–51.

Keilani, F. and Eckstein, C. (2021) 'Berliner Verwaltung: Im Chaos haben sich viele eingerichtet', Neuer Zürcher Zeitung, 1 November, Available from: www.nzz.ch/international/wieso-laeuft-doch-ld.1652124 [Accessed 29 November 2022].

Kenkel, K.M. and Destradi, S. (2019) 'Explaining emerging powers' reluctance to adopt intervention norms: Normative contestation and hierarchies of responsibility', *Revista Brasileira de Política Internacional*, 62(1).

Kenkel, K.M. and Martins, M.T. (2016) 'Emerging powers and the notion of international responsibility: Moral duty or shifting goalpost?', *Brazilian Political Science Review*, 10(1): e0003.

Kenkel, K.M. and Stefan, C.G. (2016) 'Brazil and the responsibility while protecting initiative: Norms and the timing of diplomatic support', *Global Governance*, 22: 41.

Kermani, S. (2022) 'Afghanistan gurdwara attack: Sikhs say "We don't feel safe"', BBC News, 18 June, Available from: www.bbc.com/news/world-asia-61852956 [Accessed 24 November 2022].

Khan, O.H. (2021) *Strengthening Regional Trade Integration in South Asia*, Singapore: Springer.

Khilnani, S. , Kumar, R. , Mehta, P.B. , Menon, P. , Raghavan, S. , Saran, S. , Nilekani, N. and Varadarjan, S. (2012) *NonAlignment 2.0: A Foreign and Strategic Policy for India in the Twenty First Century*, Centre for Policy Research, 29 February, Available from: https://cprindia.org/briefsreports/nonalignment-2-0-a-foreign-and-strategic-policy-for-india-in-the-twe nty-first-century [Accessed 22 November 2022].

Khobragade, V. (2016) 'India–Nepal relations: Engagement and estrangement', *World Affairs: The Journal of International Issues*, 20(3): 146–63.

Kiddey, R. (2019) 'Reluctant refuge: An activist archaeological approach to alternative refugee shelter in Athens (Greece)', *Journal of Refugee Studies*, 33(3): 599–621.

Kindleberger, C.P. (1973) *The World in Depression, 1929–1939*, Berkeley, Los Angeles, CA: University of California Press.

Kine, P. (2022) 'Biden leaves no doubt: "Strategic ambiguity" toward Taiwan is dead', Politico, 19 September, Available from: www.politico.com/news/2022/09/19/biden-leaves-no-doubt-strategic-ambiguity-toward-taiwan-is-dead-00057658 [Accessed 28 November 2022].

King, C., Ferraro, G., Wisner, S.C., Etienne, S., Lee, S. and Bartels, S.A. (2021) '"MINUSTAH is doing positive things just as they do negative things": Nuanced perceptions of a UN peacekeeping operation amidst peacekeeper-perpetrated sexual exploitation and abuse in Haiti', *Conflict, Security & Development*, 21(6): 749–79.

Kinkartz, S. (2022) 'Germany's Social Democrats, Russia, and past mistakes', Deutsche Welle, 22 April, Available from: www.dw.com/en/germanys-social-democrats-russia-and-the-failures-of-the-past/a-61556022 [Accessed 28 November 2022].

Kirkpatrick, D.D. and El-Naggar, M. (2011) 'Qaddafi's grip falters as his forces take on protesters', The New York Times, 21 February, Available from: www.nytimes.com/2011/02/22/world/africa/22libya.html [Accessed 7 August 2022].

Kirste, K. and Maull, H.W. (1996) 'Zivilmacht und Rollentheorie', *Zeitschrift für Internationale Beziehungen*, 3(2): 283–312.

Klingst, M. (2014) 'USA-Besuch: Steinmeier auf "Mission Neuanfang"', Zeit Online, 27 February, Available from: www.zeit.de/politik/ausland/2014-02/steinmeier-usa-besuch-kerry [Accessed 28 November 2022].

Koenig, N. (2011) 'The EU and the Libyan crisis – In quest of coherence?', *The International Spectator*, 46(4): 11–30.

Koenig, N. (2014) 'Between conflict management and role conflict: The EU in the Libyan crisis', *European Security*, 23(3): 250–69.

Koeth, W. (2016) 'Leadership revised: How did the Ukraine crisis and the annexation of Crimea affirm Germany's leading role in EU foreign policy?', *Lithuanian Annual Strategic Review*, 14(1): 101–16.

Kruck, A., Oppermann, K. and Spencer, A. (2018a) 'Introduction: Mistakes and Failures in International Relations', in A. Kruck, K. Oppermann and A. Spencer (eds) *Political Mistakes and Policy Failures in International Relations*, Cham: Palgrave Macmillan, pp 1–29.

Kruck, A., Oppermann, K. and Spencer, A. (eds) (2018b) *Political Mistakes and Policy Failures in International Relations*, Cham: Palgrave Macmillan.

Kuimova, A. and Wezeman, S.T. (2021) 'Transfers of major arms to Afghanistan between 2001 and 2020', Stockholm International Peace Research Institute (SIPRI), 3 September, Available from: www.sipri.org/commentary/topical-backgrounder/2021/transfers-major-arms-afghanistan-between-2001-and-2020 [Accessed 24 November 2022].

Kundnani, H. (2014) *The Paradox of German Power*, London: Hurst & Co.

Kundnani, H. and Pond, E. (2015) 'Germany's real role in the Ukraine crisis: Caught between East and West', *Foreign Affairs*, 94(2): 173–7.

Kurbjuweit, D. (2022) 'Scholz' Fernsehansprache: Engagierte Beiseitesteherei', Spiegel Online, 8 May, Available from: www.spiegel.de/politik/deutschl and/olaf-scholz-rede-zum-8-mai-engagierte-beiseitesteherei-kommen tar-a-e20305bc-48db-4310-bb2f-15a66aa492aa [Accessed 9 May 2022].

La Nación (2008) 'Chávez: las FARC no son terroristas', 12 January, Available from: www.lanacion.com.ar/el-mundo/chavez-las-farc-no-son-terroris tas-nid978386 [Accessed 26 November 2022].

Lake, D.A. (1993) 'Leadership, hegemony, and the international economy: Naked emperor or tattered monarch with potential?', *International Studies Quarterly*, 37(4): 459–89.

Lake, D.A. and Powell, R. (1999) *Strategic Choice and International Relations*, Princeton, NJ: Princeton University Press.

Lanz, D. and Mason, S. (2012) *Switzerland's Experiences in Peace Mediation*, The Finnish Institute of International Affairs Report, 32.

Larsen, H.B.L. (2014) *Great Power Politics and the Ukrainian Crisis: NATO, EU and Russia after 2014*, Copenhagen: Danish Institute for International Studies.

Larson, D.W. and Shevchenko, A. (2010) 'Status seekers: Chinese and Russian responses to US primacy', *International Security*, 34(4): 63–95.

LatinNews (2003) 'FARC attempts to regain initiative', *Latin American Regional Report – Andean Group*, 9 September.

LatinNews (2005) 'Weekly report 15 March 2005', *Latin American Weekly Report*, WR-05-11.

LatinNews (2008a) 'Brazil: Lula reshapes foreign policy', *Weekly Report*, 4 December.

LatinNews (2008b) 'Weekly report 24 July 2008', *Latin American Weekly Report*, WR-08-29.

LatinNews (2009a) 'Colombia reassesses its foreign policy priorities', *Latin America Regional Report – Andean Group*, 03/2009.

LatinNews (2009b) Latin American Weekly Report – 12 March 2009, WR-09-10.

Laub, Z. (2017) 'The US War in Afghanistan', Council on Foreign Relations, Available from: www.cfr.org/timeline/us-war-afghanistan [Accessed 24 November 2022].

Leader Maynard, J. and Haas, M.L. (eds) (2023) *The Routledge Handbook of Ideology and International Relations*, Abingdon, New York: Routledge.

Legro, J.W. (2005) *Rethinking the World: Great Power Strategies and International Order*, Ithaca, NY, London: Cornell University Press.

Leira, H. (2013) ' "Our entire people are natural born friends of peace": The Norwegian foreign policy of peace', *Swiss Political Science Review*, 19(3): 338–56.

Lewis, B.P. and Linder, D.E. (1997) 'Thinking about choking? Attentional processes and paradoxical performance', *Personality & Social Psychology Bulletin*, 23(9): 937–44.

Lindsay, J.M. (1992) 'Congress and foreign policy: Why the Hill matters', *Political Science Quarterly*, 107(4): 607–28.

Lindsay, J.M. (2018) 'Invitation to Struggle: Congress, the President, and US Foreign Policy', in D.S. Hamilton and T. Tiilikainen (eds) *Domestic Determinants of Foreign Policy in the European Union and the United States*, Washington, DC: Center for Transatlantic Relations and Finnish Institute of International Affairs, pp 145–61.

Long, T. (2022) *A Small State's Guide to Influence in World Politics*, New York: Oxford University Press.

Lowe, C.J. (1967) *The Reluctant Imperialists: British Foreign Policy 1878–1902*, London: Routledge & Kegan Paul.

Maass, R. (2015) 'India donates Mi-25 helicopters to Afghanistan', UPI, 23 December, Available from: www.upi.com/Defense-News/2015/12/23/India-donates-Mi-25-helicopters-to-Afghanistan/1591450899641 [Accessed 23 November 2022].

Mackenzie, J. and Pawlak, J. (2011) 'EU stops short on Libya no-fly zone, air strikes', Reuters, 11 March, Available from: www.reuters.com/article/us-libya-eu-summit-idUKTRE72A6DI20110311 [Accessed 9 August 2022].

Magnoli, D. (2004) 'Notícias do Haiti', Folha de S. Paulo, 30 September, Available from: www1.folha.uol.com.br/fsp/opiniao/fz3009200407.htm [Accessed 18 June 2022].

Majumder, S. (2015) 'Why India is concerned about Nepal's constitution', BBC News, 22 September, Available from: www.bbc.com/news/world-asia-india-34313280 [Accessed 25 November 2022].

Malik, S. and Gani, A. (2014) 'Ukraine crisis: Deal signed in effort to end Kiev standoff', The Guardian, 21 February, Available from: www.theguardian.com/world/2014/feb/21/ukraine-crisis-president-claims-deal-with-opposition-after-77-killed-in-kiev [Accessed 28 November 2022].

Manager Magazin (2014) 'Ukraine: Merkel droht Russland mit Sanktionen', 14 March, Available from: www.manager-magazin.de/politik/deutschland/ukraine-merkel-droht-russland-mit-sanktionen-a-958697.html [Accessed 28 November 2022].

Mann, J. (2013) *The Obamians: The Struggle inside the White House to Redefine American Power*, New York: Viking.

Maris, G. and Manoli, P. (2022) 'Greece, Germany and the Eurozone crisis: Preferences, strategies and power asymmetry', *German Politics*, 31(2): 281–301.

Marlow, I. (2018) 'India's diplomat shortage leaves it far behind China', The Economic Times, 31 August, Available from: https://economictimes.ind iatimes.com/news/politics-and-nation/indias-diplomat-shortage-leaves-it-far-behind-china/articleshow/65617912.cms?from=mdr [Accessed 24 November 2022].

Marthoz, J.-P. (2012) The Challenges and Ambiguities of South Africa's Foreign Policy, Norwegian Peacebuilding Resource Center (NOREF), September, Available from: www.files.ethz.ch/isn/153069/1d25c90556f0a 6f66548551220c882e8.pdf [Accessed 6 February 2023].

Martins Filho, J.R. (2006) 'As forças armadas brasileiras e o plano Colômbia', in C. Castro (ed) *Amazônia e Defesa Nacional*, Rio de Janeiro: FGV, pp 13–29.

Martins y Miguel, F. (2010) 'De olho em vaga na ONU, Lula abre embaixada até em ilha', O Tempo, 14 September, Available from: www.otempo.com. br/politica/de-olho-em-vaga-na-onu-lula-abre-embaixada-ate-em-ilha-1.368544 [Accessed 26 November 2022].

Matzner, S.H. (2018) 'The Politics of Intervention', University of Edinburgh Thesis, Available from: https://era.ed.ac.uk/bitstream/han dle/1842/33279/Matzner2018.pdf?sequence=1&isAllowed=y [Accessed 28 November 2022].

Maull, H.W. (2000a) 'Germany and the use of force: Still a "civilian power"?', *Survival*, 42(2): 56–80.

Maull, H.W. (2000b) 'German foreign policy, post-Kosovo: Still a "civilian power"?', *German Politics*, 9(2): 1–24.

Maull, H.W. (2011) 'Deutsche Außenpolitik: Orientierungslos', *Zeitschrift für Politikwissenschaft*, 21(1): 95–119.

Maull, H.W. (2012) 'Außenpolitische Entscheidungsprozesse in Krisenzeiten', *Politik und Zeitgeschichte*, 10: 34–40.

Maull, H.W. (2017) 'The politics of the EU', *Asian Journal of Comparative Politics*, 2(1): 55–69.

Mazenotti, P. and Lourenço, I. (2010) 'Lula teve boa relação com o Congresso nos oito anos de governo', Agência Brasil, 31 December, Available from: http://memoria.ebc.com.br/agenciabrasil/noticia/2010-12-31/lula-teve-boa-relacao-com-congresso-nos-oito-anos-de-governo [Accessed 26 November 2022].

McDermott, M.L. (1998) 'Race and gender cues in low-information elections', *Political Research Quarterly*, 51(4): 895–918.

MEA (Ministry of External Affairs, India) (no date) *India and Afghanistan: A Development Partnership*, Available from: https://mea.gov.in/Uploads/Publ icationDocs/176_india-and-afghanistan-a-development-partnership.pdf [Accessed 24 November 2022].

MEA (2011) 'Text of Agreement on Strategic Partnership between the Republic of India and the Islamic Republic of Afghanistan', 4 October, Available from: https://mea.gov.in/bilateral-documents.htm?dtl/5383/Text+of+Agreement+on+Strategic+Partnership+between+the+Repub lic+of+India+and+the+Islamic+Republic+of+Afghanistan [Accessed 23 November 2022].

MEA (2014) 'Speech by External Affairs Minister at the meeting of International Contact Group (ICG) on Afghanistan in New Delhi', 16 January, Available from: www.mea.gov.in/Speeches-Statements.htm?dtl/22755/Speech+by+External+Affairs+Minister+at+the+meeting+of+International+Contact+Group+ICG+on+Afghanistan+in+New+Delhi [Accessed 24 November 2022].

MEA (2015) 'Statement by External Affairs Minister on calling attention motion on "Situation in Nepal and State of Indo-Nepal Relation" in Rajya Sabha', 3 December, Available from: www.mea.gov.in/Speeches-Statements.htm?dtl/26104/Statement_by_External_Affairs_Minister_on_Calling_Attention_Motion_on_Situation_in_Nepal_and_State_of_IndoNepal_Relation_in_Rajya_Sabha_December_03_20 [Accessed 25 November 2022].

MEA (2017) 'Joint Statement on the 2nd Strategic Partnership Council Meeting between India and Afghanistan', 11 September, New Delhi, Available from: https://mea.gov.in/bilateral-documents.htm?dtl/28936/Joint_Statement_on_the_2nd_Strategic_Partnership_Council_Meeting_between_India_and_Afghanistan_New_Delhi_September_11_2017 [Accessed 24 November 2022].

MEA (2020a) 'EAM's remarks at Afghanistan 2020 Conference on November 2020', Available from: www.mea.gov.in/Speeches-Statements.htm?dtl/33235/EAMs_Remarks_at_Afghanistan_2020_Conference_on_24_November_2020 [Accessed 24 November 2022].

MEA (2020b) 'Official spokesperson's response to media queries on the issuance of a Joint Declaration between the Afghan and US Governments in Kabul and signing of the US–Taliban Agreement in Doha', 29 February, Available from: www.mea.gov.in/response-to-queries.htm?dtl/32442/Official_Spokespersons_response_to_media_queries_on_the_the_issuance_of_a_Joint_Declaration_between_the_Afghan_and_US_Gover nments_in_Kabul_and_signing [Accessed 24 November 2022].

MEA (2021a) 'Prime Minister participates in G20 Extraordinary Summit on Afghanistan', 12 October, Available from: www.mea.gov.in/press-relea ses.htm?dtl/34384/Prime_Minister_participates_in_G20_Extraordinary_Summit_on_Afghanistan [Accessed 24 November 2022].

MEA (2021b) 'Statement by External Affairs Minister at the UNSC debate on the UN Assistance Mission in Afghanistan', 22 June, Available from: www.mea.gov.in/Speeches-Statements.htm?dtl/33937/Statement_by_External_Affairs_Minister_at_the_UNSC_Debate_on_the_UN_Assistance_Mission_in_Afghanistan_June_22_2021 [Accessed 24 November 2022].

MEA (2022) 'Indian Foreign Service', Available from: www.mea.gov.in/indian-foreign-service.htm [Accessed 24 November 2022].

Mearsheimer, J.J. (2001) *The Tragedy of Great Power Politics*, New York: W.W. Norton.

Mehta, A.K. (2020) 'Political Dynamics in Nepal and Security Implications', in S. Kumar (ed) *India's National Security Annual Review 2019*, New Delhi: Routledge, pp 124–141.

Meiser, J.W. (2015) *Power and Restraint: The Rise of the United States, 1898–1941*, Washington, DC: Georgetown University Press.

Meltzer, H., Bebbington, P., Brugha, T., Farrell, M., Jenkins, R. and Lewis, G. (2000) 'The reluctance to seek treatment for neurotic disorders', *Journal of Mental Health*, 9(3): 319–27.

Menezes, H. and Vieira, M. (2022) 'Explaining Brazil as a rising state, 2003-2014: The role of policy diffusion as an international regulatory instrument', *Journal of International Relations and Development*, 25: 107–28.

Mercer, J. (2005) 'Prospect theory and political science', *Annual Review of Political Science*, 8(1): 1–21.

Merkur.de (2011) 'Deutschland hofft nach Tod Gaddafis auf neues Zeitalter für Libyen', 20 October, Available from: www.merkur.de/welt/merkel-gadaffi-tod-ein-wichtiger-libyer-zr-1455683.html [Accessed 28 November 2022].

MFA (Ministry of Foreign Affairs, Pakistan) (2019) 'Record of weekly press briefing by spokesperson on 17 January 2019', 17 January, Available from: https://mofa.gov.pk/record-of-weekly-press-briefing-by-spokesperson-on-17-january-2019-2 [Accessed 24 November 2022].

MHA (Ministry of Home Affairs) (India) (2021) 'Owing to prevailing security situation in Afghanistan. All Afghan nationals henceforth must travel to India only on e-Visa', Press Information Bureau, 25 August, Available from: www.mha.gov.in/sites/default/files/AfghanEvisa_25082021.pdf [Accessed 24 November 2022].

Michael, A. (2013) *India's Foreign Policy and Regional Multilateralism*, Houndmills, Basingstoke, New York: Palgrave Macmillan.

Miglani, S. (2016) 'Afghans push India for more arms, despite Pakistan's wary eye', Reuters, 23 August, Available from: www.reuters.com/article/us-afghanistan-india-defence-idUSKCN10X29W [Accessed 24 November 2022].

Milne, S. (2011) 'If the Libyan war was about saving lives, it was a catastrophic failure', The Guardian, 26 October, Available from: www.theguardian. com/commentisfree/2011/oct/26/libya-war-saving-lives-catastrophic-fail ure [Accessed 28 November 2022].

Ministério da Defesa (2022) 'Histórico brasileiro no concerto das nações', Available from: www.gov.br/defesa/pt-br/arquivos/lai/relacoes-interna cionais/historico_brasileiro_no-concerto_das_nacoes.pdf [Accessed 18 June 2022].

Ministério das Relações Exteriores (2008) 'Notícias do Itamaraty (Entrevista do Ministro Celso Amorim ao jornal O Estado de S. Paulo)', 15 March, Available from: www.gov.br/mre/pt-br/centrais-de-conteudo/publicac oes/discursos-artigos-e-entrevistas/ministro-das-relacoes-exteriores/entr evistas-mre/entrevista-concedida-pelo-ministro-das-relacoes-exteriores-embaixador-celso-amorim-ao-jornal-o-estado-de-sao-paulo-brasilia-df-16-03-2008 [Accessed 26 November 2022].

Ministério das Relações Exteriores (2008a) 'Entrevista coletiva Luiz Inácio Lula da Silva, por ocasião de encontro com a Senadora Ingrid Betancourt', 8 November, Available from: www.gov.br/mre/pt-br/centrais-de-conteudo/ publicacoes/discursos-artigos-e-entrevistas/presidente-da-republica/pre sidente-da-republica-federativa-do-brasil-entrevistas/entrevista-coletiva-concedida-pelo-presidente-da-republica-luiz-inacio-lula-da-silva-por-ocas iao-de-encontro-com-a-senadora-ingrid-betancourt-sao-paulo-5-12-2008 [Accessed 26 November 2022].

Ministério das Relações Exteriores (2008b) 'Para Pinheiro Guimarães, AL precisa de um Plano Marshall', Available from: https://www.gov.br/mre/ pt-br/centrais-de-conteudo/publicacoes/discursos-artigos-e-entrevistas/ secretaria-geral/entrevistas/para-pinheiro-guimaraes-al-precisa-de-um-plano-marshall-entrevista-secretario-geral-embaixador-samuel-pinhe iro-guimaraes-ao-jornal-valor-economico-14-07-2008 [Accessed 24 March 2023].

Ministry of Defence (India) (2015) 'Upgradation of defence equipment in Afghanistan', Available from: http://164.100.24.220/loksabhaquestions/ annex/6/AU2165.pdf [Accessed 3 February 2023].

Mintz, A. and DeRouen, K.R. (2010) Understanding Foreign Policy Decision Making, Cambridge: Cambridge University Press.

MINUSTAH (La Mission des Nations Unies pour la stabilisation en Haïti) (2022) 'Composition militaires', Available from: https://minustah.unmissi ons.org/composition-militaires [Accessed 13 June 2022].

Miskimmon, A. (2012) 'German foreign policy and the Libya crisis', German Politics, 21(4): 392–410.

Mitra, D. (2021a) "India's cold feet in granting Afghans emergency visas disheartening: Ambassador', The Wire, 13 December, Available from: https://thewire.in/diplomacy/afghanistan-ambassador-india-emerge ncy-visa-taliban [Accessed 24 November 2022].

Mitra, D. (2021b) 'India's new visa policy for Afghans is in limbo, leaving thousands tense', The Wire, 7 September, Available from: https://thew ire.in/south-asia/indias-new-visa-policy-for-afghans-is-in-limbo-leaving-thousands-tense [Accessed 24 November 2022].

Mitra, S.K. (2003) 'The reluctant hegemon: India's self-perception and the South Asian strategic environment', Contemporary South Asia, 12(3): 399–417.

Miyamoto, S. (2008) 'A política externa e operações de paz', Revista Brasileira de Estudos Políticos, 98: 361–94.

Molina, G.P. (2021) 'The failure of "Plan Colombia" and of US–Colombian counterinsurgency under President Álvaro Uribe', Strife Journal, 15/16: 61–70.

Moravcsik, A. (1997) 'Taking preferences seriously: A liberal theory of international politics', International Organization, 51(4): 513–53.

Moravcsik, A. and Schimmelfennig F. (2019) 'Liberal Intergovernmentalism', in A. Wiener, T.A. Börzel and T. Risse (eds) European Integration Theory, 3rd edition, Oxford: Oxford University Press, pp 64–84.

Mullen, R.D. (2016) 'India–Afghanistan Relations', in S. Ganguly (ed) Engaging the World, Oxford: Oxford University Press, pp 105–30.

Muni, S.D. (2015a) 'India's Nepal policy needs caution, not grandstanding', The Wire, 23 September, Available from: https://thewire.in/diplom acy/indias-nepal-policy-needs-caution-not-grandstanding [Accessed 25 November 2022].

Muni, S.D. (2015b) 'Nepal's new constitution: Towards progress or chaos?', Economic & Political Weekly, L(40): 15–19.

Münkler, H. (2015) Macht in der Mitte: Die neuen Aufgaben Deutschlands in Europa, Hamburg: Edition Körber-Stiftung.

Murtazashvili, J.B. (2016) 'Afghanistan in 2015: A year of fragmentation', Asian Survey, 56(1): 187–98.

Mützenich, R. (2015) 'Deutschland – Vom Trittbrettfahrer zur Führungsmacht wider Willen?', Zeitschrift für Außen- und Sicherheitspolitik, 8(1): 273–87.

Narlikar, A. (2010) New Powers: How to Become One and How to Manage Them, London: Hurst & Co.

Niedermeier, P. (2011) 'German policy on Libya: Right on substance, short on style', American Institute for Contemporary German Studies (AICGS), 25 March, Available from: www.aicgs.org/2011/03/german-policy-on-libya-right-on-substance-short-on-style [Accessed 28 November 2022].

Nolte, D. (2010) 'How to compare regional powers: Analytical concepts and research topics', *Review of International Studies*, 36(4): 889–993.

Nordlinger, E.A. (1996) *Isolationism Reconfigured: American Foreign Policy for a New Century*, Princeton, NJ: Princeton University Press.

NPR (2011) 'Germany draws criticism for sitting out Libya effort', 11 May, Available from: www.npr.org/2011/05/11/136177993/germany-draws-criticism-for-sitting-out-libya-effort?t=1660037495411 [Accessed 28 November 2022].

Nymalm, N. and Plagemann, J. (2019) 'Comparative exceptionalism: Universality and particularity in foreign policy discourses', *International Studies Review*, 21(1): 12–37.

OAS (Organization of American States) (2006) 'Statement on Haiti (Core Group)', 11 January, Available from: www.oas.org/en/media_center/press_release.asp?sCodigo=CG1-ENG.

Oliveira, E. and Damé, L. (2008) 'Lula afirma que a instabilidade na América do Sul é sinal de vida', O Globo, 24 May: 4.

Olson, M. (1965) *The Logic of Collective Action: Public Goods and the Theory of Groups*, Cambridge, MA: Harvard University Press.

Oltermann, P. (2015) 'Jürgen Habermas's verdict on the EU/Greece debt deal – full transcript', The Guardian, 16 July Available from: www.theg uardian.com/commentisfree/2015/jul/16/jurgen-habermas-eu-greece-debt-deal [Accessed 28 April 2016].

O'Neill, B. (2001) 'Risk aversion in international relations theory', *International Studies Quarterly*, 45(4): 617–40.

Opitz, C., Pfeifer, H. and Geis, A. (2022) 'Engaging with public opinion at the micro-level: Citizen dialogue and participation in German foreign policy', *Foreign Policy Analysis*, 18(1): 1–20.

Oppermann, K. (2012) 'National role conceptions, domestic constraints and the new "normalcy" in German foreign policy: The Eurozone crisis, Libya and beyond', *German Politics*, 21(4): 502–19.

Oppermann, K. and Spencer, A. (2016) 'Studying fiascos: Bringing public and foreign policy together', *Journal of European Public Policy*, 23(5): 643–52.

Oppermann, K., Brummer, K. and van Willigen, N. (2017) 'Coalition governance and foreign policy decision-making', *European Political Science*, 16(4): 489–501.

Oswald, V. (2005) 'Desafio renovado no Haiti: ONU prorroga missão chefiada pelo Brasil. General Heleno deverá ser substituído', O Globo, 23 June: 32.

Paliwal, A. (2017) *My Enemy's Enemy: India in Afghanistan from the Soviet Invasion to the US Withdrawal*, Noida: HarperCollins.

Palshikar, S. (2015) 'The BJP and Hindu nationalism: Centrist politics and majoritarian impulses', *South Asia: Journal of South Asian Studies*, 38(4): 719–35.

Pandit, R. (2021) 'Afghan soldiers, military cadets undergoing training in India stare at an uncertain future', The Times of India, 17 August, Available from: https://timesofindia.indiatimes.com/india/afghan-soldiers-military-cadets-undergoing-training-in-india-stare-at-an-uncertain-future/articles how/85386667.cms [Accessed 23 November 2022].

Pant, H.V. (2008) Contemporary Debates in Indian Foreign and Security Policy: India Negotiates Its Rise in the International System, New York, Basingstoke: Palgrave Macmillan.

Pant, H.V. (2010) 'India in Afghanistan: A test case for a rising power', Contemporary South Asia, 18(2): 133–53.

Pant, H.V. and Paliwal, A. (2019) 'India's Afghan dilemma is tougher than ever', Foreign Policy, 19 February, Available from: https://foreignpolicy.com/2019/02/19/indias-afghan-dilemma-is-tougher-than-ever [Accessed 24 November 2022].

Parajulee, R.P. (2000) The Democratic Transition in Nepal, Lanham, MD: Rowman & Littlefield.

Pardesi, M.S. (2015) 'Is India a great power? Understanding great power status in contemporary international relations', Asian Security, 11(1): 1–30.

Parkes, A. (2019) 'Considered chaos: Revisiting Pakistan's "strategic depth" in Afghanistan', Strategic Analysis, 43(4): 297–309.

Paterson, W.E. (2011) 'The reluctant hegemon? Germany moves centre stage in the European Union', Journal of Common Market Studies, 39(1): 57–75.

Patrick, S. (2002) 'Multilateralism and Its Discontents: The Causes and Consequences of US Ambivalence', in S. Patrick and S. Forman (eds) Multilateralism and US Foreign Policy: Ambivalent Engagement, Boulder, CO, London: Lynne Rienner Publishers, pp 1–44.

Patrick, S. (2010) 'Irresponsible stakeholders: The difficulty of integrating rising powers', Foreign Affairs, 89(6): 44–53.

Payandeh, M. (2011) 'The United Nations, military intervention, and regime change in Libya', Virginia Journal of International Law, 52(2).

Pelinka, A., Bischof, G. and Gehler, M. (2017) Austrian Foreign Policy in Historical Context, Abingdon: Routledge.

Pennock, J.R. and Chapman, J.W. (eds) (1972) Coercion, Chicago, IL: Aldine Atherton Inc.

Pierce, R. (1991) 'The Executive divided against itself: Cohabitation in France, 1986–1988', Governance, 4(3): 270–94.

Pinsker, R. (2003) 'Drawing a line in the Taiwan Strait: "Strategic ambiguity" and its discontents', Australian Journal of International Affairs, 57(2): 353–68.

Plagemann, J. and Destradi, S. (2019) 'Populism and foreign policy: The case of India', Foreign Policy Analysis, 15(2): 283–301.

Plagemann, J., Destradi, S. and Narlikar, A. (eds) (2020) India Rising: A Multilayered Analysis of Ideas, Interests, and Institutions, New Delhi: Oxford University Press.

Pollack, J.D. (1996) 'China's Taiwan strategy: A point of no return?', *The China Journal*, 36: 111–16.

Port, E.R., Montgomery, L.L., Heerdt, A.S. and Borgen, P.I. (2001) 'Patient reluctance toward Tamoxifen use for breast cancer primary prevention', *Annals of Surgical Oncology*, 8(7): 580–5.

Portari, D. and Garcia, J.C. (2010) 'Entrevista – Celso Amorim', Instituto de Pesquisa Econômica Aplicada (IPEA), 13 July, Available from: www.ipea. gov.br/desafios/index.php?option=com_content&view=article&id=25:ent revista-celso-amorim&catid=30&Itemid=23 [Accessed 14 February 2023].

Posen, B.R. (2014) *Restraint: New Foundation for US Grand Strategy*, Ithaca, NY: Cornell University Press.

Prys, M. (2010) 'Hegemony, domination, detachment: Differences in regional powerhood', *International Studies Review*, 12(4): 479–504.

Pubby, M. (2015) 'India delivers 3 Cheetal helicopters to Afghanistan', The Economic Times, 13 July, Available from: https://economictimes.indiati mes.com/news/defence/india-delivers-3-cheetal-helicopters-to-afghanis tan/articleshow/47038529.cms?from=mdr [Accessed 23 November 2022].

Puhl, J. (2022) 'Poland's prime minister on Ukraine war and energy crisis: "Germany's policies have done tremendous damage to Europe"', Spiegel International, 9 September, Available from: www.spiegel.de/intern ational/poland-s-prime-minister-on-ukraine-war-and-energy-crisis-a-aabb65a3-e0ba-4ba8-9f0c-1c967874e8b5 [Accessed 31 October 2022].

Putnam, R.D. (1988) 'Diplomacy and domestic politics: The logic of two-level games', *International Organization*, 42(3): 427–60.

Quaid, K.A. and Morris, M. (1993) 'Reluctance to undergo predictive testing: The case of Huntington Disease', *American Journal of Medical Genetics*, 45(1): 41–5.

Rabello, J.B. (2010) 'PT e FARC, uma antiga relação ideológica que encontrou abrigo no governo brasileiro', O Estado de S. Paulo, Blog, 24 July, Available from: https://politica.estadao.com.br/blogs/joao-bosco/ pt-e-farcs-uma-antiga-relacao-ideologica-que-encontrou-abrigo-no-gove rno-brasileiro [Accessed 26 November 2022].

Rae, R. (2021) *Kathmandu Dilemma: Resetting India–Nepal Ties*, New York: Vintage Books.

Rainio-Niemi, J. (2014) *The Ideological Cold War: The Politics of Neutrality in Austria and Finland*, Hoboken, NJ: Taylor & Francis.

Raj, Y. (2019) '"Why isn't India there": Trump signals military presence in Afghanistan', Hindustan Times, 3 January, Available from: www.hindust antimes.com/world-news/why-isn-t-india-there-trump-signals-military-presence-in-afghanistan/story-2SLEVZZ8xj7yJxeevkeOsN.html [Accessed 24 November 2022].

Rajagopalan, R. (2008) *Fighting Like a Guerrilla, The Indian Army and Counterinsurgency*, London: Routledge.

Rathbun, B.C. (2007) 'Uncertain about uncertainty: Understanding the multiple meanings of a crucial concept in International Relations theory', *International Studies Quarterly*, 51(3): 533–57.

Rathbun, B.C. and Pomeroy, C. (2022) 'See no evil, speak no evil? Morality, evolutionary psychology, and the nature of international relations', *International Organization*, 76(3): 656–89.

Redd, S.B. and Mintz, A. (2013) 'Policy perspectives on national security and foreign policy decision making', Policy Studies Journal, 41: S11–S37.

Renshon, J. and Renshon, S.A. (2008) 'The theory and practice of foreign policy decision making', *Political Psychology*, 29(4): 509–36.

Reulmann, S. (2022) 'Gutmann: Höhere Erwartungen an Deutschland', ZDF Heute, 11 September, Available from: www.zdf.de/nachrichten/poli tik/us-botschafterin-gutmann-kritik-bundesregierung-100.html [Accessed 31 October 2022].

Reuters (2010) 'Brazil's Lula to leave with record-high popularity', 16 December, Available from: www.reuters.com/article/us-brazil-lula-poll-idUSTRE6BF4O620101216 [Accessed 7 June 2022].

Reuters (2014) 'Finland warns Russia sanctions could spell "economic crisis"', 6 August, Available from: www.euractiv.com/section/europe-s-east/news/finland-warns-russia-sanctions-could-spell-economic-crisis [Accessed 28 November 2022].

RFI (Radio France Internationale) (2010) 'Gabon says ties with France are no longer exclusive', 19 August, Available from: www.rfi.fr/en/africa/20100819-gabon-says-ties-france-are-no-longer-exclusive [Accessed 29 November 2022].

RFI (2012) 'Gabon opposition angered by Hollande meeting Ali Bongo', 5 July, Available from: www.rfi.fr/en/africa/20120705-gabon-opposit ion-angered-hollande-meeting-ali-bongo [Accessed 29 November 2022].

Rhinard, M. (2009) 'European cooperation on future crises: Toward a public good?', *Review of Policy Research*, 26(4): 439–55.

Rinke, A. (2011) 'Eingreifen oder nicht? Warum sich die Bundesregierung in der Libyen-Frage enthielt', *Internationale Politik*, 4: 44–52.

Rinke, A. (2014a) 'Ukraine-Krise: Warum Merkel auf Sanktionen gegen Russland pocht', Manager Magazin, 11 September, Available from: www.manager-magazin.de/politik/artikel/a-991103.html [Accessed 28 November 2022].

Rinke, A. (2014b) 'Wie Putin Berlin verlor: Moskaus Annexion der Krim hat die deutsche Russland-Politik verändert', Internationale Politik, 33–45.

Rinke, A. (2015) 'Vermitteln, verhandeln, verzweifeln: Wie der Ukraine-Konflikt zur westlich-russischen Dauerkrise wurde', Internationale Politik, 2015(January/February): 8–21.

Risse, T. (2000) '"Let's argue!" Communicative action in world politics', *International Organization*, 54(1): 1–39.

Risse, T. and Sikkink, K. (1999) 'The Socialization of International Human Rights Norms into Domestic Practices: Introduction', in K. Sikkink, S.C. Ropp and T. Risse (eds) *The Power of Human Rights: International Norms and Domestic Change*, Cambridge: Cambridge University Press, pp 1–38.

Risse-Kappen, T. (1995) *Bringing Transnational Relations Back In: Non-State Actors, Domestic Structures and International Institutions*, Cambridge: Cambridge University Press.

Rodman, P.W. (1985) 'The Imperial Congress', *The National Interest*, 1: 26–35.

Rohlfing, I. (2014) *Case Studies and Causal Inference: An Integrative Framework*, Basingstoke: Palgrave Macmillan.

Rosecrance, R. (1976) *America as an Ordinary Country: US Foreign Policy and the Future*, Ithaca, NY: Cornell University Press.

Rosen, S. and Tesser, A. (1970) 'On reluctance to communicate undesirable information: The MUM effect', *Sociometry*, 33(3): 253–63.

Rosenfelder, L. and Teevs, C. (2020) 'Rot-rot-grüner Senat: Wie Corona die Schwächen der Berliner Politik offenlegt', Spiegel Politik, 4 October, Available from: www.spiegel.de/politik/deutschland/corona-in-berlin-wie-die-krise-die-schwaechen-von-rot-rot-gruen-offenlegt-a-fa0eda09-3a68-4fa3-a254-654c8e8a5d75 [Accessed 29 November 2022].

Rossi, C. (2003) 'Brasil não vai considerar FARC como grupo terrorista', Folha de S. Paulo, 3 February, Available from: www1.folha.uol.com.br/folha/mundo/ult94u52304.shtml [Accessed 26 November 2022].

Rovner, J. (2020) 'Intelligence in the Biden administration', War on the Rocks, 25 November, Available from: https://warontherocks.com/2020/11/intelligence-in-the-biden-administration [Accessed 28 November 2022].

Rovner, J. (2022) 'How long can Biden muddle through on China?', War on the Rocks, 26 January, Available from: https://warontherocks.com/2022/01/how-long-can-biden-muddle-through-on-china [Accessed 28 November 2022].

Roy, S. (2015) 'Make seven changes to your Constitution: India tells Nepal', The Indian Express, 24 September, Available from: https://indianexpress.com/article/world/neighbours/make-seven-changes-to-your-constitution-address-madhesi-concerns-india-to-nepal [Accessed 25 November 2022].

Roy, S. (2020) 'India attends intra-Afghan talks in Doha, Jaishankar says peace process must be Afghan-led', The Indian Express, 12 September, Available from: https://indianexpress.com/article/india/india-to-attend-intra-afghan-talks-in-doha-today-jaishankar-to-join-virtually-6592958 [Accessed 24 November 2022].

RTVE (2008) 'Ingrid Betancourt, rescatada por el Ejército colombiano que tendió una trampa a las FARC', RTVE.es, 2 July, Available from: www.rtve.es/noticias/20080702/ingrid-betancourt-rescatada-ejercito-colombiano-tendio-trampa-farc/111351.shtml [Accessed 22 August 2022].

Russett, B. (1985) 'The mysterious case of vanishing hegemony; or, is Mark Twain really dead?', *International Organization*, 39(2): 207–31.

Sander, L. (2008) 'Lula critica as FARC, mas evita classificação', *Folha de S. Paulo*, 16 January, Available from: www1.folha.uol.com.br/fsp/mundo/ft1601200802.htm [Accessed 26 November 2022].

Sartori, G. (1970) 'Concept misformation in comparative politics', *American Political Science Review*, 64(4): 1033–53.

Sartori, G. (1984) 'Guidelines for Concept Analysis', in G. Sartori (ed) *Social Science Concepts: A Systematic Analysis*, Beverley Hills, CA, London, New Delhi: SAGE, pp 15–95.

Sawatzky, N.A. (2022) *Understanding the Impact of Emotional Stress on Crisis Decision Making*, Cham: Springer International Publishing, Palgrave Macmillan.

Schafer, M. and Crichlow, S. (2010) *Groupthink Versus High-Quality Decision Making*, New York, Chichester: Columbia University Press.

Schaffer, T.C. and Schaffer, H.B. (2016) *India at the Global High Table: The Quest for Regional Primacy and Strategic Autonomy*, Washington, DC: Brookings Institution Press.

Scharpf, F.W. (1997) 'Economic integration, democracy and the welfare state', *Journal of European Public Policy*, 4(1): 18–36.

Schäuble, W. (2010) 'Wie Europa gestärkt aus der Krise kommt', Available from: www.wolfgang-schaeuble.de/index.php?id=36&textid=1375&page=2 [Accessed 28 April 2016].

Schelling, T.C. (1966) *Arms and Influence*, New Haven, CT: Yale University Press.

Schild, J. (2013) 'Leadership in hard times: Germany, France, and the management of the Eurozone crisis', *German Politics and Society*, 31(1): 24–47.

Schimmelfennig, F. (2015) 'Liberal intergovernmentalism and the Euro area crisis', *Journal of European Public Policy*, 22(2): 177–95.

Schlieben, M. (2011) 'Guido Westerwelle: Großer Parteichef, miserabler Minister', Zeit Online, 4 April, Available from: www.zeit.de/politik/deutschland/2011-04/westerwelle-kommentar/komplettansicht [Accessed 28 November 2022].

Schmitz, G.P. and Wittrock, P. (2014) 'Alle schauen auf Merkel', Spiegel Online, 3 March, Available from: www.spiegel.de/politik/ausland/krim-krise-merkel-setzt-bei-putin-auf-diplomatie-a-956704.html [Accessed 28 November 2022].

Schneider, H. (2011) 'Obama, Merkel disagree on Libya, economics. But they're working on it', The Washington Post, 7 June, Available from: www.washingtonpost.com/politics/obama-merkel-disagree-on-libya-economics-but-theyre-working-on-it/2011/06/07/AGjrHRLH_story.html [Accessed 28 November 2022].

Schoeller, M.G. (2017) 'Providing political leadership? Three case studies on Germany's ambiguous role in the Eurozone crisis', *Journal of European Public Policy*, 24(1): 1–20.

Scholz, O. (2022) 'Policy statement by Olaf Scholz, Chancellor of the Federal Republic of Germany and Member of the German Bundestag, 27 February 2022 in Berlin', Die Bundesregierung [The Federal Government], 27 February, Available from: www.bundesregierung.de/breg-en/search/policy-statement-by-olaf-scholz-chancellor-of-the-federal-republic-of-germany-and-member-of-the-german-bundestag-27-february-2022-in-berlin-2008378 [Accessed 31 October 2022].

Schreier, M. (2012) *Qualitative Content Analysis in Practice*, Los Angeles, CA: SAGE.

Schumacher, T. (2020) 'The EU and its neighbourhood: The politics of muddling through', *JCMS: Journal of Common Market Studies*, 58(S1): 187–201.

Schweller, R.L. (2006) Unanswered Threats: Political Constraints on the Balance of Power, Princeton, NJ, Oxford: Princeton University Press.

Schweller, R.L. and Pu, X. (2011) 'After unipolarity: China's visions of international order in an era of US decline', *International Security*, 36(1): 41–72.

Seibel, W. (2015) 'Arduous learning or new uncertainties? The emergence of German diplomacy in the Ukrainian crisis', *Global Policy*, 6(1): 56–72.

Senado Federal (2004) *Diário do Senado Federal n. 80 de 2004*, Brasília.

Senado Noticias (2009) 'José Nery defende moção de repúdio à instalação de bases norte-americanas na Colômbia', 26 August, Available from: www12.senado.leg.br/noticias/materias/2009/08/26/jose-nery-defende-mocao-de-repudio-a-instalacao-de-bases-norte-americanas-na-colombia [Accessed 24 July 2022].

Sengupta, S. (2020) 'Deciphering India's Foreign Policy on Climate Change', in J. Plagemann, S. Destradi and A. Narlikar (eds) *India Rising: A Multilayered Analysis of Ideas, Interests, and Institutions*, New Delhi: Oxford University Press, pp 167–94.

Shambaugh, D. (2011) 'Coping with a conflicted China', *The Washington Quarterly*, 34(1): 7–27.

Sharma, C.K., Destradi, S. and Plagemann, J. (2020) 'Partisan federalism and subnational governments' international engagements: Insights from India', *Publius: The Journal of Federalism*, 50(4): 566–92.

Sil, R. and Katzenstein, P.J. (2010) 'Analytic eclecticism in the study of world politics: Reconfiguring problems and mechanisms across research traditions', *Perspectives on Politics*, 8(2): 411–31.

Simon, H.A. (1955) 'A behavioral model of rational choice', *The Quarterly Journal of Economics*, 69(1): 99–118.

Simon, H.A. (1979) 'Bounded Rationality', in K.N. Waltz (ed) *Theory of International Politics*, Long Grove, IL: Waveland Press Inc, pp 15–18.

Singh, B. (2016) 'India's neighbourhood policy: Geopolitical fault line of its Nepal policy in the post-2015 Constitution', *Journal of International Area Studies*, 23(1): 59–75.

SIPRI (Stockholm International Peace Research Institute) (2022) 'Database arms transfers 2020–2021', Available from: https://armstrade.sipri.org/armstrade/html/export_values.php [Accessed 4 October 2022].

Slhessarenko, S. (2004) 'Pronunciamento de Serys Slhessarenko em 12/05/2004', Senado Federal, 12 May, Available from: https://legis.senado.leg.br/diarios/ver/826?sequencia=89 [Accessed 14 February 2023].

Smith, D. (2022) 'Biden's Taiwan vow creates confusion not clarity – and raises China tensions', The Guardian, 23 May, Available from: www.theguardian.com/us-news/2022/may/23/biden-taiwan-china-strategic-ambiguity-us-foreign-policy [Accessed 28 November 2022].

Snidal, D. (1985) 'The limits of hegemonic stability theory', *International Organization*, 39(4): 579–614.

Soares de Lima, M.R. and Hirst, M. (2006) 'Brazil as an intermediate state and regional power: Action, choice and responsibilities', *International Affairs*, 82(1): 21–40.

Spektor, M. (2010) 'Brazil: The Underlying Ideas of Regional Policies', in D. Flemes (ed) *Regional Leadership in the Global System: Ideas, Interests and Strategies of Regional Powers*, Farnham: Ashgate, pp 191–206.

Sperling, J. (2022) 'German Multilateralism after the Cold War', in K. Larres, H. Moroff and R. Wittlinger (eds) *Oxford Handbook of German Politics*, Oxford: Oxford University Press, pp 561–88.

Spiegel Online (2011a) 'A serious mistake of historic dimensions: Libya crisis leaves Berlin isolated', 28 March, Available from: www.spiegel.de/international/germany/a-serious-mistake-of-historic-dimensions-libya-crisis-leaves-berlin-isolated-a-753498.html [Accessed 28 November 2022].

Spiegel Online (2011b) 'Germany's Libya contribution: Merkel Cabinet approves AWACS for Afghanistan', 23 March, Available from: www.spiegel.de/international/world/germany-s-libya-contribution-merkel-cabinet-approves-awacs-for-afghanistan-a-752709.html [Accessed 28 November 2022].

Spiegel Online (2011c) 'Krieg in Libyen: Mehr als hundert Deutsche am Nato-Einsatz beteiligt', 9 September, Available from: www.spiegel.de/poli tik/deutschland/krieg-in-libyen-mehr-als-hundert-deutsche-am-nato-eins atz-beteiligt-a-785381.html [Accessed 28 November 2022].

Spiegel Online (2011d) 'Krieg in Libyen: Nato verzichtet auf deutsche Bomben-Hilfe', 29 June, Available from: www.spiegel.de/politik/deutschl and/krieg-in-libyen-nato-verzichtet-auf-deutsche-bomben-hilfe-a-771 347.html [Accessed 28 November 2022].

Spiegel Online (2011e) 'Libyen-Kurs: Rösler fällt Westerwelle in den Rücken', 26 August, Available from: www.spiegel.de/politik/deutschland/libyen-kurs-roesler-faellt-westerwelle-in-den-ruecken-a-782678.html [Accessed 28 November 2022].

Spiegel Online (2011f) 'Luftkrieg in Libyen: General Maggie ruft zum Kampf', 30 March, Available from: www.spiegel.de/politik/ausland/luftkr ieg-in-libyen-general-maggie-ruft-zum-kampf-a-753849.html [Accessed 28 November 2022].

Spiegel Online (2011g) 'Post-Gaddafi-Ära: Berlin hofft in Libyen auf zweite Chance', 23 August, Available from: www.spiegel.de/politik/ausland/ post-gaddafi-aera-berlin-hofft-in-libyen-auf-zweite-chance-a-781641. html [Accessed 28 November 2022].

Spiegel Online (2012a) 'Unreliable partners? Germany's reputation in NATO has hit rock bottom', 17 May, Available from: www.spiegel.de/internatio nal/world/criticism-of-germany-s-military-role-in-the-nato-alliance-a-833503.html [Accessed 24 March 2023].

Spiegel Online (2012b) 'Merkel zur Schuldenpolitik: "Keine Euro-Bonds, solange ich lebe"', 26 June, Available from: www.spiegel.de/politik/ausl and/kanzlerin-merkel-schliesst-euro-bonds-aus-a-841115.html [Accessed 28 November 2022].

Spiegel Online (2014) 'Ukraine und Russland wollen über Waffenruhe verhandeln', 2 July, Available from: www.spiegel.de/politik/ausland/ukra ine-und-russland-wollen-ueber-waffenruhe-verhandeln-a-978889.html [Accessed 28 November 2022].

Spiegel Online (2015) 'Ukraine-Konflikt: Merkel, Putin, Hollande einigen sich auf Telefonat', 6 February, Available from: www.spiegel.de/politik/ ausland/ukraine-konflikt-merkel-putin-hollande-einigen-sich-auf-telefo nat-a-1017252.html [Accessed 28 November 2022].

Spiegel Online (2016) 'Westerwelle als Außenminister: Der Vielgescholtene, 18 March, Available from: www.spiegel.de/politik/deutschland/westerwe lle-gestorben-sein-aussenpolitisches-dilemma-a-1083152.html [Accessed 28 November 2022].

Spiegel Online International (2011) 'Currency crisis: German Central Bank opposed to Merkel's Euro course', 26 September, Available from: www.spie gel.de/international/europe/currency-crisis-german-central-bank-oppo sed-to-merkel-s-euro-course-a-788352.html [Accessed 29 April 2016].

Spiegel Online International (2015) '"The Fourth Reich": What some Europeans see when they look at Germany', 23 March, Available from: www.spiegel.de/international/germany/german-power-in-the-age-of-the-euro-crisis-a-1024714.html [Accessed 28 April 2016].

Standish, R. (2015) 'Guns, lies, and videotape: The war in Eastern Ukraine is back on in full', Foreign Policy, 26 January, Available from: https://foreig npolicy.com/2015/01/26/guns-lies-and-videotape-the-war-russia-putin-nato-in-eastern-ukraine-is-back-on-in-full [Accessed 28 November 2022].

Stargardter, G. (2018) 'General behind deadly Haiti raid takes aim at Brazil's gangs', Reuters, 29 November, Available from: www.reuters.com/article/ us-brazil-violence-insight/general-behind-deadly-haiti-raid-takes-aim-at-brazils-gangs-idUSKCN1NY0GM [Accessed 14 June 2022].

Steinbruner, J.D. (1974) *The Cybernetic Theory of Decision: New Dimensions of Political Analysis*, Princeton, NJ: Princeton University Press.

Steinmeier, F.-W. (2014) 'Vorwort von Bundesaußenminister Dr Frank-Walter Steinmeier', *Zeitschrift für Außen- und Sicherheitspolitik*, 8(1): 1–3.

Stokke, K. (2012) 'Peace-building as small state foreign policy', *International Studies*, 49(3–4): 207–31.

Stolte, C. (2015) *Brazil's Africa Strategy: Role Conception and the Drive for International Status*, New York: Palgrave Macmillan.

Strange, S. (1987) 'The persistent myth of lost hegemony', *International Organization*, 41(4): 551–74.

Strasheim, J. and Bogati, S. (2016) 'Nepal's quest for federalism: A driver of new violence', GIGA Focus Asia, 1, Available from: www.giga-hamburg. de/en/publications/giga-focus/nepal-s-quest-for-federalism-a-driver-of-new-violence [Accessed 24 November 2022].

Strøm, K., Müller, W.C. and Smith, D.M. (2010) 'Parliamentary control of coalition governments', *Annual Review of Political Science*, 13(1): 517–35.

Stuenkel, O. (2014) 'Can Brazil defend democracy in Venezuela?', Carnegie Endowment for International Peace, 9 April, Available from: https://carneg ieendowment.org/2014/04/09/can-brazil-defend-democracy-in-venezu ela/h7m0 [Accessed 22 July 2015].

Süddeutsche Zeitung (2011) 'Die Deutschen und der Krieg in Libyen – Westerwelle vollzieht Kehrtwende bei Nato-Militäreinsatz', 28 August, Available from: www.sueddeutsche.de/politik/die-deutschen-und-der-krieg-in-libyen-westerwelle-vollzieht-kehrtwende-bei-nato-militaereins atz-1.1135764 [Accessed 28 November 2022].

Swami, P. (2015) 'Afghanistan calls on India to step up military assistance', The Indian Express, 13 September, Available from: https://12ft.io/proxy?q=https%3A%2F%2Findianexpress.com%2Farticle%2Findia%2Findia-news-india%2Fafghanistan-calls-on-india-to-step-up-military-assistance%2F [Accessed 24 November 2022].

Szabo, S.F. (2014) 'Germany's commercial realism and the Russia problem', *Survival*, 56(5): 117–28.

Tagesspiegel (2011) 'Nach Libyen-Resolution: Deutschland erwägt offenbar Awacs-Einsatz in Afghanistan', 18 March, Available from: www.tagesspiegel.de/politik/deutschland-erwagt-offenbar-awacs-einsatz-in-afghanistan-7028860.html [Accessed 13 November 2022].

Taneja, K. (2017) 'India and the Afghan Taliban: Can Delhi contribute to an Afghan political reconciliation?', The Diplomat, 30 November, Available from: https://thediplomat.com/2017/11/india-and-the-afghan-taliban [Accessed 24 November 2022].

Tarapués Sandino, D.F. (2012) 'Colombia y Brasil en la lucha contra el crimen transnacional: Una revisión a sus posturas, acciones y estrategias de seguridad', in E.P. Buelvas, S. Jost and D. Flemes (eds) *Colombia y Brasil: ¿Socios estratégicos en la construcción de Suramérica?*, Bogotá: Editiroal Pontificia Universidad Javeriana, pp 423–52.

Terra (2009) 'Uribe virá ao Brasil agradecer ajuda em libertações das FARC', 9 February, Available from: www.terra.com.br/noticias/mundo/america-latina/uribe-vira-ao-brasil-agradecer-ajuda-em-libertacoes-das-farc,5688803f3f40b310VgnCLD200000bbcceb0aRCRD.html [Accessed 25 July 2022].

Tewari, R. (2017) 'Upset Madhesis say India no longer backs their agenda', The Print, 1 September, Available from: https://theprint.in/politics/upset-madhesis-say-india-no-longer-backs-agenda/8920/#:~:text=Another%20leader%20of%20the%20RJP,do%3B%20we%20have%20no%20option [Accessed 25 November 2022].

Tewes, H. (2002) *Germany, Civilian Power and the New Europe*, London: Palgrave Macmillan UK.

Thakur, R. (2013) 'R2P after Libya and Syria: Engaging emerging powers', *The Washington Quarterly*, 36(2): 61–76.

Thakur, R. (2016) 'The responsibility to protect at 15', *International Affairs*, 92(2): 415–34.

Tharoor, S. (2017) *The Paradoxical Prime Minister: Narendra Modi and His India*, New Delhi: Aleph.

t' Hart, P. (1990) *Groupthink in Government: A Study of Small Groups and Policy Failure*, Amsterdam and Rockland, MA: Swets & Zeitlinger.

Thies, C.G. (2017) 'Role theory and foreign policy analysis in Latin America', *Foreign Policy Analysis*, 13(3): 662–81.

Thiessen, M.A. (2022) 'Biden's flip-flop on defending Taiwan makes America look weak', The Washington Post, 24 March, Available from: https://www.washingtonpost.com/opinions/2022/05/24/biden-flipflop-defending-taiwan-undermines-deterrence/ [Accessed 28 November 2022].

Times of India, The (2015a) 'India has not imposed any blockade on Nepal: Sushma Swaraj', 8 December, Available from: https://timesofindia.indiatimes.com/india/india-has-not-imposed-any-blockade-on-nepal-sushma-swaraj/articleshow/50084655.cms [Accessed 25 November 2022].

Times of India, The (2015b) 'UN chief calls for lifting of blockade on Indo–Nepal border', 12 November, Available from: https://timesofindia.indiatimes.com/india/un-chief-calls-for-lifting-of-blockade-on-indo-nepal-border/articleshow/49747847.cms [Accessed 25 November 2022].

Times of India, The (2022) 'PM Narendra Modi continues to be most popular global leader with approval rating of 74%', 8 December. Available from: https://timesofindia.indiatimes.com/india/pm-narendra-modi-continues-to-be-most-popular-global-leader-with-approval-rating-of-74-survey/articleshow/93527036.cms [Accessed 6 February 2023].

Tisdall, S. (2011) 'Germany blocks plans for Libya no-fly zone', The Guardian, 15 March, Available from: www.theguardian.com/world/2011/mar/15/germany-blocks-libya-no-fly-zone [Accessed 14 February 2023].

TOLOnews (2016) 'India moves to scale up military aid to Afghanistan', 1 December, Available from: https://tolonews.com/afghanistan/india-moves-scale-military-aid-afghanistan [Accessed 24 November 2022].

TOLOnews (2019) 'Germany wants India to play a bigger role in Afghanistan', 19 July, Available from: https://tolonews.com/afghanistan/germany-wants-india-play-bigger-role-afghanistan [Accessed 24 November 2022].

Torres, S. (2011) 'General Ham visits Ramstein AOC responsible for Operation Odyssey Dawn air campaign', Ramstein Air Base, 23 March, Available from: www.ramstein.af.mil/News/Article-Display/Article/304432/general-ham-visits-ramstein-aoc-responsible-for-operation-odyssey-dawn-air-camp [Accessed 28 November 2022].

Traynor, I. (2010) 'Markets tremble as Angela Merkel plays for time over Greece rescue deal', The Guardian, 26 April, Available from: www.theguardian.com/business/2010/apr/26/markets-greece-rescue-imf-package [Accessed 28 April 2016].

Traynor, I. and Watt, N. (2011) 'Libya no-fly zone plan rejected by EU leaders', The Guardian, 11 March, Available from: www.theguardian.com/world/2011/mar/11/libya-no-fly-zone-plan-rejected [Accessed 9 August 2022].

Tversky, A. and Kahneman, D. (1974) 'Judgment under uncertainty: Heuristics and biases', Science, 185(4157): 1124–31.

UCDP (Uppsala Conflict Data Program) (2022a) 'Afghanistan', Available from: https://ucdp.uu.se/country/700 [Accessed 24 November 2022].

UCDP (2022b) 'Colombia', Available from: https://ucdp.uu.se/country/100 [Accessed 5 August 2022].

UCDP (2022c) 'FLRN', Available from: https://ucdp.uu.se/actor/765 [Accessed 26 November 2022].

UCDP (2022d) 'Government of Colombia – FARC', Available from: https://ucdp.uu.se/statebased/623 [Accessed 5 August 2022].

Uken, M. (2022) 'Swift und Waffenlieferungen: Und Deutschland trödelt hinterher', Zeit Online, 26 February, Available from: www.zeit.de/poli tik/2022-02/swift-waffenlieferungen-deutschland-ukraine [Accessed 31 October 2022].

UN (United Nations) (2005) '60/1. 2005 World Summit Outcome', UN General Assembly, Available from: www.un.org/en/development/desa/population/migration/generalassembly/docs/globalcompact/A_RES_6 0_1.pdf [Accessed 26 November 2022].

UN (2015) 'Unanimously adopting Resolution 2202 (2015), Security Council calls on parties to implement accords aimed at peaceful settlement in Eastern Ukraine', 17 February, Available from: https://press.un.org/en/2015/sc11785.doc.htm [Accessed 26 November 2022].

UNASUR (Union of South American Nations) (2009) 'Declaración de Santiago de Chile', Available from: http://sedici.unlp.edu.ar/bitstr eam/handle/10915/45638/UNASUR_-_Declaraci%C3%B3n_de_San tiago_de_Chile__4_p._.pdf?sequence=2&isAllowed=y [Accessed 26 November 2022].

UN Peacekeeping (2022a) 'MINUSTAH Fact Sheet', Available from: https://peacekeeping.un.org/en/mission/minustah [Accessed 13 June 2022].

UN Peacekeeping (2022b) 'Troop and police contributors', Available from: https://peacekeeping.un.org/en/troop-and-police-contributors [Accessed 13 June 2022].

UN Peacemaker (2015) 'Package of measures for the implementation of the Minsk agreements', Available from: https://peacemaker.un.org/sites/peacemaker.un.org/files/UA_150212_MinskAgreement_en.pdf [Accessed 28 November 2022].

UNSC (United Nations Security Council) (2004a) 'Resolution 1529 (2004)', Available from: https://digitallibrary.un.org/record/516210 [Accessed 26 November 2022].

UNSC (2004b) 'Resolution 1542 (2004)/adopted by the Security Council at its 4961st meeting, on 30 April 2004', Available from: https://digitallibr ary.un.org/record/520532 [Accessed 26 November 2022].

UNSC (2011a) 'Resolution 1970 (2011)', United Nations Security Council, Available from: https://documents-dds-ny.un.org/doc/UNDOC/GEN/N11/245/58/PDF/N1124558.pdf?OpenElement [Accessed 30 March 2023].

UNSC (2011b) 'Resolution 1973 (2011)', United Nations Security Council, Available from: https://digitallibrary.un.org/record/699777?ln=en [Accessed 26 November 2022].

UNSC (2011c) '6498th meeting', Available from: www.securitycouncilreport.org/atf/cf/%7B65BFCF9B-6D27-4E9C-8CD3-CF6E4FF96FF9%7D/Libya%20S%20PV%206498.pdf [Accessed 26 November 2022].

Upreti, B.C. (2016) 'India–Nepal relations: Complexities, misperceptions and irritants', *Indian Foreign Affairs Journal*, 2(11): 107–13.

US Department of State (2020) 'Agreement for bringing peace to Afghanistan', 29 February, Available from: www.state.gov/wp-content/uploads/2020/02/Agreement-For-Bringing-Peace-to-Afghanistan-02.29.20.pdf [Accessed 3 February 2023].

van Dongen, R. (2003) 'US places high value on Uribe's safety', *The Washington Times*, Available from: https://2001-2009.state.gov/m/ds/rls/22161.htm [Accessed 6 August 2022].

Varadarajan, S. (2010) 'The danger in India's Nepal policy', The Hindu, 16 August, Available from: www.thehindu.com/opinion/columns/siddharth-varadarajan/The-danger-in-Indias-Nepal-policy/article13101110.ece [Accessed 21 April 2011].

Vaughn, J. and Dunne, T. (2014) 'Leading from the front: America, Libya and the localisation of R2P', *Cooperation and Conflict*, 50(1): 29–49.

Veja (2011) 'Uribe reclamou de "imperialismo brasileiro" e disse que Lula não honrou promessas', 17 February, Available from: https://veja.abril.com.br/mundo/uribe-reclamou-de-imperialismo-brasileiro-e-disse-que-lula-nao-honrou-promessas [Accessed 6 August 2022].

Verbeek, B. (2017) *Decision-Making in Great Britain during the Suez Crisis: Small Groups and a Persistent Leader*, London: Routledge.

Villa, R.A.D. and Viana, M.T. (2010) 'Security issues during Lula's administration: From the reactive to the assertive approach', *Revista Brasileira de Política Internacional*, 53(spe): 91–114.

von Rohr, M. (2022) 'Das verspielte Vertrauen des Olaf Scholz', Spiegel Politik, 16 May, Available from: www.spiegel.de/politik/deutschland/news-olaf-scholz-die-gruenen-nrw-wahl-ukraine-krieg-nato-wladimir-putin-a-a94b4414-c9b9-4a79-97f3-f7f1cbfcb9a9 [Accessed 28 November 2022].

Waltz, K.N. (1979) *Theory of International Politics*, New York: Random House.

Whelpton, J. (2005) *A History of Nepal*, Princeton, NJ: Cambridge University Press.

Wiener, A. (2014) *A Theory of Contestation*, Berlin, Heidelberg: Springer.

Wire, The (2020) 'India loath to welcome US–Taliban agreement but notes all Afghans have hailed deal', 1 March, Available from: https://thewire.in/diplomacy/india-notes-all-afghans-have-welcomed-us-taliban-pact-but-wont-itself-welcome-deal [Accessed 24 November 2022].

Wire, The (2021) 'India calls for "inclusive dispensation" in Afghanistan a day after Taliban seizes Kabul', 16 August, Available from: https://thewire.in/diplomacy/india-calls-for-inclusive-dispensation-in-afghanistan-a-day-after-taliban-seizes-kabul [Accessed 24 November 2022].

World Bank, The (2022) 'Population, total – India', 22 November, Available from: https://data.worldbank.org/indicator/SP.POP.TOTL?locations=IN [Accessed 22 November 2022].

Wu, X., Ramesh, M. and Howlett, M. (2015) 'Policy capacity: A conceptual framework for understanding policy competences and capabilities', *Policy and Society*, 34(3–4): 165–71.

Yahuda, M. (2013) 'China's new assertiveness in the South China Sea', *Journal of Contemporary China*, 22(81): 446–59.

Yu, R. (2015) 'Choking under pressure: The neuropsychological mechanisms of incentive-induced performance decrements', *Frontiers in Behavioral Neuroscience*, 9: 19.

Zakaria, F. (1998) *From Wealth to Power: The Unusual Origins of America's World Role*, Princeton, NJ: Princeton University Press.

Zartman, I.W. and Faure, G.O. (2006) *Escalation and Negotiation in International Conflicts*, Cambridge: Cambridge University Press.

Zeit Online (2010) 'Militär: Bundeswehr droht Kahlschlag bei Rüstungsprojekten', 7 July, Available from: www.zeit.de/politik/deutschland/2010-07/bundeswehr-sparliste-waffen [Accessed 28 November 2022].

Zeit Online (2011) 'Hilfsaktion: Regierung plant Bundeswehreinsatz in Libyen', 7 April, Available from: www.zeit.de/politik/ausland/2011-04/libyen-bundeswehr-einsatz?page=5&utm_referrer=https%3A%2F%2Fwww.google.com%2F [Accessed 28 November 2022].

Zeit Online (2015) 'Konflikte: Ischinger warnt vor Tabuisierung von Waffenlieferungen an Ukraine', 14 March, Available from: www.zeit.de/news/2015-03/14/konflikte-ischinger-warnt-vor-tabuisierung-von-waffenlieferungen-an-ukraine-14081813 [Accessed 28 November 2022].

Zeit Online (2022) 'Deutschland für gezielte Einschränkung von Swift', Sanktionen gegen Russland, 26 February, Available from: www.zeit.de/politik/ausland/2022-02/russland-sanktionen-swift-zahlungsverkehr-ukraine-krieg [Accessed 13 November 2022].

Zilla, C. (2011) *Brasilianische Außenpolitik – Nationale Tradition, Lulas Erbe und Dilmas Optionen*, Berlin.

Index

www.ingramcontent.com/pod-product-compliance
Lightning Source LLC
Chambersburg PA
CBHW070619030426
42337CB00020B/3852